THE MEANING OF HESED IN THE HEBREW BIBLE: A NEW INQUIRY

HARVARD SEMITIC MUSEUM
HARVARD SEMITIC MONOGRAPHS

edited by
Frank Moore Cross

Number 17

THE MEANING OF HESED IN THE HEBREW BIBLE: A NEW INQUIRY

by
Katharine Doob Sakenfeld

SCHOLARS PRESS
Missoula, Montana

THE MEANING OF HESED IN THE HEBREW BIBLE: A NEW INQUIRY

by

Katharine Doob Sakenfeld

Published by
SCHOLARS PRESS
for
The Harvard Semitic Museum

Distributed by

SCHOLARS PRESS
P.O. Box 5207
Missoula, Montana 59806

THE MEANING OF HESED IN THE HEBREW BLBLE: A NEW INQUIRY

by

Katharine Doob Sakenfeld

Library of Congress Cataloging in Publication Data
Sakenfeld, Katharine Doob 1940–
The meaning of hesed in the Hebrew Bible.

(Harvard Semitic monographs ; 17 ISSN 0073-0637)
A revision of the author's thesis, Harvard University.
Bibliography: p.
Includes index.
1. Hesed (The word) 2. Bible. O.T.—Theology.
I. Harvard University. Semitic Museum.II. Title.
II. Series.
BS525.S22 1978 222'.1'044 78-3861
ISBN 0-89130-231-X

1 2 3 4 5 6
Printed in the United States of America

CONTENTS

LIST OF ABBREVIATIONS

AB	Anchor Bible
ANET	J. B. Pritchard, ed., *Ancient Near Eastern Texts*
ATD	*Das Alte Testament Deutsch*
BA	*Biblical Archaeologist*
BANE	G. E. Wright, ed., *The Bible and the Ancient Near East*
BASOR	*Bulletin of the American Schools of Oriental Research*
BDB	F. Brown, S. R. Driver, and C. A. Briggs, *A Hebrew and English Lexicon of the Old Testament*
BH	*Biblia Hebraica*
BK	*Biblischer Kommentar*
CB	Century Bible
CBQ	*Catholic Biblical Quarterly*
EvTh	*Evangelische Theologie*
GK	*Gesenius' Hebrew Grammar* as Edited and Enlarged by E. Kautzsch. Translated by A. E. Cowley.
HkzAT	Handkommentar zum Alten Testament
HTR	*Harvard Theological Review*
HUCA	*Hebrew Union College Annual*
IB	Interpreter's Bible
JBL	*Journal of Biblical Literature*
JNES	*Journal of Near Eastern Studies*
JSS	*Journal of Semitic Studies*
KAT	Kommentar zum Alten Testament
KHCzAT	Kurzer Hand-Commentar zum Alten Testament
OTL	Old Testament Library
RB	*Revue Biblique*
VT	*Vetus Testamentum*
WC	Westminster Commentaries
ZAW	*Zeitschrift für die Alttestamentliche Wissenschaft*
ZTK	*Zeitschrift für Theologie und Kirche*

PREFACE

This inquiry into the biblical usage of the Hebrew word *ḥesed* was first undertaken in 1970 and was presented to Harvard University as a doctoral dissertation. The original study was done under the direction of Professor G. Ernest Wright, who suggested the topic and provided the advice and encouragement so important to the completion of that work. The bulk of revisions in the present version were unfortunately completed after his death. I am indebted also to Professor Frank Moore Cross for his suggestions on many points of detail. Miss Carol Cross has typed several versions of the manuscript, and I am grateful for her painstaking work.

My special thanks go to my husband Helmar, whose confidence at every stage that the work could and should be completed was in itself an act of *ḥesed* in the biblical sense of the word.

K. D. S.
Princeton, New Jersey
January 1977

CHAPTER I
INTRODUCTION

The Present State of Research

The modern study of the Hebrew word *ḥesed* began with the work of Nelson Glueck,[1] and his analysis still dominates the brief statements about the word found in most handbooks and commentaries. Glueck opened his discussion of the secular meaning of *ḥesed* by briefly itemizing all the various personal relationships within which *ḥesed* was practiced. His list included relatives and related tribes, host and guest, allies and their relatives, friends, ruler and subject, and finally "those who have gained merit by rendering aid, and the parties thereby put under obligation."[2] His preliminary list suggested that *ḥesed* was practiced only by those in close relationship to each other, and he then proceeded to discuss in some detail the various passages which illustrated each of these types of relationship. All the relationships were subsumed under the general category of "mutual relationships of rights and duties," and *ḥesed* in his summary of secular usage was defined as "conduct in accord

---

1. Originally presented as a doctoral dissertation at Jena in 1926, published as *Das Wort* ḥesed *im alttestamentlichen Sprachgebrauche als mensliche und göttliche gemeinschaftgemässe Verhaltungsweise* (Giessen: Alfred Töpelmann, 1927). Published in English as Ḥesed *in the Bible*, tr. by Alfred Gottschalk (Cincinnati: The Hebrew Union College Press, 1967). Citations will be based on the German edition. A comprehensive collection of the subsequent literature is summarized without critical comment in Gerald LaRue's Introduction to the English edition of Glueck's work. A number of the writers cited by LaRue do not make any substantial new contribution to the scholarly debate about *ḥesed* and will not be included in the summary of research here.

2. Glueck, *Ḥesed*, p. 3.

with" such a relationship.[3] On the basis of his examination of secular usage, Glueck concluded that "the constituent parts of the comprehensive term *ḥesed*...are principally reciprocity, then mutual service, uprightness, friendliness, brotherliness, duty, faithfulness and love" and that "in the older sources, the common usage of *ḥesed* never means an arbitrary demonstration of grace, kindness, favor or love."[4]

In his analysis of the religious usage of *ḥesed* Glueck concluded that it was to be done by "all men, as co-equal members of human society." He recognized that conduct of men toward each other and relationship of men to God were both inseparably a part of *ḥesed*. *Ḥesed* was distinguished from mercy on the grounds that "*ḥesed* is obligatory."[5]

In theological usage Glueck regarded *ḥesed* as the action of God toward those in covenant with him - a patriarch, the king, all Israel. He continued to emphasize its mutual or reciprocal character. The reciprocity apparently consisted in the human partner's loyalty to Yahweh; although Glueck himself noted that such religious usage was restricted to "prophetic and related literature," he assumed that it applied everywhere. He regarded *ḥesed* as action due to those in relation to God because of their loyalty, action God was obligated to perform. He saw that God's *ḥesed* was regarded as a gift rather than a right, but he saw this as a latent, "spiritualized," and "more or less developed" theme which only occasionally received open expression.[6] He apparently did not regard this view as a possibility in secular usage. Nor did he feel any tension between religious usage applied to all mankind and theological usage restricted to those in covenant.

Criticisms of Glueck's analysis of specific passages are scattered throughout the body of this work, and it is the

---

3. *Ibid*., p. 3 and *passim*; *ḥesed* "als die einem Rechts-Pflicht-Verhältnis entsprechende Verhaltungsweise."

4. *Ibid*., p. 21: "...vor allem Gegenseitigkeit, denn Gegenleistung, Aufrichtigkeit, Freundlichkeit, Brüderlichkeit, Pflicht, Treue, und Liebe."

5. *Ibid*., p. 34.

6. *Ibid*., p. 52.

reevaluation of many individual texts which leads eventually to differing conclusions. At this introductory point only a very general critique is appropriate. Essentially, Glueck was correct in his observation that *ḥesed* is done within a relationship, and this is his great contribution. However, by simply listing the relationships descriptively rather than attempting to define larger analytic groupings, he left the impression that any relationship at all - except possibly that of an open enemy - could be one in which (secular) *ḥesed* was done by both parties. More serious, his definition of *ḥesed* as "conduct in accordance with..." suggests that any and all proper action with respect to the other party done by individuals or groups in relationship to one another was called *ḥesed*. Closer analysis suggests that only certain types of action were called *ḥesed*, and a major thrust of this work will be to lay out the particular circumstances within a relationship under which the use of the word *ḥesed* was in fact appropriate. Finally, Glueck's emphasis on "obligation" in terms of "customary law" or the "laws of human society" cannot be sustained in detail. It will be argued here that there is certainly "obligation" present - or preferably, "responsibility" - but it is not in the nature of a requirement which is punished or punishable by society. Hence *ḥesed* is not a legal right but a moral right and as such can also be a gift. Glueck's need to refute the traditional translation of *ḥesed*, *Gnade* in German and loving-kindness in English after Coverdale, led him to a false dichotomy between obligatory action and action freely done.

A dissertation with overall conclusions very close to those of Glueck was completed by Boone M. Bowen in 1938.[7] Bowen completed his research without knowledge of Glueck's work, however, and only added comparisons and contrasts in the final stage of his work. Unlike Glueck, who brought together material from all periods and sources as it fitted topically, Bowen arranged his texts to provide an extremely detailed author-by-author analysis of usage. By this procedure he was able to give a picture of the historical development of the word.

---

7. "A Study of *ḥsd*" (Yale University: unpublished Ph.D. dissertation, 1938).

Nevertheless, he preserved small categories even where no distinctive usage could be perceived, and this approach precluded the grouping of related texts to show more general types of usage. It also tended to suggest differences in usage which may have been a matter of accident, since there were so few examples from any single source.[8] Bowen's source analysis itself followed in the old literary critical tradition which was current at the time he wrote. This further compounds the difficulty in using his work in the Pentateuchal texts and in Samuel as well, since he allows for far less ambiguity of source, fluidity of usage, oral transmission, or redactional activity than is generally accepted today.

Meanwhile W. F. Lofthouse, building on Glueck's work, had proposed a basic distinction between *ḥēn* and *ḥesed* based on the presence or absence of a tie or claim.[9] While Lofthouse' distinction was essentially correct, he failed to give sufficient attention to the sub-types of usage of *ḥēn*, and hence he tied *ḥēn* too much to the absence of any bond whatsoever.[10] Lofthouse observed that *ḥēn* passes from a superior to an inferior but made no specific comment on whether this feature applies to *ḥesed*. He did recognize stronger and weaker parties within a covenant relationship but only in terms of action taken to

---

8. The distinctions in secular usage between J, E, and the "Saul" source, for example, ought probably to be attributed to difference in subject matter rather than to difference in orientation of the author. The J usage is restricted to familial relationships, but these are a main subject of the patriarchal traditions and the word occurs only twice. The king-subject relation, most common in the "Saul" source, was not appropriate for J's material. What Bowen should have investigated in more detail is how these relationships resemble and differ from one another, and whether any difference in the use of *ḥesed* could be discerned for groupings of relational categories.

9. "*Ḥēn* and *Ḥesed* in the Old Testament," *ZAW* 51, N.F. 10 (1933) 29-35, esp. 32-33.

10. For critical comment on this aspect of his work, see Chapter IV, p. 162 and n.20.

restore a broken relationship.[11]

Lofthouse was only the first of a steady stream of scholars to support, modify, or reject Glueck's work. The studies covered briefly in the following paragraphs appeared in 1944, 1946, 1949 (2), 1952, 1954, and 1957. These represent only a sampling of what has been said; the items selected are either major specialized studies or in two instances (Snaith, Robinson) widely cited general works which comment on *ḥesed*.

Norman Snaith chose "covenant-love" as his translation for *ḥesed*, distinguishing it from *ʾahăbâ* as "election-love."[12] His analysis of the original meaning of *ḥesed* as "that attitude of loyalty and faithfulness which both parties to a covenant should observe towards each other"[13] is very close to Glueck's view, although Snaith associated his position especially with the work of Lofthouse. Two methodological weaknesses limit the usefulness of Snaith's work. First, he allows undue weight to statistical observations in establishing the range of meaning of the word. The difficulty is that set expressions typical of a liturgical formula or particular author bias the results. To take a single example, the expression *hbryt whḥsd* occurs seven times. Of these, two are in Dt. 7:9,12 composed by the Deuteronomic historian, and one in I Kings 8:23 is in the address to Yahweh opening a prayer composed by the same hand. Although Snaith might not have recognized these three as a pattern of a single author, he should have noted that II Chr. 6:4 is simply a quotation from I Kings 8:23 and that Dan. 9:4 and Neh. 1:5; 9:23 are simply a prayer-address reuse of Dt. 7:9. In short, these cannot be regarded as seven independent associations of *ḥesed* with covenant. The same problem applies to many of the other figures he cites. A second and equally serious weakness

11. "*Ḥēn* and *Ḥesed*," p. 34. The difficulty with his suggestion is that *ḥesed* as action designed to restore a broken relationship appears only in theological texts. In secular texts, by contrast, *ḥesed* is regularly and even explicitly based on the relationship's good repair.

12. *Distinctive Ideas of the Old Testament* (London: The Epworth Press, 1944), pp. 94-130.

13. *Ibid.*, p. 99.

is Snaith's tendency to see *ḥesed* everywhere once a general meaning has been established. Hence he has special headings entitled "The 'Chesed' of God in Amos," ...in Micah, ...in (I) Isaiah, even though the word does not appear at all in Amos or I Isaiah and in Micah's own work only with human subject. The subject of Snaith's book is "Distinctive Ideas," but this approach should not lead to the application of the Hebrew word itself where it does not even occur. This is not to say that the word could not have been used by these prophets; but Snaith's implication to his readers that the *word ḥesed* was central to their recorded thought is misleading to say the least.

H. Wheeler Robinson, without mention of Glueck, likewise suggested the importance of "the element of loyalty, of moral obligation, of social bond, which the Hebrew word includes."[14] He preferred the translation "grace" for divine *ḥesed* since it was implicitly (and after the exile explicitly) the basis for God's forgiveness, his persistent faithfulness to the people despite their disobedience. As a human quality, Robinson suggested that *ḥesed* is that "supreme moral value" which prompts a man to help his neighbor even though no strictly legal obligation could be enforced.[15] The specific recognition of non-enforceable obligations engendered by social bonds is a step beyond Glueck, despite the generalization to "moral value" and any "neighbor." Robinson's treatment was too brief, however, to provide any extended exegesis of passages supporting his suggestion.

Uku Masing first suggested the importance of the superior-inferior character of the parties in a relationship when *ḥesed* was performed,[16] thus rejecting Glueck's idea of mutual

---

14. *Inspiration and Revelation in the Old Testament* (Oxford: Clarendon Press, 1946), p. 57.

15. *Ibid.*, p. 84-85.

16. "Der Begriff *Ḥesed* im alttestamentlichen Sprachgebrauch," *Charisteria Iohanni Kõpp: octogenario oblata*, Papers of the Estonian Theological Society in Exile (Holmiae, 1954), pp. 27-63. A critique of Masing's etymological theory is presented below, p. 19. His association of *ḥesed* with Indian

reciprocity. Masing began from the perspective that in most cases *ḥesed* was done by the politically or socially superior individual, as king to subject, master to servant, father to child, man to woman. He explained the numerous exceptions to this pattern by reference to the specially altered status of one of the parties in relationship. Thus, Joseph as Pharaoh's official was superior to his father, David is a commoner when Hushai does *ḥesed* for him. But not all examples can be handled in this way, notably Abraham and Sarah. Masing did not see that throughout the examples it is circumstantial superiority rather than the superiority of formal status which is important. From this perspective reciprocity need not be utterly rejected, for it occurs when there is a reversal of circumstances, as Masing himself recognized in the case of Rahab and the spies.[17]

A study by Glenn Yarbrough concluded that *ḥesed* was the "constant warmth of feeling" which constitutes the essence of loyal friendship.[18] Except in this emotive nuance his work relies heavily on Glueck and is quite superficial.

Felix Asensio argued for the meaning of "mercy-feeling" which leads to "mercy-work" over against the emphasis of Glueck on duty or obligation.[19] His emphasis was on the generosity, grace, and benevolence which he found essential to *ḥesed*. Methodologically the writer is uncomfortable with Asensio. He apparently regarded the Greek and Latin translational traditions as an important clue or at least as prominent confirmation of his analysis of the Hebrew usage. Thus he could not allow adequately for historical development, since he generalized the value of the Greek and Latin renderings to the Hebrew word without regard either for possible internal development

---

potlach rituals is not tenable.

17. *Ibid.*, p. 49.

18. "The Significance of *Ḥesed* in the Old Testament" (unpublished Ph.D. dissertation, Southern Baptist Theological Seminary, 1949).

19. *Misericordia et Veritas, el Ḥesed y 'Emet divinos, su influjo religioso-social en la historia de Israel*, in *Analecta Gregoriana* 48, Sec. 3, no. 19 (Rome: Apud Aedes Universitatis Gregorianae, 1949).

of the Hebrew usage or for the history of the versions themselves.[20] Asensio allowed for *ḥesed* to become obligatory in the presence of an oath (Abraham and Abimelech) and also in Nehemiah; yet he insisted that in the divine covenant with men mercy (as emotion and action) is the central feature. In most secular usage, likewise, he did not regard *ḥesed* as obligatory in any sense at all. It would seem that Asensio too was caught up in the dichotomy established by Glueck and was attempting to swing the pendulum to the other side.

Hans Joachim Stoebe also set his results over against those of Glueck.[21] Although his study was particularly concerned with *ḥesed*, he began his work with an analysis of *ḥēn* and *raḥămîm* on the supposition that apparent synonyms within a language are not identical in meaning and can be distinguished by comparative study. Stoebe pointed out that *ḥēn* is normally oriented toward the object of action (i.e. the recipient) whereas *raḥămîm* is oriented toward the subject (i.e. the actor). He argued that *ḥesed* has in common with *raḥămîm* its actor-orientation. Since *ḥesed* (singular) is the "A" word whenever paired with *raḥămîm* in poetry, Stoebe concluded that *ḥesed* is the dominant *(übergeordnete)* concept meaning good-hearted sentiment or kindness *(gütige Gesinnung oder Freundlichkeit)*, while *raḥămîm* is the concrete working out of this sentiment.[22] He

---

20. Asensio did not make use of critical editions of the Greek or Latin. While a review of the critical Greek actually shows little manuscript variation in the translation of *ḥesed* or *ʾĕmet* specifically, greater care in citation might be expected from one who placed such emphasis on the evidence in question.

21. *Bedeutung und Geschichte des Begriffes ḥäsäd* (Münster: unpublished doctoral dissertation, 1951). See also Stoebe's brief summary, published as "Die Bedeutung des Wortes *Ḥäsäd* im Alten Testament," *VT* 2 (1952) 244-254. Neither work refers to Asensio. Stoebe's article "Gnade, I" *(Evangelisches Kirchenlexikon*, ed. by Heinz Brunotte and Otto Weber [Göttingen: Vandenhoeck & Ruprecht, 1956], I, 1604-05) is even more abbreviated, devoting only a single paragraph to *ḥesed*.

22. "Die Bedeutung des Wortes *Ḥäsäd*," pp. 247-248.

further argued that the plural of *ḥesed*, which appears in relatively late texts, refers to concrete acts and observed that it is used as a "B" word in parallel with *raḥămîm* (2x out of 3 examples). Also in the late period *ḥesed* and *ṭūb/ṭōb* appear together.[23] From this set of observations Stoebe concluded that the original meaning of *ḥesed* must have been "good-heartedness, kindness" *(Güte, Freundlichkeit)* and that the word shrank in meaning under the influence of *raḥămîm*, rather than expanding as most scholars had assumed.[24] In reaching this proposal for an original meaning, Stoebe thus assumed that *ṭōb* gradually displaced *ḥesed* in late usage. He suggested that the use of the root *ṭwb* for *ḥesed* some 130x each in the Targums and Syriac confirmed this analysis.[25] But he did not analyze *ṭōb* in detail, and this word would seem to have throughout the spectrum of biblical materials just the meaning he suggests for *ḥesed*. Yet by Stoebe's own premise this ought not to be so, since he argues that *ṭwb* replaced *ḥesed* only in the late period. He also fails to treat in this connection two important early texts in which *ṭōb* and *ḥesed* appear together (I Sam. 2:6; Micah 6:8).

Stoebe turned to specific exegetical study to confirm his conclusions. In the history of Judges through Kings he found that the word had the meaning good-heartedness, kindness, and further stood for what one expected or deserved, something based in magnanimous readiness to help another.[26] Perhaps this

---

Developed in his *Bedeutung und Geschichte des Begriffes ḥäsäd*, p. 47.

23. *Bedeutung und Geschichte des Begriffes ḥäsäd*, pp. 18-34.

24. "Die Bedeutung des Wortes *Ḥäsäd*," p. 248.

25. *Die Bedeutung und Geschichte des Begriffes ḥäsäd*, pp. 54-56. Whether with respect to *raḥămîm* it is legitimate to assume that the "A" word must govern the "B" word in poetry is a question unto itself. The writer would be hesitant to allow the sweeping conclusions for meaning which Stoebe appears to make from the A-B positioning. For a possible alternate interpretation of the Targumic and Syriac usage, see below, p. 16.

26. "Die Bedeutung des Wortes *Ḥäsäd*," pp. 248-249.

specification is what Stoebe regarded as the distinction from *ṭōb* used more generally, but he makes no comment. Even the longer study does not develop any of these passages in detail, probably because the "definition" established in the preceding lexical section is so general that it obviously applies to all the passages. The possibility of more detailed nuancing is not addressed. Stoebe suggested that the theological use of *ḥesed* was a special development introduced by the J writer as a revision of an old liturgical formula (Ex. 34).[27] This attribution seems consonant with the high degree of creativity assigned to J by von Rad and others, but the present writer finds it difficult to imagine what form the old liturgical usage could have had without the inclusion of *ḥesed*.[28]

In 1957 Sidney Hills presented a paper on *ḥesed*[29] which, along with Glueck's work, has been particularly useful for the present study. Since Hills' paper has not been published, his major points will be quoted (with his permission) from his 16-page manuscript in the order in which they appear:

With human subject:

1. The word *ḥesed* denotes action and not a psychological state.
2. *Ḥesed* denotes unilateral assistance for the helpless, granted without compensation or condition, not a mutual exchange: [there may be] two successive unilateral acts in opposite directions.
3. *Ḥesed* denotes essential and often indispensable assistance, not extra privilege.
4. *Ḥesed* denotes action determined not by law or custom but by personal decision: [it is] non-legal, fundamentally unlike law or custom.
5. *Ḥesed* denotes actions which may be promised with or without confirmation by a promissory oath (or

---

27. *Ibid.*, pp. 249-250.

28. See discussion of liturgical formulae, Chapter III, pp. 112-122.

29. "The *Ḥesed* of Man in the Old Testament" and Part II "The *Ḥesed* of God," delivered before the Biblical Colloquium, meeting in Pittsburgh, November 29, 1957.

covenant); only exceptionally is *ḥesed* related to a previous covenant relationship.

6. *Ḥesed* denotes action that is not optional but rather obligatory on moral grounds.
7. *Ḥesed* denotes action which requires special moral qualities: viz. initiative, courage, constancy, and trustworthiness.
8. *Ḥesed* denotes extra-legal acts or good-works deserving special recognition and reward; their omission brings moral condemnation.
9. *Ḥesed* denotes action which has its source in God. He desires and commands it, recognizes and rewards it, and punishes its omission.

In theological usage, the *ḥesed* of God, like the *ḥesed* of man:

1. denotes action, not a psychological state.
2. usually denotes unilateral help for the helpless without compensation or condition.
3. denotes essential assistance, not mere privilege.
4. is essentially distinct from judicial or legal action. God grants *ḥesed* not as a divine judge but as a personal friend and benefactor who fulfills his responsibility to the helpless whoever they may be, without regard to their merit and often in direct contradiction to his own law.
5. may or may not be confirmed by promissory oath or covenant.
6. possesses certain marvellous characteristics: all-pervading initiative, irresistible power, never-failing constancy.
7. is worthy of highest praise, and is to be rewarded not by reciprocal *ḥesed* but by love and obedience.

Several aspects of the present study received their impetus from Hills' suggestions, and the writer is grateful for Hills' permission to build upon his brief work. A few points of particular concern may be mentioned here.

In the area of human usage, Hills' view of the relationship between covenant and *ḥesed* requires closer analysis and refinement. While constancy and trustworthiness are certainly a part of *ḥesed*, courage and initiative are occasionally but not essentially present. Hills' evaluation of the "religious" use of *ḥesed* (summed up in point 9) does not take into account the special problems and theological context of such usage. In theological usage the implication that covenant-based usage is rare must be called into question. Also, initiative and power surely characterize God's actions generally in the Old Testament, not merely his *ḥesed*. And finally, the "rewarding" of God's *ḥesed* is a strange use of words. Response to his *ḥesed* would seem more appropriate terminology.

Hills performed a great service for the study of *ḥesed* in his recognition that *ḥesed* is done by the situationally superior party for one who is completely lacking in present resources or future prospects. In this point the present work attempts to build and expand upon his insight. The objections to his presentation suggested in the preceding paragraph will be dealt with in some detail in the course of the study.

On the matter of covenant it should be noted that Hills has himself fluctuated in his view of the relationship between *bᵉrît* and *ḥesed*. In a second presentation on the problem,[30] he argued that *bᵉrît* could entail either a *ḥesed* type of covenant ("no coercion") or a covenant between more or less equals ("mutual exchange of benefits with possible coercion"). He failed to see, however, that any parity treaty could fit both of his types. It is only when coercion is possible but is not exercised that the action is called *ḥesed*. Part of Hills' difficulty lies in the vague fluidity of meaning he attaches to the term *bᵉrît*. He sees it implied in the Sarah-Abraham and in the Cup-bearer-Joseph relationships, for example. This is occasioned by his apparent assumption in the 1960 paper that every act of *ḥesed* must result in (or be founded in) a *bᵉrît*. He wrote that "*ḥesed* denotes that initial act of extraordinary kindness or love" by which a superior creates a bond *(bᵉrît)*, also further acts within the bond and the "inward disposition which motivates the acts." While there are a very few texts

---

30. "*Ḥesed* and *Berîth* and their Interrelationships," outline of talk presented to the Biblical Colloquium, meeting at Drew University (Madison, N.J.), November 25, 1960.

in which *ḥesed* might be regarded as the initial act creating a bond, it will here be argued that such usage was secondary and exceptional - *ḥesed* was properly used primarily for acts performed within an existing relationship.[31]

Even this brief summary of modern studies in *ḥesed* makes clear the wide variety of shading which is possible in the interpretation of a word which has no obvious English equivalent and which exhibits great flexibility in usage within the biblical tradition. The extent and variety of material published on *ḥesed* ensures that little can be said which is completely new. Nevertheless, there is certainly room for a new combination of the existing suggestions for the many individual passages, especially in light of the new understanding of treaty types which has blossomed from the initial efforts of George Mendenhall.[32] The recombination of many small points can lead to a fresh synthesis, and it is this objective which the present study seeks to accomplish.

---

31. The writer learned indirectly that by 1970 Hills believed there was no connection at all between *ḥesed* and *bᵉrît*. This position (if the extreme statement of it is accurate) is as difficult to accept as his earlier attempt to associate a *bᵉrît* with every instance of *ḥesed*. "*Bᵉrît*" is only one of many socially or legally recognized human relationships, all of which, it will be argued, may provide a context for "doing *ḥesed*."

For another rejection of any connection between *bᵉrît* and *ḥesed*, see Alfred Jepsen, "Gnade und Barmherzigkeit im Alten Testament," *Kerygma und Dogma* 7 (1961) 261-271. Jepsen attempts to refute Glueck's emphasis on duty, but he goes to an extreme in arguing that the concept of obligation is completely absent. His insistence that *ḥesed* is never directed from men to God in prophetic usage is also to be rejected. (See Chapter V.)

32. See *Law and Covenant in Israel and the Ancient Near East* (Pittsburgh: The Biblical Colloquium, 1955). For a recent review and survey of the literature on the subject, see Dennis J. McCarthy, *Old Testament Covenant* (Richmond, Va.: John Knox Press, 1972).

Plan of the Investigation

After a preliminary consideration of evidence from the translations of the Greek and versions, the cognate languages, and Hebrew inscriptions, the main body of the study will focus upon the individual biblical occurrences of the term. The overall format of Chapters II through V will be a text-by-text analytical presentation of the biblical evidence. The traditional distinction of "secular," "theological," and "religious" usages is observed. Chapter II deals with secular usage in pre-exilic prose narrative texts; Chapter III, with theological usage in pre-exilic prose narrative texts; Chapter IV, with all post-exilic prose narrative texts (secular, religious, and theological).[33] The religious and theological usage in prophecy comprises Chapter V; only religious and theological examples occur. Throughout Chapters II-V texts from the Psalms are introduced wherever relevant. Chapter VI summarizes the materials from Psalms, Proverbs, and related texts which have not been previously presented; a brief conclusion provides a review of the results of the investigation. It should be noted that within each chapter or major subsection the texts are arranged in an order which best brings out their interrelationship and contributes to the overall development of the argument for the particular section. This means that a strict ordering by chronology or even by author is not observed; however, date and authorship do receive attention insofar as differentiation of usage can be discerned.

Evidence from Translations of Greek and Versions

The Greek and versions are of course useful and even essential in identifying and solving textual problems in the contexts in which *ḥesed* appears. Establishment of the text has been undertaken in each case prior to any analysis of usage; results of text critical work are presented in the discussion of many passages dealt with in the study. Here, however, our concern is for the contribution which the specific translational terms used for *ḥesed* may make to an understanding of the

---

33. There are no examples of religious usage in pre-exilic prose narrative.

Hebrew word.

The Greek ἔλεος is the normal equivalent for *ḥesed* used by the Septuagint translators. The usual range of meaning of ἔλεος in Classical usage was mercy or sympathy, and this is a focus of meaning for *ḥesed* which appears to emerge in exilic theological usage and become dominant in the intertestamental period.[34] The Greek translators were using a term which best fit the Hebrew meaning as they knew it; but it does not follow that that meaning had always been the central content of *ḥesed*.[35] The meaning in earlier periods of Hebrew writing can only be ascertained by study of the texts themselves.

The central meaning will be seen to be different in earlier texts, and there is evidence for the possibility that the translators themselves felt the inappropriateness of the term they were using. Δικαιοσύνη, most often used for *ṣdq*, *ṣdqh*, is used for *ḥesed* in 5 of 11 examples in Genesis and 2 of 4 examples in Exodus.[36] The distribution of the two Greek words shows no pattern, however; even in an identical repetition of a phrase in Gen. 24 there is no consistency. Possibly the relative rarity of *ṣdq/ṣdqh* in these two books[37] allowed the translator here greater flexibility in his choice of words. Still his apparent arbitrariness is difficult to understand.

The Greek of Proverbs is the second major area of variance from ἔλεος. Here ἐλεημοσύνη is used for 7 of 13 occurrences of

---

34. See Isa. 54:8; also Bultmann's discussion of "ἔλεος ἐλεέω A. The Greek Usage and B. The OT and Jewish Usage" in *Theological Dictionary of the New Testament* (ed. by Gerhard Kittel, tr. and ed. by Geoffrey W. Bromiley; Grand Rapids, Mich.: Wm. B. Eerdmans Publishing Company, 1964), II, 477-482, esp. 477 and 481 and texts cited therein. The Latin *misericordia* presumably follows the Greek tradition.

35. It is a methodological weakness of Asensio's work that he does not recognize this fact.

36. Gen. 19:19; 20:13; 21:23; 24:27; 32:10 (11); Ex. 15:13; 34:7.

37. *Ṣdq* does not appear at all; *ṣdqh* appears only 3x, all in Genesis and all translated by δικαιοσύνη.

ḥesed.[38] Of the remaining six examples, one uses δικαιοσύνη, two use a participial verb form ἐλεήμων, and one reads a different Hebrew *(ḥsr)*. Since ἐλεημοσύνη and ἔλεος are closely related in Greek,[39] the variation may be stylistic. However, the fact that this Greek word is elsewhere used for *ṣdq/ṣdqh* (12x) should not be overlooked. Possibly the connection between *ḥsd* and *ṣdq/ṣdqh* was not forgotten, even though the overlapping nuances were not originally those suggested by the Greek rendering.[40]

The Peshitta normally uses *ṭybwtʾ* ("goodness, kindness; a favor or benefit") as the translational equivalent of *ḥesed*. This term, like the Greek, only approximates certain aspects of the content of the Hebrew term and is especially appropriate for late Hebrew usage. Nevertheless, it is possible that the selection of a noun from the root *ṭwb* is a late reflection of a much older tradition of Hebrew-Aramaic semantic equivalence which may even have extended to Akkadian as well. This equivalence, if it existed, would have been found in a specialized application of *ḥesed* and nouns derived from *ṭwb* to treaty contexts and particularly to the friendly behavior expected of parties in a treaty relationship. The appearance of *ṭwb* along with *ḥesed* in the treaty context of II Sam. 2:6 (Chapter III, p. 110) and in the lawsuit context of Micah 6:8 (Chapter V, pp. 188-189) may possibly support such a hypothesis, but there is no certain evidence and the proposal must remain conjectural.

Evidence from Other Semitic Languages

A thorough search of appropriate lexica has yielded no material which can be of any substantial help for our understanding of the biblical usage of *ḥesed*. There is no evidence

---

38. Prv. 8:3; 14:22; 15:27 (16:6); 19:22; 20:28a; 21:21; 31:27 (26). Cf. LXX of Gen. 47:29 which also uses this Greek noun.

39. See Bultmann, "ἐλεημοσύνη," *Theological Dictionary of the New Testament*, II, 485-486.

40. The connection between the Hebrew terms lay not in the area of sympathy or mercy but in nuances of morally right behavior, relationally appropriate behavior, and salvific (delivering) action. See esp. Chapters V, VI.

for the appearance of the root in Akkadian, Amorite, or Ugaritic texts.

The root is well known in Targumic Aramaic and in Syriac, but here it usually has the nominal meaning of "a shameful thing" and the verbal usage "to jeer, blaspheme, disgrace." Where meanings in the range of "kindness, love" occur they have been generally recognized to be under Hebrew influence.[41] There are a few Old Testament occurrences of *ḥesed* which appear to be Aramaisms. The two most generally cited are Prov. 25:10 and Lev. 20:17.[42] The text of Prov. 14:34 is problematic but may be related to the text of 25:10.

Two Arabic roots have been related to Hebrew *ḥesed*. Arabic *ḥasada*, "to envy," with a nominal form meaning "that which is a cause of corruption or evil,"[43] is clearly an etymologically correct root for correspondence with the Hebrew and Aramaic words. The range of meaning approximates that of the common Aramaic and Syriac usage. Yet as early as 1829 the Arabic *ḥašada* was suggested as possibly related to Hebrew *ḥesed*.[44] The basic meaning of this second Arabic root is "to collect together," as to aid a person or to entertain a guest.[45] Etymologically, this root cannot by normal equivalence be regarded as a cognate since Arabic *š* regularly represents only proto-semitic *ś*, never *s*. Nevertheless, it has continually been cited in the literature because of its supposed closer

---

41. So, for example, Theodor Nöldeke, *Neue Beiträge zur semitischen Sprachwissenschaft* (Strassburg: K. J. Trübner, 1910), p. 93.

42. See Max Wagner, *Die lexikalischen und grammatikalischen Aramaismen im alttestamentlichen Hebräisch* (Beiheft 96, *ZAW*; Berlin: Alfred Toepelmann, 1966), pp. 56-57, and sources cited therein.

43. Edward Lane, *An Arabic-English Lexicon* (London: Williams and Norgate, 1863-1893), Book I, part 2, p. 567b-c.

44. Wilhelm Gesenius, *Thesaurus Philologicus Criticus Linguae Hebraeae et Chaldaeae Veteris Testamenti* (Lipsiae, sumtibus typisque Fr. Chr. Guil. Vogelii, 1829), I, 502.

45. Lane, Book I, Part 2, p. 574c.

resemblance in meaning to the Hebrew usage of *ḥesed*.[46] Those holding this view have generally sidestepped the linguistic difficulty by appealing to the confusion between *śîn* and *samekh* in the orthography of Biblical Hebrew.[47] A Hebrew root *ḥśd* would of course correspond properly to the Arabic *ḥšd*, so it is argued that the Hebrew root must originally have been *ḥśd*. The difficulty with such a solution is that the *śîn-samekh* confusion in Biblical Hebrew is attested only sporadically. There are no recognized instances of the systematic revision in consonantal orthography of a well-known root. If the root had originally been with *ś* one would *expect* the change to *s* to appear in Aramaic and especially in Syriac so that the earlier root there also should have been *ḥśd*. But the argument for original *ś* applied to Hebrew has not generally been extended to those languages, presumably because the present meaning of the root *ḥsd* there relates to the meaning of the etymologically correct correspondent *ḥasada* in Arabic.

Masing noticed this weakness in the usual argument and thus attributed even the Aramaic-Syriac *ḥsd* to original *ḥśd*. He attempted to support this change by arguing further that the Aramaic root *ḥšd*, "to be suspicious," is the equivalent for the Arabic *ḥsd*. This latter correspondence is strictly correct etymologically, since proto-semitic *s* and *š* roots normally fall together into Arabic *s*. To account for the new variables he had introduced, however, Masing hypothesized that a positive meaning of *ḥsd* similar to the biblical range existed in pre-Christian religious Aramaic (alongside the negative sense reserved for secular literature) but that cultural break caused only the negative sense to be preserved in Church Syriac. Correspondingly, he hypothesized that the negative sense was common in secular Hebrew of the biblical period and is unknown to us only because the preserved texts are sacred ones.[48] Such

---

46. So Glueck, pp. 67-68. See also U. Masing, "Der Begriff *Ḥesed*," pp. 33-34.

47. This argument was advanced by Friedrich Schulthess, *Homonyme Wurzeln im Syrischen* (Berlin: Reuther and Reichard, 1900), p. 32 and is cited by Glueck and Masing.

48. "Der Begriff *Ḥesed*," p. 33.

speculation seems almost fanciful and in any case does not advance the strictly linguistic discussion.

In short, the writer can see no valid basis for evading the more obvious correspondence of the Hebrew *ḥsd* with its Aramaic and Arabic counterparts, even though the range of meaning is very different. The better argument lies with those who assume that the root has simply developed very different meanings in the cognate languages.[49] Yet is must be said that any effort to extrapolate from the meanings now preserved to a hypothetical original meaning of the root can only be an exercise of the imagination. Our task is to study the meaning of the word as it occurs in the texts which are actually before us.

The only non-Hebrew inscriptional example of this root known to the author is the occurrence of *ḥsyd* in line 7 (first line of column II) of the Neo-Punic dedicatory inscription from the temple at Maktar in Numidia.[50] The first two columns concern the building of the temple, while the remainder consists of a series of personal names. Unfortunately, the number of

---

49. So Nöldeke, *Neue Beiträge*, p. 93. N. Snaith also takes this position (*Distinctive Ideas*, p. 97). In support of his view he cites several words which can have opposite or at least very different meanings within individual languages, as well as on a comparative basis. While no number of additional examples can ever prove the individual case, the viability of the approach which preserves the correct etymology is clearly demonstrated.

50. Maktar A: First published by Philippe Berger, "Mémoire sur la grande inscription dédicatoire et sur plusieurs autres inscriptions néo-puniques du temple d'Hathor-Miskar à Maktar," *Mémoires de l'Académie des Inscriptions et Belles-lettres*, Vol. XXXVI, Part 2 (Paris: Impr. nat., 1899). Discussed also by Charles Clermont-Ganneau, *Recueil d'Archéologie Orientale* (Paris, 1900), II, pars. 57 and 3; and by Mark Lidzbarski, *Ephemeris für semitische Epigraphik* (Giessen: Alfred Toepelmann, 1902), I, pp. 45-52. Restudied most recently by J. G. Février, "La grande inscription dédicatoire de Mactar," *Semitica* VI (1956) 15-31.

obscured or debatable letters, along with the frequency of unknown words where the text is legible, has left the exact translation of the opening columns very much in doubt.

The line with which we are concerned is particularly ill preserved. The words *ḥsyd tm* in the middle of the line are agreed upon by all, but there are breaks on both sides so that the sense cannot be reconstructed satisfactorily. Lidzbarski regards the two words as possibly an epithet referring to the deity in whose honor the temple was constructed.[51] Février proposes that the *sml* at the beginning of the line be understood as a statue of some Roman functionary who was a benefactor of Maktar. The phrase *ḥsyd tm* would then refer to this individual, whose name Février finds in the next letters of the line.[52]

Despite the attractiveness of these words in a dedicatory context, the reading should perhaps be held in abeyance. There are apparently no word dividers or spaces and the text is broken both before and after this group of letters. Neo-Punic did not regularly use *yôd* as a vowel letter, although its occurrence was more frequent than in Punic texts.[53] Nevertheless, it does appear possible that we have here a single example of the use of the root *ḥsd* in a late inscriptional text, and further that its range of meaning may be more comparable to the biblical usage than to the Aramaic. Although the text is late and unclear, and although the usage could conceivably be dependent upon late Hebrew, one cannot discount the possibility that there was a Canaanite dialectal development of the root which was comparable to Hebrew usage but by reason of chance has not appeared in texts thus far discovered.

Evidence from Hebrew Inscriptions

To date no certain example of the root *ḥsd* in any form has been identified in published Hebrew inscriptions. However, F. M. Cross had suggested a conjectural reading of *ḥesed* in line 4

---

51. Lidzbarski, *Ephemeris*, I, p. 50.

52. Février, "La grande inscription," p. 20.

53. Z. Harris, *A Grammar of the Phoenician Language* (New Haven: American Oriental Society, 1936), p. 19.

of the Neḥemyahu ostracon from Arad.[54] The first word of that line, *wʿt*, concludes the epistolary introductory formula. The letter itself then begins: *hṭ* [*ʾt ḥ*]*ṡdk*: "extend your *ḥesed*..."[55] In Biblical Hebrew *nṭh* is used with *ḥesed* in the hi. in Esr. 7:28; 9:9 and in the qal in Gen. 39:21. Unfortunately, the inscription as whole is in such severe disrepair that the thrust cannot be determined with certainty; nor can the recipient be identified except for his name, Malkiyahu. From the use of "sons" in the introductory formula it is apparent that the letter concerns persons in either a familial or a political relationship. If the latter is the case (cf. references to *ʾdm* = Edom?), then a subordinate is asking for *ḥesed* from a political superior. Either of these situations would comport well with the parameters for the secular use of the word *ḥesed* developed in the next chapter. But since the content of the request cannot be ascertained (and since the occurrence itself is conjectural) the ostracon cannot contribute anything additional to the picture of usage available from the biblical texts.

---

54. Personal communication, June 1970. The ostracon was first published by Yohanan Aharoni, "Three Hebrew Ostraca from Arac," *Eretz Israel* 9 (1969) 10-21 (Hebrew), English translation in *BASOR* 197 (February, 1970) 16-41. Aharoni dates the ostracon to 701 B.C.; Cross prefers a late seventh century dat ing on paleographical grounds.

55. It should be reemphasized that the reading is tentative. Cross would wish to see glossy photographs before developing the suggestion for publication.

CHAPTER II

THE SECULAR USE OF *ḤESED* IN PRE-EXILIC PROSE

Introduction

The pre-exilic narrative uses of *ḥesed* with a human subject fall into two broad types: Section A of this chapter describes those acts of *ḥesed* which are based implicitly on intimate personal relationships, that is, situations where close personal relationships are plainly evident and where no reason or basis for the act of *ḥesed* is explicitly stated. Section B describes a second type, acts of *ḥesed* which are based on some prior action which may be explicitly named and which may also be called *ḥesed*. In this type there may be some relationship between the two parties involved, but it is not intimate or personal and it may even be hostile. The story of the relationship between David and Jonathan is a special "mixed" type discussed in Section C.

The chapter covers texts from a wide span of centuries, including texts from the J and E strands of the patriarchal narratives,[1] a variety of sources used by the Deuteronomic historian, and texts from that historian's own hand.[2] The decision to group together these texts from such divergent periods was made only after it became clear that any effective analytic categories within this time span regularly cut across all subgroupings made by date or author.[3] The post-exilic texts do

---

1. J probably took its written form during the period of the United Monarchy; it is presumably antecedent to E, which has been dated by Alan W. Jenks ("The Elohist and North Israelite Traditions" [unpublished Th.D. dissertation, Harvard University, 1965]) to the reign of Jeroboam or shortly thereafter.

2. That is, from Dtr^1, following the analysis of F. M. Cross, Jr., "The Structure of the Deuteronomic History," *Perspectives in Jewish Learning* III (1967) 9-24. These are dated to the reign of Josiah in the last quarter of the seventh century. See also Cross's *Canaanite Myth and Hebrew Epic* (Cambridge, Mass.: Harvard University Press, 1973), pp. 274-289.

3. As has been noted in Chapter I, Bowen did a strict

show a distinctive pattern of usage and are treated separately in Chapter IV.

Although the analysis is built up inductively from a passage-by-passage study of the texts, the very ordering of the passages is of course affected by conclusions reached during the course of the research. Hence it seems only fair to the reader to summarize at the outset the understanding of *ḥesed* to which the inductive study leads. The chapter attempts to show that there are four features normally present in situations in which the word *ḥesed* is appropriate. The first two form a pair held in tension: (1) the human actor always has some recognizable responsibility for the person who is to receive *ḥesed*, either because of an obvious personal relationship or because of some previous action; yet (2) situationally the actor is always quite free not to perform the act of *ḥesed* - no pressure can be brought on him and no reprisal is available within the legal system. Two additional factors are (3) that the act of *ḥesed* usually fulfills an important need for the recipient and (4) that it is something which he cannot possibly do for himself and often is something which no one but the actor can do for him.

With this brief summary of the anticipated results we may turn directly to the study of the texts in which human *ḥesed* appears.

A. Ḥesed *Based Implicitly on Intimate Personal Relationships*

The first group of texts to be dealt with may be described as those in which the personal relationship between the parties involved forms the direct yet implicit basis for the doing of *ḥesed*. That is, there is a specific relationship between the parties; it is close and personal, and it can be named or described in familial or political terms. At the same time, this relationship is not in any of these cases cited as the basis or reason for the act of *ḥesed*. In each text the request for or statement of intended *ḥesed* is made without statement of any

---

period-and-author analysis, but the small distinctions in usage among the pre-exilic secular texts which he noted are not analytically significant.

basis for the request; since the basis is assumed, it apparently lies in the relationship between the parties which is implicit in the situation.

Genesis 20:13

> Then when God had me wander about (away) from my father's house I said to her, "this is your *ḥesed* which you shall do for me: at every place to which we come say, 'he is my brother.'"

The only textual question in the verse concerns the plural verb *hitʿû* used with *ʾĕlōhîm*. The Samaritan Pentateuch reads the singular form. The Greek and versions translate with a singular verb, but it seems probable that they would do so *ad sensum*. Readings in which *ʾĕlōhîm* is associated with a plural predicate or adjective are found elsewhere, although rarely, in early narrative (e.g. Gen. 35:7; Jos. 24:19). The Israelite use of *ʾĕlōhîm* (the Canaanite plural for *ʾĒl*, already fixed in the Amarna period) in the sense of "God" reflects the Canaanite religious usage in which a god was honored by use of the plural in the sense of "totality of manifestations" or even "totality of the gods."[4] Hence the use of a plural verb or adjective may be very old and may have survived as a matter of taste or preference in certain circles. The plural form is probably to be regarded as the earlier reading.

The verse is a part of the Elohistic narrative of Abraham and Sarah at Gerar. Abraham explains to Abimelech that he had deceived him about Sarah's marital status because he feared for his own life (vs. 11). Sarah's role was one of complicity as this narrator presents it. In vs. 2 Abraham says "she is my sister," and in vs. 5 Abimelech states that the two both claimed to be brother and sister. In the Yahwistic narrative (Gen. 12:10-20) the story elements essential to the understanding of Abraham's instruction to Sarah remain basically unchanged - except that the term *ḥesed* is not used. This striking instance of the absence of the word where we might most clearly expect it should serve as a warning: the actual occurrences of the word do not exhaust the instances in which the

---

4. W. F. Albright, *From the Stone Age to Christianity* (Baltimore: The Johns Hopkins Press, 1940), p. 161.

term might have been appropriate.

Speiser has argued that the wife-sister relationship involved in these passages[5] had its source in Hurrian customs which had long since been forgotten in the process of social change and hence were no longer meaningful to the narrators.[6] It is only in the E text that there is any clear indication that Sarah was actually in a sisterly (as well as wifely) relationship to Abraham (vs. 12). If only the J narrative were available, one would necessarily conclude that the entire episode involved a deception, pure and simple. But in either case it is clear that the "implicit" relationship is at least that of marriage, and perhaps of blood kinship as well.

For Glueck this passage provided an important key to the understanding of *ḥesed*, particularly because of the "requirement" form of the first part of Abraham's statement: "This is your *ḥesed* which you 'must' do...." He saw the basis of the narrative in duty-oriented conduct based in reciprocity which obligated all members of a family to assist one another.[7] Coming to the same text from a different perspective, Hills interprets the imperfect verbal form with the coloring "can and ought to do," thus supporting his argument that "*Ḥesed* denotes an action that is not optional but rather obligatory on moral grounds."[8] Although the two positions appear similar on the surface, they emerge from very different basic perceptions of the text. For Glueck, Abraham was asking nothing more of Sarah than she might normally be expected to do. For Hills, however, the act far exceeded what the law might require.

It will be necessary to examine a long series of texts before making judgment between these contrasting interpretations.

---

5. Cf. also Gen. 26:6-11, although that passage does not bear directly on the understanding of *ḥesed*.

6. E. A. Speiser, *Genesis* (AB; Garden City: Doubleday & Company, Inc., 1964), pp. 91-94. See his "The Wife-Sister Motif in the Patriarchal Narratives," *Biblical and Other Studies* (Lown Institute Studies I), ed. by Alexander Altmann (Cambridge: Harvard University Press, 1963), pp. 15-28.

7. Glueck, p. 5.

8. "*Ḥesed* of Man," p. 7.

Yet certain descriptive statements can be made about each passage which will provide a basis for general analysis of usage after the texts have been presented. In Gen. 20:13 it is obvious first of all that Abraham and Sarah are in a kinship relationship. Further, Abraham does not give any justification for the request he makes.[9] Third, in the particular circumstances - at least as Abraham perceives them - Sarah's non-compliance will mean certain death for Abraham. And there is no other person who can perform this particular act. Thus, if she does not respond favorably Abraham himself will have no recourse. Finally, it should be noted that while the anticipated result of the requested *ḥesed* may not have endangered Sarah personally, it did represent a potentially serious threat to her current marital relationship. Although she might well desire to preserve Abraham's life, it was nevertheless not an easy thing which was asked of her.

II Samuel 3:8

> Abner became furious at Ishbaal's words and said, "am I a dog's head? At this moment I am doing *ḥesed* with the household of your father Saul, to his brothers and his friends, in that I have not delivered you into David's power; yet today you have accused me of a fault concerning a woman!"

No Greek manuscripts represent the MT phrase *ʾăšer lîhûdâ*, and oddly only the Lucianic minuscules and the Old Latin show any indication of the existence of an alternate reading to replace this phrase.[10] This peculiar textual situation is probably beyond reconstruction but fortunately does not seriously

---

9. Note that the imperative *ʾimrî* can readily be understood as a request, just as is the *ʾimrî-nāʾ* of the J version (12:13). It is only the prior construction using a nominal sentence with relative clause which suggests a command or demand on Abraham's part.

10. Minuscules boc_2e_2: εμαυτω σημερον εποιησα παντα ταυτα (και εποιησα ελεον...). Old Latin: *ipse mihi feci haec omni qui*. The Chronicler gives no help, since he omits the entire story in order to present David as gaining the kingship over all Israel immediately.

affect the meaning of the passage. If the phrase is to be retained, it serves only to emphasize Abner's point of his loyalty to the Saulides over against David.[11]

Abner has set up Ishbaal as king in the northern part of the country, in competition with David (see II Sam. 2:8-11 *et seq*.). Abner had become the most powerful individual within the Saulide camp, and now Ishbaal accuses him of intimacy with one of Saul's concubines. Such an act may have been associated with a move toward the assuming of kingship for himself.[12] In any case, Abner's response makes abundantly clear that he is primarily responsible for preserving the political fortunes of Ishbaal and his family.

The implicit relationship in this situation is described by Glueck as one between ruler and subject.[13] While this is obviously the most immediate feature of the relationship, Abner's statement suggests that the description should be broadened to cover political ties to the whole family as a contending faction: Abner's *ḥesed* is with the Saulides and their supporters, not with Ishbaal alone - and if one reads the text literally, not with Ishbaal at all except as he happens to be one among the Saulides. Abner had of course been the commander

---

11. George Caird explains the phrase as a scribal interpolation stemming from a misreading of *klb* as the tribe Caleb which had been incorporated into Judah (*The First and Second Books of Samuel: Introduction and Exegesis* [IB; New York: Abingdon Press, 1953], p. 1057). If this were the case, one could imagine that such a gloss might remain in manuscript margins until the Greek and versional traditions were established. Yet it is difficult to suppose that the use of *r'š* would so easily mislead a scribe well acquainted with the Hebrew idiomatic usage of *klb*.

12. So John Bright, *A History of Israel*[2] (Philadelphia: Westminster Press, 1972), p. 192. This view was suggested long ago by W. Robertson Smith, *Kinship and Marriage in Early Arabia* (first published 1885; reprinted with additional notes by the author and Ignaz Goldziher, ed. by Stanley A. Cook; London: Adam & Charles Black, 1903), p. 110.

13. Glueck, pp. 50-51.

of Saul's army, and although the emphasis here is on the political relationship the ties were perhaps strengthened in that he was a relative of Saul as well.[14]

Abner goes on to take an oath that he will act in accordance with God's word to David that he will wrest the kingdom away from Saul's household and establish David as king over both Israel and Judah. Commentators in the strict literary critical tradition have been concerned that no earlier prophecy to this effect could have been known to Abner. The anointing by Samuel (I Sam. 16:1-13) is supposedly secret and further is from a different source ("early," as opposed to the present passage which is in the "late" source).[15] The problem cannot be solved, but as Hertzberg suggests, there is no real need to find a specific antecedent event. Abner's reference may best be understood as reflective of the author's predisposition in setting down the narrative. God has planned that David will achieve ascendancy over all Israel, and this is coming to pass.[16]

There is an additional difficulty in making historical sense of the passage. If Abner's taking of the concubine[17] was intended as a political action, his plan does not seem very coherent. Why should he make a move to assume power and then at once (just because of Ishbaal's remark) turn around and offer to make a covenant whereby David would rule over the entire territory? To achieve this objective he needed only to give

---

14. I Sam. 14:50. Whether Abner was Saul's cousin (so Josephus, *Antiquities* VI.vi.6) or his uncle cannot be determined from this verse alone. Each possibility requires some emendation of texts, but the latter choice is less complicated.

15. E.g. Caird, *Samuel*, p. 1058. He appears to follow Pfeiffer's attempt to solve the problem by "omitting" vss. 9-10 and 18b.

16. Hans Wilhelm Hertzberg, *I & II Samuel: A Commentary* (OTL; tr. by J. S. Bowden from 2d rev. German ed., 1960; Philadelphia: Westminster Press, 1964), p. 258.

17. Reading with the Lucianic Greek and regarding MT and Egyptian as haplographic in vs. 7, it is stated quite explicitly that he did so.

Ishbaal over to David. And even if his visit to the concubine was a personal matter, his oath to go over to David certainly seems to be an overreaction to Ishbaal's accusation. One suspects that in order to move his story along the narrator has brought together events which may not have been in a cause-effect sequence. The lack of any specific antecedent for Yahweh's promise to David further confirms this interpretation.

The content of *ḥesed* in Abner's reply is difficult to assess, both because it consists in *not* doing something (rather than in a particular positive action) and also because in his anger Abner elects to abandon his doing of *ḥesed*. Nevertheless certain features of the situation can be delineated with some confidence. Here again the implicit relationship appears to be the basis for Abner's not giving Ishbaal over to David. Since the *ḥesed* is with Saul's household, to *his* brothers and *his* friends, it is quite possibly based in Abner's relationship to Saul, who is already dead. Abner alone has the power to maintain Ishbaal's position, against increasingly difficult odds (cf. 3:17); and once Abner decides to give the kingdom to David, Ishbaal can do nothing. Thus from two different perspectives Abner is acting from a position of freedom. Saul is no longer living to witness the action, and Ishbaal is wholly dependent upon Abner. Thus even though Ishbaal is "king," Abner as subject is the person who really holds the power in this particular situation. If Abner is speaking truthfully, his use of *ḥesed* suggests that it is his moral responsibility involved in his relation to Saul (rather than his own desire for kingship) which has motivated his support of Ishbaal, so that the affair with the concubine should rightly be understood as a personal matter. Furthermore, Abner's continued support of Ishbaal as the Saulides were growing weaker can scarcely have been politically expedient. It could certainly be disadvantageous to be the most powerful man on the losing side - hence, practically speaking, his decision to sue David for peace. Yet for the narrator Abner's inexpedient support of Ishbaal (his *ḥesed*) was important enough that its abandonment is given an unlikely explanation rather than none at all.

In dealing with this text, one is tempted to regard *ḥesed* as an abstract quality because *ḥesed* persists over a period of time. But despite the negative form of the text the *ḥesed* may be described positively as whatever ongoing political and military maneuvers were necessary to the maintaining of Ishbaal. An attitude is inevitably involved, but the focus of the *ḥesed* is in the concrete action which Abner has taken on Ishbaal's behalf.

II Samuel 16:17

> And Absalom said to Hushai, "Is this your *ḥesed* with your friend? Why didn't you go with your friend?"

When Absalom attempted to take the throne, David fled from Jerusalem. His "friend" (15:37: a royal official)[18] Hushai attempts to accompany him, but David asks him to return to the city and, feigning allegiance to Absalom, to serve in a counterespionage function. Hushai acclaims Absalom and receives a stinging reply in return. Absalom plays on the title "friend," reversing its usage and implying that Hushai above all should have gone with the fleeing monarch. He perceives Hushai's abandoning of David as the failure to do *ḥesed*. Yet by this ingenious turn of phrase the narrator of course suggests to the reader that Hushai's action is in fact his *ḥesed* for David. David's life depends upon Hushai's act of *ḥesed*. Hushai is doing just what David requested of him, although David could not have required it of him.

Although the example of *ḥesed* appears in its negative form, the salient characteristics of the situation are still clear. The basis for Absalom's expectation that *ḥesed* should have been performed lies in the implicit personal relationship between David and Hushai, in this case the close political relationship of king and high-ranking member of government. The inability of the fleeing king to exercise any control over Hushai's action is also apparent from the circumstances. From Absalom's viewpoint, Hushai has elected not to help David; and with

---

18. The term *rēʿeh hammelek* appears as an official title in the Solomonic list of I Kings 4:5. On the identification of the office, see Roland de Vaux, *Ancient Israel: Its Life and Institutions* (New York: McGraw-Hill Book Company, Inc., 1961), pp. 122-123.

Absalom's victory, David will have no recourse even if he survives. From the advice given to Absalom (ch. 17) it is quite clear that there is no intention of letting David live. The lack of any other significant source of help for David is implicit in Hushai's high position. No one else would be respected enough to have any chance of being heard over against Ahitophel. David in flight from Jerusalem could do nothing if Hushai, circumstantially free to do as he pleased, failed to meet his moral responsibility to help the king in need.

Ḥesed weʾĕmet

In the next text for consideration we first encounter the phrase *ḥesed weʾĕmet*. The translation adopted for this compound may best be discussed before the text is introduced. This expression occurs in fifteen instances.[19] In addition, slight modifications of the *ḥesed weʾĕmet* form by the addition of prepositions or suffixes appear in another six cases.[20] The distribution of the phrase clusters in early narrative sources and in Psalms and Proverbs. Obviously the paired usage was well established both for everyday speech and for liturgical contexts, and this very fact makes it difficult to determine what nuance, if any, the addition of *weʾĕmet* placed upon the term *ḥesed*. No pattern for the use of the phrase rather than the single word is apparent in the narrative materials. The phrase appears both in secular usage and with God as subject. With God as subject it appears in both liturgical (Ex. 34:6) and narrative (II Sam. 2:6; 15:20) materials. Conceivably the Elohistic narrative source and the sources for the Deuteronomic history reserved the use of the phrase for God's actions. It is true that in the Samuel narrative the compound appears in each of the two texts which have God as subject (II Sam. 2:6; 15:20) and that *ḥesed* appears alone in all other cases. But for the Elohist we have no examples of narrative usage with God as subject, so that here the argument is strictly from silence

---

19. Gen. 24:49; 47:29; Ex. 34:6; Jos. 2:14; II.Sam. 2:6; 15:20; Ps. 25:10; 61:8; 85:11; 86:15; 89:15; Prv. 3:3; 14:22; 16:6; 20:28.

20. Gen. 24:27; Ps. 40:11,12; 57:4; 115:1; 138:2. Cf. also Gen. 32:11.

and can bear little weight.[21] And the J usage is not consistent: two of three secular uses are compound; two of five uses with God as subject are compound. There are no apparent circumstances peculiar to the situations in which the single or compound expressions are used. Thus it seems probable that the compound usage involves some optional nuancing or emphasis.

A survey of the passages from these same sources in which *ʾĕmet* appears independently can give some indication of the direction of this nuancing. In the immediate context of the passage next to be considered Abraham's servant speaks of Yahweh "who led me *b^e derek ʾĕmet* to take the daughter of my lord's brother for his son." (Gen. 24:48) The meaning is probably both literal and figurative; hence, "by the direct path" (Speiser) or "by the right way" (RSV) or "along a reliable course."

In Ex. 18:21 Moses is instructed to choose men to help him by adjudicating the less difficult cases. They are to be bribe-haters, God-fearers, and also *ʾanšê ʾĕmet*, men who are "trustworthy" (RSV) or "reliable."

In Gen. 42:16 Joseph announces his decision to hold all his brothers in prison except one who would return for Benjamin: "Thus shall your words be tested, (as to) whether there is *ʾĕmet ʾitt^e kem*." On the overt level the meaning is clearly "whether you are truthful" (cf. use of the verbal form, vs. 22). The truthfulness is to be counted as a sign that they are not spies. But Joseph already knows that the story is true, and he alone knows that he will know immediately whether the person brought to him is really the brother or not. Thus the real test he sets is concerned for his brothers' trustworthiness; and the narrator uses the test to show the transformation which takes place in the brothers. Reuben comments on their guilt concerning Joseph (vs. 22) and they proceed immediately to fetch Benjamin without any thought of another deception.

Finally, in Jotham's parable the bramble says, "if *beʾĕmet* you are anointing me...." (Judges 9:15). Jotham reuses the phrase as the basis for his indictment of the Shechemites: "if

---

21. It should also be noted that the liturgical formula in the decalogue (Ex. 20:6 = Dt. 5:10) uses simply *ḥesed*.

you acted *b'mt wbtmym* when you made Abimelech king...if you acted *b'mt wbtmym* with Jerubbaal..." (vss. 16, 19). Once again the connotations are of action "in good faith" (RSV), trustworthiness, honesty, reliability.[22]

Although none of these passages uses *'ĕmet* in a construction precisely like that of the compound with *ḥesed*, the examples do make clear that the sureness, certainty, or trustworthiness of a specific act or ongoing behavior is the central content of *'ĕmet*. In its use with *ḥesed*, then, *'ĕmet* should be understood as an optional emphasis on the concern (in the case of a request) or assurance (in the case of a statement) that the *ḥesed* will be done despite the lack of control over the act which is inherent in the very use of the term *ḥesed*. When the compound usage appears with a verb the nuance can best be translated "be sure to do *ḥesed*." In a non-verbal construction, the meaning is "sure *ḥesed*," that which can be relied upon or counted upon.[23]

Genesis 24:49

> And now, if you are definitely (surely) going to do *ḥesed* with my lord, tell me; and if not, tell me, that I may know how to proceed. (lit: that I may turn to the right or to the left)

Abraham's servant, commissioned to find a wife for Isaac from among Abraham's own kin, has been taken into the home of Bethuel and Laban in the far distant homeland. He reports his mission and explains the sign which he asked of Yahweh by which he knew that Rebekah should be selected as the bride. He has

---

22. We shall have occasion to return to this text in connection with the discussion of *ḥesed* in Judges 8:35 (see below, p. 57).

23. Note that this interpretation differs from the usual suggestion of "constancy," which in English generally connotes continuance over a period of time. The emphasis in these texts cannot be in this direction, since each example involves a once-for-all action. Where the concern is for an ongoing series of actions, "reliable" may be used with the nuance of constancy (continuous and continual). See, for example, Gen. 32:10-12 and especially Gen. 24:27, discussed in Chapter III.

asked Yahweh to do *ḥesed* for Abraham by prospering his mission,[24] now he asks the kinsmen to do *ḥesed* for his master by letting him take the girl. The reply is promptly given: "The matter is from Yahweh; it is not for us to approve or disapprove.

In this beautifully constructed and presented narrative from the Yahwistic source, it is striking that throughout all the servant's mission the focus remains on Abraham and his need for a suitable daughter-in-law. The point is made subtly but clearly by the servant's repeated use of "Yahweh, God of my master Abraham" and by the consistent understanding that *ḥesed* (both divine and human) is to be done for Abraham, not for the servant.

The request that Laban let Rebekah go is a request for *ḥesed* based in the relationship of kinship: thus the *ḥesed* is for Abraham, not for the servant who has no connection with Laban except through Abraham. Although kinship is quite explicit in the narrative, since it is the whole reason for the long journey, it nevertheless remains implicit in the request for *ḥesed*. No basis for the request is actually stated. The *ḥesed* is appropriately for Abraham in other ways as well. The servant has nothing to lose if Laban refuses the request; he is simply freed from his oath (24:41). For Abraham, however, the request involves the essential features of the possibility for fulfillment of the destiny which God has promised him. Isaac must stay in Canaan (because the promise was tied to the land), yet he should have a wife from the homeland.[25] Of course neither Abraham nor his servant will be in a position to take action if the prospective bride is not allowed to travel to Canaan. The possibility that this mission is Abraham's last opportunity to make the appropriate arrangements for Isaac further highlights this lack of alternative in the event of

---

24. See discussion of theological usage in Chapter III, pp. 102-104.

25. See in this connection the suggestion of Speiser (*Genesis*, p. 94, cf. p. 183) that the purity of the wife's background was important for the theological function of the biblical genealogies.

failure. The opening of the narrative suggests that Abraham may not live until the servant returns, and the obscure circumstances of the arrival back in Canaan (with no mention of Abraham) also suggest that at one stage in the history of the narrative Abraham may have died before the return.[26]

In review, the request of *ḥesed* is based in the implicit kinship relationship. In this instance the life of the individual in need is not at issue. The need is still essential, however, from Abraham's viewpoint (and from the theological perspective of the narrator). There can be no external compulsion of Laban's response, either by Abraham personally or (apparently) by the legal structure, and there is seemingly no possibility for an alternate source of assistance.

Genesis 47:29

> The time of Israel's death grew near, and he summoned his son Joseph and said to him, "If you really wish to please me[27] place your hand under my thigh, and you shall be sure to do *ḥesed* with me: do not bury me in Egypt; when I lie with my fathers you shall carry me out of Egypt and bury me in their burial place."

As Jacob is about to die he makes provision for his remains to be removed to the land of promise. In its own way this narrative emphasizes the importance of the tie of the patriarchal

---

26. Gerhard von Rad, *Genesis: A Commentary* (OTL; tr. by John H. Marks from the 1956 German ed.; Philadelphia: Westminster, 1961), pp. 249, 254; Speiser, *Genesis*, p. 185. The oath sworn with the hand under the thigh occurs in only one other passage, Gen. 24 (J), where it is clearly associated with a deathbed request (see below, p. 38). Since independent confirmatory evidence is lacking, the use of this congruence as an additional support for a deathbed interpretation of Abraham's action (Speiser, *Genesis*, p. 183, cf. Otto Procksch, *Die Genesis übersetzt und erklärt*[3] [KAT I; Leipzig: A. Deichertsche Verlagsbuchhandlung, 1924], p. 268) must be regarded as speculative.

27. Adopting Speiser's translation of the Hebrew idiom "if I have found favor in your eyes..." (*Genesis*, p. 354).

promises to the land of Canaan, just as did Abraham's requirement that Isaac remain in Canaan. Joseph is asked to swear that he will fulfill his father's request; the hand under the thigh is associated with the oath. This version of the event is essentially from the hand of J, although some have argued that the detail concerning the burial place of the fathers is a modification towards the P version in 49:29-33 (cf. Gen. 23, the narrative from P of the purchase of the Cave at Machpelah).[28] Whether the text has been changed slightly is immaterial for our discussion, since both the J and the P traditions draw attention to the importance of the patriarchal association with Canaan. Indeed, this theme is reduplicated with the tradition of the carrying to Canaan of Joseph's remains as well (Ex. 13:19; cf. Jos. 24:32).

Jacob's deathbed request is one which by its very nature he could not accomplish for himself and could not control whether or not it was ever done, since it is absolutely clear that the recipient will first be dead. In the case of Abraham, by contrast, prior death was possible and perhaps likely, yet not fully certain. The implicit basis for Jacob's request is the father-son relationship. The phrase "if you are really pleased with me" serves only as a polite form; it should not be understood as the basis either for the request or for Joseph's affirmative response. One may wonder why Joseph was selected. Although nothing is said directly, it seems apparent that Joseph as the main power holder among the brothers is the son most likely (if not uniquely) to be able to fulfill the request. The great concern which the Egyptians show over Jacob's death (mummification, mourning, accompanying the burial party to Canaan) is best attributed to Jacob's position as father of

---

28. So John Skinner, *A Critical and Exegetical Commentary on Genesis*^{2} (ICC; Edinburgh: T. & T. Clark, 1930), p. 503. Apparently the argument is that "their burial place" is not consistent with J's "my grave which I dug for myself" in 50:5 and the accompanying narrative of the mourning at Atad. The absence of any reference to the relatives in the J burial narrative may support this suggestion; but it is impossible to establish certainty about such a minor detail.

Joseph who was second only to Pharaoh. The Egyptians would expect Joseph to take charge of the funeral arrangements. Joseph was not only the most likely candidate for the request; once the request was agreed to he was the only hope for its fulfillment. Presumably no one else knew of the request, so that Joseph had only to do nothing and the matter would remain forever unknown. Thus Joseph's act of *ḥesed* once again displays the characteristics we have seen in the previous examples: a personal (here familial) relationship as the implicit basis for an action which only a particular person can readily perform and whose performance the person requesting the action cannot compel.

In this case, however, we have an added feature: the oath. This oath, exacted of Joseph in connection with the request for *ḥesed*, has been problematic for past interpreters. Glueck admits that, according to his understanding of *ḥesed*, "no special oath should have been necessary....It was the only possible conduct of a son toward his father, since father and son are both of the same flesh and blood."[29] Hills regards the oath as optional and describes it as "an additional element desirable as reinforcing a simple promise."[30] If *ḥesed* is to be understood as an act which the recipient has no power to attempt to compel, the importance of reinforcement through what may be called "divine control" in the form of an oath becomes apparent. The type of circumstances in which an oath is required is by no means fully consistent. Nevertheless, with respect to the question of control the oath situations do fall roughly into two groups. Although the majority of these texts have not yet been discussed, they should be anticipated briefly at this juncture. The present text is the best example of the first type of situation, namely one in which the *ḥesed* is to be performed or completed after the death of the person making the request.

The second example of this usage is in connection with the formally similar oath which Abraham required of his servant in the passage discussed just above. It will be recalled at once

---

29. Glueck, p. 5.

30. "*Ḥesed* of Man," p. 6.

that Abraham did not use the term *ḥesed* in connection with his request so this example might simply be omitted. Yet the overall narrative makes clear that *ḥesed* is involved from the servant's point of view. Rebekah's family is to do *ḥesed* with Abraham, God is to do *ḥesed* with Abraham, and the servant is the agent by which all this can take place. The point here is that an oath is exacted in a situation where it is possible that Abraham will no longer be alive when the act is performed. The action involves someone else, but the person making the request may be dead.

The third instance of this type involves the last section of the famed conversation between David and Jonathan in I Sam. 20. The text of the chapter is extraordinarily difficult; but if we may follow the Masoretic pointing of vs. 17, then it is Jonathan who asks David to swear that he will do *ḥesed* with Jonathan's household if Jonathan dies.[31] Although David is also requested to do *ḥesed* with Jonathan if he lives, the oath may perhaps be especially associated with the possibility of Jonathan's death.

The second circumstance in which an oath is requested is essentially the request for *ḥesed* where there is relatively little assurance that the request will be complied with. The two cases are that of Rahab and the spies (Jos. 2:12-14) and that of Abraham and Abimelech (Gen. 21:23). Perhaps more important is the fact that the *ḥesed* requested is to extend into or be done in the future. In this respect these situations are parallel to the three already outlined. In other instances in which *ḥesed* is requested, the action is presumably to take place at once, so that the action itself is immediate confirmation of the person's intent to comply with the request.

---

31. The promise in the event of Jonathan's death must be textually reconstructed. See below, p. 85, where the textual problems are discussed in detail. The LXX reads the unpointed Hebrew of vs. 17 "And Jonathan swore again," which is also textually possible. In this case, Jonathan's oath would repeat his oath of vs. 13; the passage then would be less germane to the question of when an oath may be added to a request for *ḥesed*, since the oath would be not requested but offered.

It is only when the action is to be delayed that an oath is requested as well.[32] Thus although the reinforcement by oath perhaps ought not to be necessary (because of an existing relationship) and although it may be optional, there are nevertheless particular circumstances in which it is especially likely to be used. These can be humanly understood as occasions of future uncertainty.

It may also be noted that each of the three instances of secular usage of the phrase *ḥesed we'ĕmet* in the early narrative is found in association with one of the five oath passages. In Gen. 24:49, as has already been indicated, the connection is only indirect as the servant relays his commission to Laban. In Gen. 47:29 and Jos. 2:14, the usage is quite straightforward. Since the phrase becomes standardized, one hesitates to generalize from such a small number of examples. Still, the nuance of "be sure to do..." would appear to receive further confirmation from the association with the oath context.

II Samuel 2:5

> And David sent messengers to the men of Jabesh Gilead and said to them, "May you be blessed by Yahweh because you have done this *ḥesed* with your lord, with Saul, in burying him."

The translation essentially follows the MT. Sorting of the Greek traditions is difficult: B is missing and the other Old Greek exemplars appear to follow readings of the Byzantine and Catena text types. The cx minuscules for the hexaplaric type appear to have suffered internal corruption in the first

---

32. The oath nevertheless is not recorded in every case in which future *ḥesed* is requested. One exception is Gen. 40:14, in which the butler would presumably fulfill Joseph's request three days later, yet Joseph does not ask him to swear. The second is I Kings 2:7 in which David asks Solomon to do *ḥesed* with the sons of Barzillai. Either the oath was optional or else it was not included in the narrative. It is of interest that the butler forgets Joseph for a long time and that we are never told anything of what happens to the sons of Barzillai, but the silence of the text cannot fairly be used to support the interpretation.

part of the verse. The Greek pluses "anointed of the Lord" (cf. 1:14) and "and Jonathan his son" (cf. 21:12) are clearly expansionistic. It is possible that *ḥsd ʾlhym* (cf. 9:3) and *hḥsd hzh* were variants which became conflated in the Greek tradition. Probably *hḥsd hzh* was the original reading and *ʾlhym* intruded under the influence of *ʾlyhm* earlier in the line. The Greek ἡγουμένος found in slightly variant forms throughout the traditions is not a regular representation of the Hebrew *ʾnšy* and calls to mind the Hebrew *bʿly ybyš glʿd* of 21:12[33] which refers to this same event. If *bʿly* were the original reading in 2:5, the *ʾnšy* of the Hebrew could be readily explained by its appearance in vs. 4b. However, in 21:12 the Greek reads τῶν ἀνδρῶν for *bʿly*, just where one would expect ἡγουμένος or a synonym. Probably we are dealing with a series of assimilations and partial corrections in more than one tradition, but the evidence does not permit a definitive conclusion.

In this verse, as in Gen. 47:29, the content of the *ḥesed*-action is proper burial, an act which obviously must be carried out by another individual or group. In the use of the term *ḥesed* it is made clear that it was a matter of great importance that Saul be properly buried. Obviously, Saul himself had no recourse in the matter, and under the circumstances it would have been just as easy, even easier, to have left his remains in enemy hands. The relationship "your lord" is mentioned; but since it is not cited as the reason for the action the political relationship is properly regarded as "implicit" with respect to the action. It is true that Saul had performed a specific act of deliverance for the city of Jabesh-Gilead in rescuing them from the threat of Nahash and his Ammonite force (I Sam. 11). Hence it is particularly appropriate that the men of that city should have rescued Saul's corpse from Beth-shan. However, as we shall see in section B of this chapter, *ḥesed* is usually based on a prior action only when the character of the relationship between the persons cannot in itself provide a strong enough basis for the assuming of responsibility. Then a

---

33. Cf. S. R. Driver, *Notes on the Hebrew Text of the Books of Samuel* (Oxford: Clarendon Press, 1890), p. 185.

prior act is cited as the more immediate basis of the moral obligation which should/does issue in a *ḥesed* act. In this case, by contrast, the personal character of the ongoing political relationship is the important feature.

In this instance we cannot know historically whether other groups in political relationship with Saul were in a position to have retrieved his body. The tradition of I Sam. 31:6-7 suggests that Israel on both sides of the Jordan was routed with the collapse of Saul's army. Since the stealing of the bodies was clearly a difficult and risky task, whoever of Saul's friends was able and willing to do it might have been recognized as doing an act of *ḥesed* for him.

Ruth 3:10

> And [Boaz] said, "May you be blessed by Yahweh, my daughter. You have made your latter act of *ḥesed* better than the former, in that you have not gone after (the) young men, whether poor or rich."

The example of *ḥesed* in Ruth is included here because the usage has its clearest affinities with pre-exilic narrative rather than with the Chronicler (see Chapter IV), whatever date may be assigned to the present form of the book of Ruth itself.[34] Glueck noted the affinity to earlier sources in the sense of conduct "in accord with familial duties." He regarded the usage, however, as "a development beyond the ordinary use of the term in the older sources, since *ḥesed* in Ruth is more deliberate, subjectively willed, and not simply an attitude of obligation."[35] But what Glueck sees as a new development is essentially that combination of responsibility and freedom

---

34. The long and continuing debate over the date and purpose of the book need not be catalogued here. The introductions to recent commentaries give an indication of the division of opinion and arguments for various positions. See for example, John Gray, *Joshua, Judges, and Ruth* (CB; London: Thomas Nelson and Sons Ltd., 1967), pp. 398-402; W. Rudolph, *Das Buch Ruth, Das Hohe Lied, Die Klagelieder* (KAT XVII 1-3; Gütersloh: Gütersloher Verlagshaus Gerd Mohn, 1962), pp. 26-29.

35. Glueck, p. 6.

which is here suggested to apply to all the examples of pre-exilic secular usage.

Ruth's "former" *ḥesed* from Boaz' viewpoint is presumably expressed in 2:11, where he tells her that he has been informed of how she left her parents and native country. This he summarizes as "what you have done *(ʿśh)* with *(ʾt)* your mother-in-law after the death of your husband." Thus it appears that Ruth's first act was one of comfort and support for Naomi. Her second act is on behalf of her dead husband, for in offering herself to Boaz Ruth is opting for fulfillment of the law of levirate. While this was understood in terms of a legal obligation for the male relative, the suggestion by the woman herself does not appear to be treated as a legal obligation. Ruth was acting on the basis of her personal relationship to her husband who after death had no recourse in the survival of his name.[36] It is evident that neither of her actions was required: Naomi dismissed both daughters-in-law with a blessing, and Orpah's departure is understood as the natural course of events.[37] A foreigner was not expected to go to great lengths to carry on the husband's name. In both instances Ruth's action was based in the moral obligation of familial relationships. In both instances, she was free not to fulfill the responsibility while at the same time being uniquely in the position to do so. In the first instance, her position as the unique source of comfort and help for the aging Naomi is heightened by the departure of Orpah. And in the latter action, of course, the widow alone can bear a son to carry the husband's name.[38]

---

36. For *ḥesed* done for a person already dead, cf. Gen. 47:29; possibly Gen. 24:49 (see discussion of passage); II Sam. 2:5; 9:1,3,7.

37. On the use of *ḥesed* at the departure, see Chapter III, pp. 108ff.

38. The importance of the survival of the family line and an example of a very different act of *ḥesed* to achieve this same objective is found in the texts relating to David and Jonathan discussed in section C of this Chapter.

Summary of Section A

From the examination of seven texts in which an act of *ḥesed* may be described as based implicitly in a personal relationship between the parties involved, four characteristics of the particular situations for which the word *ḥesed* is appropriate stand out. First, the individual making the request cannot do what is needed for himself. There is no single reason for this inability; it may involve old age, death, human frailty, or political exigencies, but in every case this factor is present. To do something for someone which he could just as well do himself is not an act of *ḥesed*.

Second, the assistance requested is completely necessary. The person in need will die without it, or his line of descendants will be cut off, or his association with his homeland will be cut off. The last two items were perhaps more important for ancient man than for twentieth century thought, but their full significance even in the biblical context can be seen only in terms of the theological import which the narrators affixed to the situations.[39]

Third, the need is such that one particular person, a person in some intimate relationship to the one in need, is conspicuously, even uniquely, in a position to fulfill the need. No one else could replace Sarah or Ruth or Abner or Hushai or Laban in their respective roles. An alternate to Joseph was conceivable, but no one else could even approach his qualifications for performing the task.

Fourth, the circumstances are such that the person in need can have no control over the response of the person of whom assistance is asked. He cannot personally compel the desired response; and if he is turned down he either cannot (in the nature of the request) or will not be able (because of circumstances) to appeal within the structure of formal law or customary law. In several instances he will die if help is not

---

39. In his outline of characteristics of *ḥesed*, Hills had combined these first two features: "*Ḥesed* denotes essential and often indispensable assistance, not extra privilege." ("*Ḥesed* of Man," p. 3) The need is crucial and the person cannot fulfill it himself.

received. In the case of Abraham and Laban the person making the request is absent and the go-between is freed from obligation if the request is refused. Additionally, Abraham may die before he knows the outcome of the mission; but the key issue is his lack of control over Laban, not over the outcome in general. In yet another instance (Jacob and Joseph) the person requesting *ḥesed* must be dead before the act can be performed, and so also in the case of Saul the recipient is already dead.

This lack of control, this inability for an act of *ḥesed* to be required or compelled, can correctly be understood as the central feature of all the texts, for it is the product of the three preceding features. If a person cannot act for himself, is in urgent need, and can receive adequate assistance only from one person, then inevitably the person who can help is in full control of the situation. These features are especially clear in this group of texts because every example involves identifiable concrete action. Thus the usage here provides guidelines for the evaluation of subsequent examples for which the narrative framework is lacking.

Finally, it should be reemphasized that all the texts in this section are characterized by an intimate personal relationship between the actor and the recipient of *ḥesed*. That is, the relationships are those which may be described broadly as primary or *gemeinschaftlich* in character sociologically. Admittedly it is hardly a frequent occurrence that a complete stranger would be in a position to help a person; but it is still true that no "good Samaritan" situations are recounted as *ḥesed* in these narratives. The hypothesis that the implicit relationship is an essential feature is strengthened when the remaining texts are examined. In any situation in which there is no implicit relationship or in which it is not an intimate one (i.e. in sociologically secondary or *gesellschaftlich* type relationships), some prior act is understood as the immediate basis for the *ḥesed* action.

B. Ḥesed *Based on Prior Action*

The texts in this group may be divided into two major types: acts of *ḥesed* based on prior acts which are not called *ḥesed*, and acts of *ḥesed* based on prior acts which are called *ḥesed* (either directly or indirectly). In addition, there is a single case in which the action being performed is not referred to as *ḥesed* directly; only its antecedent action is called *ḥesed* (I Sam. 15:6). While the prior existence of implicit relationships can be identified in many (but not all) of these texts, some specific action is regarded as the more immediate basis of the *ḥesed* performed. This reference to prior action occurs when a relationship does not yet exist or when the existing relationship is not intimate, that is, when the persons involved are in a neutral or even potentially hostile stance within their relationship.

1. *Ḥesed* Based on a Prior Act not Called *Ḥesed*

Genesis 40:14

> Only remember me, the one who was with you, when it is well with you, and do *ḥesed* with me; call me to the attention of Pharaoh and get me out of this house.

Joseph completes his interpretation of the Cup-bearer's dream and without pause goes on to ask him to intercede with Pharaoh for his fellow-prisoner's release. The syntax of the opening phrase is difficult, since *ky ʾm* normally opens the apodosis clause but here is used uniquely in the protasis. Genesius-Kautzsch suggests that a protasis be supplied from context, such as "I desire nothing else...."[40] Speiser translates, "So if you still remember...please do me the kindness..." and comments, "This is an intricately construed sentence but it yields good Hebrew and excellent sense."[41] Although this construction does make the best sense out of the verse without assuming any unexpressed phrase, the interpretation of the usage still appears to be *ad hoc*.

Aside from grammatical problems, the verse presents difficulties in the understanding of *ḥesed* itself. Some aspects of

---

40. G. K. Par, 163d.

41. Speiser, *Genesis*, p. 307. He attributes this interpretation to Ernst L. Ehrlich, *Der Traum im Alten Testament* (Beiheft zur *ZAW* 73; Berlin: Alfred Töpelmann, 1953), but the writer is unable to find a discussion of the grammatical point in Ehrlich's work.

the usage are clear enough. Joseph is asking for help in attaining his freedom. He cannot speak to Pharaoh himself; the Cup-bearer will be in a unique position to bring Joseph's case to Pharaoh's attention; held in prison Joseph has no recourse if the Cup-bearer does not comply. But what is the basis for his request? The text is here classified as a request for *ḥesed* based on another action not called *ḥesed*, namely, the interpretation of the dream. Presumably the two did not have a pre-existing intimate personal relationship. Rather, Joseph's good deed established a bond between the two men, created a relationship within which Joseph could ask for *ḥesed*.

The nature of the bond is difficult to assess. Ehrlich suggests that the person receiving a dream interpretation was normally required to pay, and that Joseph asks for this help in lieu of cash.[42] Such an arrangement would suggest legal obligation rather than moral responsibility on the part of the Cup-bearer, except that the agreement (even if made in advance)[43] probably could not be enforced in a court of law. Whether or not recompense was normally required, Joseph did perform a real service for the Cup-bearer. It is not so much that he "interpreted the dream propitiously,"[44] (although he did so) as that he provided the interpretation. Oppenheim has shown that in the ancient Near East dreams believed to have some meaning were

---

42. Ehrlich, *Traum*, p. 69 and n.3. There are no biblical examples of paying for interpretations.

43. The agreement at best could only be made after the Cup-bearer told his dream, for only then would Joseph have known of the man's imminent release. Since the Cup-bearer would not have cash in any case, it seems best to regard Joseph's action as a freely performed good deed. From the narrator's viewpoint, the particular basis of the request for *ḥesed* is of little concern. His interest is that someone who knows of Joseph's ability should be present when Pharaoh needs an interpreter. The request merely adds suspense - and the Cup-bearer must not remember Joseph right away or else Joseph would no longer be readily available when Pharaoh's dreams begin.

44. Against Glueck, p. 20.

regarded as dangerous so long as they remained enigmatic.[45] Thus the telling of a dream serves a "cathartic" function and the interpreting is "therapeutic" in purpose.[46] The interpreting of the symbolic dream did not affect the coming to pass of the event; nevertheless, one could not ignore such a dream with the thought that "what will be will be." In his willingness to be of service to the two officials, Joseph discovered a possible avenue for help for himself.

The sequel to the story confirms that the Cup-bearer did in fact have some obligation because of the prior event. Two years go by. When Pharaoh's wise men fail to interpret his dreams, the Cup-bearer prefaces his story about Joseph with the remark, "I remember my faults *(ḥṭ'y)* today" (41:9). Clearly the narrator regarded the act of *ḥesed* as something the Cup-bearer ought to have done.

Judges 1:24

> And those lying in wait (keeping watch) saw a man going out from the city. And they said to him, "Show us how to enter the city and we will do *ḥesed* with you."

The Greek and versions are unanimous in the insertion of καὶ ἔλαβον αὐτόν ("and they seized him") between the watchers' seeing the man and speaking to him. The plus presumably serves to make clear what is implicit in the Hebrew narrative. Yet it is strange that there are no revisions toward the shorter text.

Albright has proposed that Judges 1:22-26 is probably an old fragment of an account of the capture of Bethel preserved from before the time the tradition was transferred from Bethel to Ai.[47] If the all-Israel tradition of the capture recorded

---

45. A. Leo Oppenheim, *The Interpretation of Dreams in the Ancient Near East* (Philadelphia: The American Philosophical Society, 1956), p. 219.

46. *Ibid.*, p. 220.

47. The two locations are only about a half mile apart, and archaeology has shown that Bethel was destroyed ca. 1250, whereas Ai was not even occupied during the period of the Conquest. The explanation accounts for the difficulty of the elaborate narrative about Ai in Jos. 7-8. See W. F. Albright,

in Joshua 7-8 is correct, then the attribution here to the house of Joseph can be regarded as an editorial adjustment by a compiler who believed that everything done under Joshua was already included in what is now our book of Joshua. The house of Joseph was the appropriate choice, since Bethel was located in Ephraim.[48]

The Israelites on watch around the city offer an unidentified man *ḥesed*. He is to tell them how to get into the city. He gives them the information; the city is razed and its inhabitants put to the sword, but the man and his family are spared.

For Glueck this passage provided a key example of *ḥesed* as mutual aid. The person who received help became obligated to act toward his helper "as toward a blood relative or ally"; the man who gave the information was considered as a member of their [Israelite] group and thus received appropriate reciprocal treatment.[49] For Hills, the passage was problematic, as a principal exception to his description of *ḥesed* as "unilateral assistance...granted without compensation or condition, not a mutual exchange."[50]

The dual qualities here proposed as essential to *ḥesed*, recognized obligation coupled with absence of external controls, can accommodate important features of both Hills' and Glueck's analyses in the understanding of this passage. It should be observed at the outset that this text is the first example in which *ḥesed* has been *offered* rather than requested. It is inevitable that this less common situation nuances the usage somewhat.

First of all, *ḥesed* here is being offered conditionally. But *ḥesed* is regularly an act which has a basis either in an implicit relationship or in a prior act. Here the prior act has not yet taken place. *Ḥesed* is not usually a mutual *(quid*

"The Israelite Conquest of Canaan in the Light of Archaeology," *BASOR* 74 (1939) 74-76.

48. G. E. Wright, "The Literary and Historical Problem of Joshua 10 and Judges 1," *JNES* 5 (1946) 108.

49. Glueck, pp. 18-19.

50. "*Ḥesed* of Man," p. 2.

pro quo) exchange, but it is usually dependent on something prior.

Second, and equally important, the offer of *ḥesed* in this situation is much more than a casual offer to spare the man whom we may imagine under interrogation. The man might well suppose he would be killed as soon as he parted with the desired information. But the very use of the word *ḥesed* by his captors[51] entails their assurance that although they do control the situation completely they will not kill him once he answers their question. The exchange is "mutual" in that both parties do gain something. Yet it is not mutual in that at the moment the relative position of the two parties is completely unbalanced. Once the man tells the spies how to enter the city, the sparing of his life does become a unilateral act on their part.

Viewed from this perspective, the situation does not involve "mutual exchange" and does not countermand that aspect of Hills' description of *ḥesed* quoted above. But *ḥesed*, we are attempting to show, is never without some sort of "basis" (i.e. it is not done outside of a relationship of responsibility) and the "condition" or "compensation" which puzzles Hills must be regarded as the act which establishes that basis. Glueck's approach, on the other hand, does not seem to be sufficiently attuned to the practical reality of the situation. He seems to imply that rendering help would automatically produce a mutual relationship with full legal obligation of both parties. But in actual life there must have been many instances when this did not take place, especially when the one party so clearly held the upper hand. Glueck overlooks the importance of the unevenness in the situation. The offering of *ḥesed* is not so much an assurance that the man will be regarded as an Israelite as it is an assurance that the attackers who hold the upper hand will keep their word.[52]

---

51. Assuming the LXX interpretation of the circumstances as correct.

52. It must be granted that the captors do not spell out their doing of *ḥesed* in the direct quotation attributed to them. But *ḥesed* where it is specified is regularly associated with a particular action. Thus it is not necessary to assume the

I Kings 20:31

> And his [Ben-hadad's] servants said to him, "Since we have heard that the Israelite kings are kings of *ḥesed*, let us put sackcloth on our loins and ropes on our heads and let us go (out) to the king of Israel: perhaps he will spare your life."

The Old Greek (B, boc_2e_2) here preserves an ancient variant in which Ben-hadad addresses his servants rather than vice versa: "And he said to his servants, 'I have heard....'" Such a variant could easily emerge with a single careless scribe, since Ben-hadad is the subject of the previous sentence. The only major orthographic change is from *šmʿnw* to *smʿty*; and this could easily have been a secondary scribal change. The MT reading is probably superior because the sense flows better into the 3d pl. usage of vs. 32. This passage probably comes from a source used by the Deuteronomic historian, although it is impossible to be certain that the particular phrasing is not his.

The construction found here is different from that of any other passage considered in this chapter.[53] The general intent is evidently "kings who do *ḥesed*," but the use of the phrase *malkê ḥesed* divorces the word from a direct connection with any particular aspect of the subsequent encounter between Ahab and Ben-hadad.[54] We must ask, then, how the narrator intends us to understand the Aramaeans' view of the Israelite kings. Are

---

establishment of a relatively permanent relationship as the basis for the particular action. To say that the man is regarded "as a member of their group" is to go beyond the evidence.

53. It is not unique, however; cf. Isa. 57:1: *ʾanšê ḥesed*.

54. The writer tentatively follows the argument of W. F. Albright ("A Votive Stele Erected by Ben-hadad I of Damascus to the God Melcarth," *BASOR* 87 [1942] 23-29) against B. Mazar ("The Aramean Empire and its Relations with Israel," *BA* 25 [1962] 106) and others that this Aramean ruler is Ben-hadad I. That debate, however, does not substantially affect the interpretation of *ḥesed* in the passage and thus need not be detailed here.

they willing to let an enemy go if he submits in due humility? Are they willing to "make a deal"? Are they merciful or are they politically astute? Where does the emphasis lie?

The Arameans' two-stage approach to Ahab suggests that all these factors are involved. The prime concern is to keep Ben-hadad alive, so the servants, dressed in sackcloth and ropes,[55] go to Ahab first. They hear what they apparently regard as a hopeful omen ("he is my brother")[56] and are commanded to bring Ben-hadad. When Ben-hadad arrives, he immediately offers geographic and economic concessions.[57] Ahab agrees to the terms, makes a covenant *(bᵉrît)* with Ben-hadad, and lets him go. Thus in the first scene we see what may be construed as supplication

---

55. Various explanations have been given for the rope on their heads. See John Gray, *I & II Kings: A Commentary* (OTL; Philadelphia: Westminster Press, 1963), p. 382. The answer is not clear, so that this action cannot be used to help determine the understanding of *ḥesed* in the passage.

56. Glueck places a great deal of emphasis on this phrase as Ahab's indication of "his readiness to establish a *ḥesed*-relationship" (p. 18). The expression may also suggest that a covenantal relationship had already existed between these kings before the war began and that Ahab was willing to recognize that fact still. Of this we know nothing historically. Gray (*I & II Kings*, p. 383) has argued for a prior covenant on the basis of the definite article with *bbryt* in vs. 34. However, none of the Greek mss read the article which is of course dependent upon the Masoretic punctators' tradition.

57. He refers to cities which his father took from Ahab's father and to economic concessions given to his father in Samaria. Nothing is known of these events, which are a source of some difficulty for Albright's Ben-hadad I theory. Albright says that the speech is stylized and that Samaria is a "concretizing" reference for the Israelite capital which had till recently been elsewhere; thus he places the events far enough back to accommodate his longer reign for Ben-hadad ("A Votive Stele," p. 27). For our purpose, however, the historical fact is not so important as that the narrator describes the event in these terms.

for mercy, whereas the second scene is apparently characterized by a hardheaded bargain.

This combination expresses in a sequential fashion the features with which we have been describing *ḥesed*. The case is like that of the spies at Bethel in that the party in need does something (here offers concessions) which provides the basis for the act of *ḥesed*. It is noteworthy that he does look for some assurance first, since (unlike the Bethel situation) *ḥesed* has not been offered. Glueck's focus on "he is my brother" is correct.[58] Ben-hadad does not come within range of Ahab until he has some assurance he will not be killed instantly. Ahab agrees that the terms offered do provide an adequate basis for releasing Ben-hadad, and he keeps his word.

Furthermore, Ahab is manifestly in a position of freedom of action. He could have killed Ben-hadad as soon as he appeared or after he had affirmed their treaty. One might argue that such an action would nullify the proposed treaty and therefore that Ahab himself stood to gain something essential and thus was mutually dependent on Ben-hadad.[59] But Ahab was now presumably in a military position to gain economic concessions by force rather than treaty. Hence he did not *have* to rely on Ben-hadad, and this factor makes the crucial difference. *Ḥesed* may be done in enlightened self-interest, but it is still the free granting of assistance (here life and freedom) to one who has no power of compulsion and no other hope for deliverance. Here as elsewhere the *ḥesed* action is onesided; it is

---

58. The writer finds Glueck's frequently repeated term "*ḥesed*-relationship" objectionable, however. That expression suggests that any act appropriate to any human relationship of "rights and duties" could be termed *ḥesed*. The writer would say rather that within human relationships certain specific actions had particular qualities (discussed in the body of the study) which placed them within the category of acts of *ḥesed*. This holds true consistently at least for the pre-exilic secular usage.

59. Unlike the spies at Bethel, who had no more use for their informant once they had gained the necessary knowledge of the weak spots in the city fortifications.

not really mutual or reciprocal. At the same time, its benevolent or gracious aspect cannot be allowed to obscure the actor's own gain. A *ḥesed* act may sometimes be disinterested or involve personal sacrifice, but this is not a necessary parameter for the use of the term.[60]

It should be noted that this entire narrative is analyzed as an example of *ḥesed* only because of the Arameans' introductory comment about "kings of *ḥesed*." Although we have shown that the story fits within the scope of *ḥesed*, there is no assurance that Arameans got exactly the treatment they expected (i.e., that the narrator regarded all the details as a precise example of *ḥesed*). Finally, even though Ahab may have done (humanly speaking) an act of *ḥesed*, the Deuteronomic historian and/or the tradition on which he drew clearly condemned the action from a religious perspective.

Judges 8:35

> And they did not do *ḥesed* with the household of Jerubbaal (Gideon) in accordance with all the good *(ṭôbâ)* which he did with Israel.

Verses 33-35 serve as the connecting link which an editor, the Deuteronomic historian or an earlier compiler,[61] places

---

60. Other instances in which the actor may serve some interest of his own in doing *ḥesed* include Sarah to Abraham, Abner to Ishbaal and (still to be discussed) David to Meribaal and to Hanun.

61. Gray, *Joshua, Judges, Ruth*, p. 315, attributes the verses to the historian. So also Wolfgang Richter, *Traditionsgeschichtliche Untersuchungen zum Richterbuch* (Bonn: Peter Hanstein verlag, 1963), p. 251, where vs. 35 is attributed to the "Deuteronomisches Geschichtswerk." Richter assumes the point without discussion and notes the all-Israel expansion. Most recently, Robert Boling argues that the core material of Judges was brought together by a "pragmatic compiler" in the eighth century and that only a few major and framing pieces were added in the Josianic and exilic phases of the Deuteronomic historian's compilation (*Judges* [AB; Garden City, N.Y.: Doubleday & Company, Inc., 1975], pp. 29-38). These verses would then belong to the pragmatic compiler (p. 169).

between the materials of chapters 8 and 9. Thus this notice is to be dated considerably later than the other passages dealt with in this chapter. The construction and usage, however, have close affinity with several earlier passages, especially Gen. 21:23 and II Sam. 10:2 which will be discussed below. Whether the identification which the tradition made between Gideon and Jerubbaal was historically valid need not concern us here.

As a tradition, this summary comment anticipates in all-Israel terms the Shechemites' cooperation in the murder of Jerubbaal's seventy sons and their crowning of Abimelech who was their kinsman but only a son by a concubine (8:29; 9:18). In 9:16b there is another statement of the central point of 8:35 which does not use the term *ḥesed*. Jotham says, "If you have done good *(ṭôbâ)* with Jerubbaal and with his household, and if you have done to him according to what his deeds deserved *(kgmwl ydyw)*...." Then he summarizes in vs. 17 that which Jerubbaal (Gideon) had done: he had fought for them and rescued them from Midian, as is narrated in chs. 6-8. In the Deuteronomic statement Jerubbaal's action is called *"ṭôbâ"* and the Israelites' response is labeled as "not *ḥesed*"; in Jotham's accusation the Shechemites' response is indicted as "not *ṭôbâ*."

This alternation between *ḥesed* and *ṭôbâ* raises the problem of the particularity of the usage of the term *ḥesed*. We have already seen[62] that there may be situations where the word *ḥesed* would be appropriate but is not used. Now we must ask whether *ṭôbâ* can be distinguished from *ḥesed* and, if this is possible, why there is an alternation of usage in this context. An examination of the occurrences of *ṭôbâ* suggests that there are two principal grammatical uses of the word. The first type is grammatically the second member of a construct chain, or a predicate nominative, or appositional, all of which usually

---

62. See above, the discussion of the J and E forms of the story in which Sarah is presented as Abraham's sister. It is possible that the absence of the word in J reduces the emphasis on the obligational aspect of Sarah's deception, but this cannot be demonstrated.

correspond to an adjectival usage in English.[63] The second usage is a substantive one, usually as the object of a verb. This may be divided into two sub-types, the first being usage in a context where doing good to a person is the only matter of concern (there is no concern about evil). This usage is relatively infrequent.[64] The second and common sub-type is the usage in a specific contrast between good and evil *(rʿh)*.[65] This usage is so widespread that it appears that the substantive usage may have become partially "tied" to this contrast. *Ṭôbâ* is also used where the particular evil action is specified but *rʿh* itself is not used.[66] This modification of the *rʿh* antithesis provides an insight to the use of *ṭôbâ* in Judges 9. In 9:16b, Jotham's "if you have done *ṭôbâ*" is saying by the obvious word association "you Shechemites have done *rʿh*." The exchange between Saul and David recorded in I Sam. 24:18-20

---

63. A frequent usage. E.g. construct: Gen. 15:15; 25:8; Ex. 3:8; Dt. 8:7; II Ki. 3:25; Dt. 1:35; 4:21; 6:18; 8:10; 11:17; Jos. 23:13, 15. Predicate nominative: Nu. 14:7; Dt. 1:25; Jd. 15:2; I Sam. 12:23; II Sam. 17:14.

64. Ex. 18:9; II Sam. 2:6; 7:28; I Ki. 8:6 = II Chr. 7:10. D. Hillers has suggested that in II Sam. 2:6 the phrase *ʾʿsh ʾtkm hṭbh hzʾt* constitutes David's request for a "treaty of friendship" with the men of Jabesh Gilead. ("A Note on Some Treaty Terminology in the Old Testament," *BASOR* 176 [1964] 47. Hillers' article is an extension to the biblical text of the findings of W. L. Moran on the Akkadian usage of *tūbtu, ṭābūtu (ṭābuttu)*, "A Note on the Treaty Terminology of the Sefîre Stelas," *JNES* 22 [1963] 173-176.) Hillers' interpretation provides new insight to what has been a difficult passage. But it is important to recognize that such isolated examples in Hebrew do not necessarily constitute a full "technical" usage, in that it is not well represented in the overall occurrences of the word. The only other example which Hillers suggests is Dt. 23:7.

65. Gen. 44:4; 50:20; Nu. 13:19; 24:13; I Sam. 24:18-20; 25:21; II Sam. 16:12; Jer. 18:10,20; Ps. 35:12; 38:21; 109:5; Prv. 17:13.

66. E.g., II Sam. 16:12.

provides the clearest parallel. There *rʿh* is contrasted with the repeated use of *ṭôbâ* and the verb *gml* is used (cf. *kgml ydyw* in Jdg. 9:16b). Thus it is possible that *ṭôbâ* was used instead of *ḥesed* in 9:16b to heighten the sarcastic emphasis on the wicked deed of the Shechemites.

A closer comparison of the two passages, however, suggests a possible alternate explanation. Conceivably the crucial distinction here is that the subjects of the actions recorded in these two verses are in fact different. It is the Shechemites who did not do *ṭôbâ* but the Israelites who failed to do *ḥesed*. When we ask what act of *ḥesed/ṭôbâ* was at stake in each case, it becomes apparent that *ḥesed* is much more readily applicable to the context where it actually appears than to the context where it does not.[67] The Shechemites' action toward the sons of Jerubbaal was to kill them; not to have done this *rʿh* would have been to leave them alive and perhaps to see to their welfare. But none of this is spelled out. The focus of attention is on the murders. Conceivably the "positive" (neutral) action could be construed as *ḥesed*, but the word usually involves positive action of deliverance or protection, as we have already seen.

The addition in 8:35, however, can be understood as a quite specific failure to provide deliverance: Israel as a whole did not rise up to rescue Jerubbaal's sons from the treachery of Abimelech and the Shechemites.[68] From this perspective the chief features of the potential act of *ḥesed* are apparent. The basis lay in the good which Jerubbaal had done for all Israel (a prior act not called *ḥesed*), especially against Midian. But the Israelites, free to act as they pleased, ignored their moral responsibility and the seventy

---

67. Although it is not wholly inappropriate for 9:16; hence the development of the preceding argument for the use of *ṭôbâ* here.

68. The verse thus does anticipate ch. 9, but the reference to all Israel is not in this instance an expansion of the Shechemites (against Richter, p. 251). Rather, the writer intends what he says, and all Israel is presented over against the Shechemites.

sons were killed. Since the Deuteronomic editor does not elaborate on his comment, there is no sure evidence that the suggested contrast between all Israel and the Shechemites is correct. Nevertheless, this analysis does bring the usage of *ḥesed* in 8:35 precisely within the situational parameters delineated from other examples.

Preliminary Summary

Although a more extended summary will be presented at the end of section B, a preliminary review of results will be given here. The responsibility in all the foregoing examples is established by the prior act. But the relationship created is not intimate or personal; hence the claim to *ḥesed* cannot be assumed but must be demonstrated by reference to the prior act. These relationships in sociological language are "secondary" rather than "primary." The parties involved remain discrete personal or political units; the relationship is not such that it welds them together as a single unit over against outsiders.[69] This same quality of relationship is found in the second sub-type of group B situations to which we now turn.

2. *Ḥesed* Based on a Prior Act Called *Ḥesed*

There are four texts in which both a request (or an offer) and the prior act on which it is based are clearly called *ḥesed*. Glueck approached these cases by identifying an underlying implicit relationship in which the first action was based.[70] Hills, however, apparently regarded the first actions in such cases as ones which initiated relationships.[71] In distinction

---

69. In any such dictinctions there are inevitably borderline cases which receive their coloration from the usage selected by the writer. The fact that the case of Saul and the Jabesh Gileadites falls formally into group A while that of Gideon and the men of Israel falls into group B exemplifies the potential fluidity in usage. Nevertheless the totality of examples in each group confirms the proposed distinction in quality of relationship.

70. Glueck, pp. 10-11, 16.

71. This position would seem to be the implication of his statement that "*ḥesed* denotes that initial act...which creates

from these two positions, the writer wishes to suggest yet a third view.

We have already seen a number of examples of *ḥesed* based on implicit but clearly intimate and personal relationships. We have also seen *ḥesed* based on actions not called *ḥesed*. In the following examples it will be argued that the prior acts are called *ḥesed* by an extension (from the usual usage of the word for a "second" or "dependent" action) to the prior action which forms the basis of the *ḥesed* offered or requested. The point is that wherever a single action is involved, *ḥesed* is always done within some specific relationship (7x, section A of this chapter). Wherever two actions are involved, the word *ḥesed* is regularly used (8x) for the *second* action but only optionally used (4x of the 8, 3x directly, 1x indirectly) for the prior action. *Ḥesed* is never used for an "initiatory" action except when it serves as the statement of a basis for a *ḥesed* action by the second party.[72] Thus Hills' definition of *ḥesed* as an initial act which establishes a relationship may apply to a few special cases but certainly cannot be regarded as a general rule. These special cases must be given explanation as such rather than being taken as the starting point for the entire discussion of the word.

But if one follows Glueck's alternative and perceives the relationships as already established, another question arises: If the existing *relationship* is central, why in these few cases is a prior *act* of *ḥesed* within the relationship cited as the basis for the new act of *ḥesed*? Glueck does not recognize the connection between these examples, in which *ḥesed* is based on a prior act called *ḥesed*, and the examples in which the prior act

---

a *sacred religious* (not legal) *bond* between the two parties..." ("*Ḥesed* and *Berīth* and their Interrelationships," p. 1).

72. There is one additional instance in which *ḥesed* is used only for the prior action (I Sam. 15:6). As will be suggested in the discussion of this passage, the second act is clearly *ḥesed* although not so called. The usage represents the full development of the "extension" process, but even here the usage is not freed from the central concern for the second action.

is not called *ḥesed*. In the latter type he perceives the emergence of a mutual relationship because of the prior action,[73] but he does not discuss the function of the first action in the cases in which it is called *ḥesed* except to suggest that being true to the duties required by the relationship entitled the first party to demand the same of the second.[74] But the "right" to ask for *ḥesed* should be inherent in the relationship itself if the relationship is centrally at issue. In only these few cases is there need to give a special "proof." The interpretation of *ḥesed* in these examples as an extended application of the word allows them to be tied more closely with the examples in which the prior action is not called *ḥesed*. It is with these situations, rather than those involving intimate personal relationships, that the texts now to be discussed have their greatest affinity.

I Kings 2:7

> (But) to the sons of Barzillai the Gileadite you shall do *ḥesed*, and they shall be among those who eat at your table. For in like manner *(kēn)* they approached me when I was fleeing from Absalom your brother.

In this first example of *ḥesed* explicitly based in a prior act called *ḥesed*, the action of Barzillai's family is called *ḥesed* by indirection only. Nevertheless, the term clearly applies to both acts. In this case, we know the background action in some detail. When David fled to Mahanaim during Absalom's revolt, Barzillai the Gileadite from Rogelim was one of three principals who brought food for the king and his entourage.[75] After Absalom had been killed and David was assessing his support in preparation for return to Jerusalem, Barzillai apparently came to escort the king as far as the Jordan. David invited him to come and live in Jerusalem, but Barzillai

---

73. Glueck, pp. 18-20.

74. *Ibid.*, p. 10.

75. II Sam. 17:27. The others named are Shobi son of Nahash of Rabbah of the Ammonites and Machir son of Ammiel from Lo-debar. Each of these men figures problematically in the discussion of *ḥesed* in subsequent passages.

protested his old age and desire to die in his own city. He suggested that Chimham[76] go with David instead, and David agreed. The word *ḥesed* is not used in connection with David's invitation in II Sam. 19. Nor is there any statement of reason for the invitation, although the reward for favor is clearly evident from the context.

The circumstances surrounding David's request in I Kings 2 are unfortunately less well known. With the exception of verses 1-4, ch. 2 is generally considered the conclusion of the Court History. As the deathbed words of David, vss. 5-9, would seem appropriate for the Court History; yet there are problems. The instructions concerning Joab and Shimei do not seem to fit with the picture of David in the preceding part of the History.[77] It is not apparent why Barzillai's family should be singled out for special attention. If David actually gave this instruction concerning Barzillai, we must suppose Solomon might have preferred to do otherwise. If Solomon attributed the command to David, he may have been using this ploy to circumvent pressures on him to remove the sons of Barzillai from royal patronage.

The expression "royal patronage" is chosen to allow flexibility in the understanding of "those who eat at the king's table," since the precise meaning of this status or privilege is not known. If the phrase is a summary equivalent for all

---

76. II Sam. 19:32-40. Chimham is not further identified, but it is generally assumed (on the basis of I Ki. 2:7) that he was a son of Barzillai.

77. I Ki. 2:1-4 is generally regarded as from the Deuteronomic historian, while the remainder of the chapter is viewed as part of the Court History (see Leonhard Rost, *Die Überlieferung von der Thronnachfolge Davids* [Stuttgart: Verlag von W. Kohlhammer, 1926], p. 89). F. M. Cross (private communication) has suggested that ch. 2 may not be part of the Court History at all because it contradicts the earlier picture of David. Thus the final instructions are placed on David's lips in order to justify and absolve Solomon's actions in consolidating his kingdom. For discussion of the possible addition or reworking of vss. 5-9, 10-12, see Gray, *I-II Kings*, pp. 15-16.

which Barzillai was declining in II Sam. 19:36, then it presumably included housing, full financial support and court privileges. Whether actually eating in the same room with the king was included is not made explicit and conceivably varied from case to case. This privilege is also accorded to Meribaal (II Sam. 9:9-11) and the expression is used also for Jehoiachin's status under Evil-Merodach (II Kings 25:29 = Jer. 52:33) and even for Baal's prophets under Jezebel (I Kings 18:8).[78] The only extra-biblical parallels which the writer has found are those cited originally by Rawlinson: the Persians' way of handling captured royalty (exemplified in Herodotus i.153,207; iii.36) and the traditional Egyptian Tale of Sinuhe.[79] But these examples are neither chronologically comparable nor precisely parallel, so that they are of little help for a more exact interpretation of the biblical usage. The biblical examples suggest that this status could be accorded to political prisoners (Jehoiachin - presuming the writer applied to a foreign situation a term familiar from his own national context), to honored supporters (Barzillai's family) or to others finding royal favor.

This assessment of a place at the king's table seems to contradict one aspect of the picture of *ḥesed* which has emerged so far, for *ḥesed* generally involves the fulfillment of need rather than the granting of special privilege. But a closer examination of the circumstances is in order. As has been noted, the term *ḥesed* does not appear in connection with David's initial establishment of these arrangements. It is only with the impending succession of Solomon that the question of *ḥesed* arises. David enjoins Solomon to have[80] the sons of

---

78. Cf. further Neh. 5:17 which probably reflects this same usage. Also I Sam. 20:5, which will be discussed below.

79. G. Rawlinson, *Five Great Monarchies of the Ancient Eastern World*^{2} (New York: Dodd, Mead, & Company [1881]), III, 193. For the appropriate section of Sinuhe see *ANET*^{2}, p. 22, where he is given "the house of a royal son" (tr. by John A. Wilson). Here, however, the meals are brought from the palace, so the parallel is only general.

80. The Hebrew is *w^{e}hāyû*, which does not reveal whether

Barzillai at his table. Why does David's act of grateful munificence become for Solomon an act of *ḥesed*? In the first instance, Solomon is asked to take on a responsibility which he would be free to drop as soon as David dies. Although the *ḥesed* is not asked for David himself, the situation is analogous to Jacob's deathbed request for burial in Canaan. The emphasis is on the assuming of responsibility to do something after the person making the request is no longer present. Furthermore, Solomon is under indirect obligation to the family of Barzillai, for although they did *ḥesed* with David directly, the eventual succession of Solomon was made possible in part through their support of David during Absalom's attempt to usurp the throne.

But what of the issue of privilege versus need? Perhaps the indirectness of Solomon's obligation and the corresponding emphasis on his responsibility overrides the appearance of privilege. However, the writer would propose tentatively that historically there was, for some reason which can no longer be recovered, a dispute about the fate of this family after the death of David. This hypothesis about the situation is supported by two points: first that Barzillai's sons are selected for mention in David's final instructions and second that this family is set in specific contrast[81] with Joab and Shimei who are condemned to execution. If there were factions opposed to the Barzillai family, then a place at the king's table might function as a sort of protective custody.[82] If Cross is correct that all this action is Solomon's own doing, only attributed to a request from David, then Solomon may actually have elected, against opposition, to protect this family for his own political advantage and incidentally because of what they had done for David. In these circumstances, regardless of Solomon's

---

this is a new policy or a continuation. It is here assumed to be a continuation because of the story of I Sam. 19.

81. Note the emphatic word order in Hebrew, with the recipients of *ḥesed* named before the verb and direct object.

82. See below, where David's action toward Meribaal both protects the Saulide and enables David to keep track of his movements.

gain, protection of the family from opposing forces would be the central objective, and in its protective function a place at the king's table could certainly be construed as *ḥesed*. These suggestions are admittedly speculative. Nevertheless, they do provide a basis for an interpretation which is consonant with the basic features of a *ḥesed* action, an action which fills a real need for the recipient and is done from a position of responsibility and freedom.

Joshua 2:12-14

> (12) "And now, swear to me by Yahweh[a]: since I have done *ḥesed* with you, you also shall do *ḥesed* with my father's household,[b] (13) And you shall preserve alive my father[c] and my mother and my brothers and my sisters[d] and you shall rescue my[e] life from death." (14) And the men said to her, "Our lives for yours!"[f] And she said,[g] "When Yahweh gives you the city you shall be sure to do *ḥesed* with me."

The translation given here is based on a reconstruction of a probably more original Hebrew text. The notes which follow outline the reasoning underlying the reconstruction.

(a) The reading *ʾĕlōhîm/ʾĕlōhèkā* of the LXX is regarded as expansionist; the shorter MT is probably original.

(b) The MT phrase "and you shall give me a sure sign" is omitted. It is represented outside the Hebrew only by two Hexaplaric manuscripts, x and $\not{s}^{m}$ (under ⋇). The phrase may have come about through (1) the adding of *ʾmt* (cf. *ḥsd wʾmt*, vs. 14),[83] then (2) a dittography *ʾmt ʾmt* (3) read later *ʾwt ʾmt* with (4) the verb and preposition added in an *ad sensum* expansion anticipating the scarlet cord of vs. 18.

(c) Here the Greek reads "my father's household" (shown in Syrohexapla under ÷). The overall phrase naming family members suggests that the Hebrew is correct; the Greek reading

---

83. Martin Noth (*Das Buch Josua*^{2} [HAT I,7; Tübingen: Verlag von J. C. B. Mohr, 1953], p. 25) regards this *ʾmt* as original here as well as in vs. 14. Its absence in the Greek tradition suggests that this was not the case. The remainder of the development postulated for this phrase is in agreement with Noth.

probably originated as dittography from the preceding phrase which would be identical as a Hebrew *Vorlage* mistake and would differ only in case ending as an inner Greek error.

(d) At this point the MT adds *wʾt kl ʾšr lhm*. The Old Greek B reads this entire phrase and also, preceding it, καὶ πάντα τον οἶκόν μου *(wʾt kl byty)*. The Lucianic tradition (gn, dpt) represents a third variation with a *Vorlage wʾt kl bytm ʾšr lhm*. These readings suggest at least two ancient variants (the MT, and the LXX^B plus) and probably a third (*wʾt kl bytm* of the Lucianic tradition), all of which were expanisonist specifications or elaborations of the preceding series of household members. The Catena (ej, svz) reading, *wʾt kl byt ʾby*, is best regarded as a secondary corruption from the preceding *byt ʾby*.

(e) The reading "my life" (τὴν ψυχήν μου = *npšy*) is found throughout the Greek tradition. Only four scattered manuscripts read with the MT "our lives"; all members of the B and boc_2e_2 families read the singular form. The Greek clearly represents an earlier reading, which in the MT has been adjusted to include the entire family. The impetus for such a change was present even in the short form of the text and could only have been increased by the insertion of "and all which are theirs" into the preceding series.

(f) The MT reads, "if you (m. pl.) do not reveal this business of ours." The entire phrase is omitted in the Old Greek. In the Syrohexapla it is shown under the asterisk. Two Lucianic manuscripts (gn) have the phrase but with a singular (presumably feminine) verb form. Within the transmission of the phrase it is likely that *tgydy* was the more original reading (cf. vs. 20) with the easy *y*⟶*w* orthographic shift to *tgydw* taking place with further reinforcement from the preceding references to family members. The entire phrase, however, is to be regarded as a secondary expansion in anticipation of vs. 20a.[84]

---

84. Noth, *Josua*, p. 24, showed this phrase and the remainder of the verse (following MT against Greek, cf. note g) in bracketed light type, indicating that he regarded it as doubly secondary. Unfortunately, he discussed neither the

(g) The reading "and she said" is found throughout the Greek traditions, over against the MT tradition in which there is instead *whyh*. Thus in the Greek Rahab speaks to the spies in the rest of the verse, whereas in the Hebrew the spies continue speaking to Rahab. The words are almost all the same but the personal endings on verb and prepositions are systematically reversed. The Greek tradition is to be regarded as original for several reasons. First, the Greek is contextually the *lectio difficilior*. Rahab has asked the spies to swear to do *ḥesed* and they have just done so. Thus the second request now seems redundant. It is more likely to have been smoothed away than to have been created within the tradition. Second, within the phrase itself the wording is different at one important point. The Greek reads τὴν πόλιν *(hʿyr)* instead of *hʾrṣ*. The reading "city" is appropriate to the immediate context, whereas the more generalized "land" reflects more a widespread expression and especially the usage in 2:8 and 2:24. Although the use of "city" could conceivably be regarded as a Hebrew *Vorlage* change in the direction of specification, a change made by replacement rather than by supplementation seems highly unlikely. Third, the Greek cannot readily be regarded as inner-Greek corruption. While the καὶ αὐτὴ εἶπεν could conceivably be accounted for by its similarity to the preceding καὶ εἶπαν αὐτῇ, a change from hypothetical εἰς ὑμᾶς to εἰς ἡμᾶς would be the expected corresponding corruption, whereas the actual reading is the singular εἰς ἐμὲ. The occurrence of "city" may have been an independent variable but taken with the use of ἐμὲ it may be regarded as further evidence that the Greek is a separate, legitimate tradition rather than an internal corruption.

Despite the evidence that the Greek reading is superior, it is still difficult to explain precisely how the corruption in the Hebrew came about. Margolis, in fact, opts for the Greek as the corrupt form because there he can give some sort of explanation. He suggests that the Hebrew *whyh* had been corrupted to *whyʾ*, "which the translator read as two words" *(whyʾ*

---

relative dates of his "secondary" additions nor the differences in Greek treatment within the bracketed sections.

ʾmrh) whereupon he was forced to change the suffixes.[85] But there is no apparent reason for the translator to have supposed an abbreviated word. Probably Margolis is correct that the *Vorlage* read at least *hyʾ*. The specific rendering αὐτὴ and the comparable usage in 2:6,8 suggest this possibility, although here one might expect that the sequence of converted tenses should have been maintained (hence *wattōʾmer*). It may be conjectured that the original reading was either *wtʾmr* or perhaps (a variant?) *whyʾ ʾmrh* which was intended grammatically to suggest a time lapse during which the spies lay down (cf. vs. 8) before Rahab's final repeat of the request and their window departure. One can only imagine how this might have been transformed to *whyh* with the corresponding change in suffixes, but as has already been suggested the tendency toward the change was inherent in the context, especially if the proposed notion of a time lapse were forgotten by the copyist. The likelihood of the change would be further increased once the secondary *ʾm...zh* clause (see above, note f) was introduced into the MT text tradition. If a scribe copied this clause while thinking of it not as a condition on the preceding oath but rather as a protasis anticipating a subsequent apodosis, the transformation of the subsequent phrase to an apodosis would be an easy error to make. While this proposed Hebrew corruption is more complex than the Greek change suggested by Margolis, in this case the more complicated solution takes better account of the total evidence.

The text critical study has shown that sections of the Hebrew text are probably relatively late and independent secondary additions. Thus the analysis will focus on the shorter text shown in the translation. Although it has been argued that Rahab is correctly the speaker in the final phrase of verse 14, it should be noted that no matter who is the speaker the phrase is only an extension of what has gone before and does not alter the circumstances or the agreement. It is important to recognize 14bα as a separate addition on textual grounds, for the blatant imposing of a condition on a person

---

85. Max Margolis, ed., *The Book of Joshua in Greek* (Paris: Librairie Orientaliste Paul Guethner, 1931), p. 25.

who requests to receive *ḥesed* would be unique and, if our interpretation is correct, possibly inappropriate.[86]

The situation in which Rahab asks for *ḥesed* based on her act of *ḥesed* again exhibits the central characteristics of *ḥesed* action. Her request is based on the assumption that the spies will get away and that (as she has already asserted she believes) Yahweh will give the city to Israel. The spies and Israel thus are in full control of the situation from Rahab's point of view. It might be argued that she has the upper hand, or at least some leverage, at this point in the story because the spies are still with her. But she has already deceived the king's guards and thus has committed herself to her course of action. She could not now betray the spies without exposing herself to punishment for the original lie. There is no one else to whom Rahab can turn for help. She and her family are certain to die if her request is not granted.

From the spies' perspective there is moral obligation to Rahab as well as freedom to ignore her request. Glueck sees the obligation as based in a host-guest relationship,[87] but one may wonder whether this obligation was regularly extended to the harlot's visitors. In any case, it seems more appropriate to see the primary focus of the obligation where the narrator himself put it, in Rahab's "*ḥesed*" to the spies. The spies are obligated by her prior action of hiding them and diverting the guards. Thus Rahab's request for *ḥesed* is congruent with the

---

86. Glueck argued that "the spies had no right to impose another condition on Rahab" (p. 10, n.2). One might infer from his note that the interpretation of *ḥesed* was the basis for deletion of 14bα, rather than corroborative evidence, but he is clearly aware of the Greek variation. Glueck does not deal with the later reference to this "condition" in vs. 20. Probably Rahab's silence about the mission should be understood as the completion of her own act of *ḥesed* and as a sign of her good faith in anticipation of her deliverance. While special requirements are not imposed as conditions for receiving *ḥesed*, breach of relationship is not tolerated (see the story of Abner above). Here it is a question of emphasis.

87. Glueck, p. 10.

understanding of the word throughout the texts.

But in what sense does the narrator use *ḥesed* as a summary word for Rahab's action in relation to the spies? First and foremost, Rahab's deception shares the quality of *ḥesed* as an action in which the actor is in full control of the situation and holds the fate of the other party in his hands. By this point there was no one else to whom the spies could turn. In this text, as in the case of Barzillai and of the two subsequent examples (Abraham and Abimelech; David and Hanun), the focus of attention in the double use of *ḥesed* is on the situational reversal of the superior and inferior parties. When the reversal of circumstances is central, the term *ḥesed* is extended to the action of each party in turn. It is this aspect of the situation which precipitates the double usage of the word.

The possible (although unlikely) host-guest relationship and the obligation which it may have imposed upon Rahab are not centrally pertinent here. If the relationship were central, she would simply ask for *ḥesed* without giving a basis. The central issue is rather her action which created an obligation for the spies. It cannot be known with certainty whether her action initiated the obligation (Hills) or whether it proved that she recognized some previously established implicit relationship which the spies were thus also obligated to recognize (Glueck). It does seem clear that the more common usage has been expanded in a dependent way. *Ḥesed* in this dependent, secondary specialization is essentially an act performed free of control which in retrospect[88] is seen as a basis for a new action which would regularly be called *ḥesed*. Because the first act is now of interest in relation to future events, the background of the action is of little importance for the appropriateness of the use of the word.

The use of the oath as additional confirmation of the moral

---

88. If Rahab was sure Yahweh would give Israel the city, she might have acted in anticipation of her future need for *ḥesed*. Usually, however, the original actor has no specific knowledge at the time that his action might be needed as the basis for a future request for assistance.

responsibility to follow through in an anticipated act of *ḥesed* has been dealt with in the discussion of Gen. 47:29. Here the oath is associated with an act which is to take place a little distance into the future. In the absence of immediate confirmation through the performance of the *ḥesed*, Rahab gains additional assurance by making the men answerable to Yahweh in the matter rather than to their consciences alone. The presence of the oath gives additional emphasis to the picture of the actor's full personal freedom in the performance of *ḥesed*. Only God is in a position to requite the person who does not perform *ḥesed* in accordance with his responsibilities.

Genesis 21:22-24

> At about that time Abimelech, with Phicol the commander of his troops, said to Abraham, "God is with you all that you do. Therefore, swear to me now by God: You surely shall not deal falsely *(šqr)* with me or with my offspring or with my posterity. In accordance with the *ḥesed* which I have done with you you shall do *(ḥesed)* with me and with the land in which you have sojourned." And Abraham replied, "I swear."

This small passage is unanimously agreed to be E. Whether it can be joined to a part of the conflate (double) aetiology of Beersheba in the following verses is not certain; but Gunkel's proposal, assigning verses 27 and 31 to the tradition of 22-24 is certainly plausible.[89]

Several major commentators, notably Gunkel, Speiser and von Rad, have regarded Abraham as the weaker party in this relationship.[90] In light of the preceding incident with Sarah

---

89. Hermann Gunkel, *Genesis übersetzt und erklärt* (HkzAT I,1; Göttingen: Vandenhoeck & Ruprecht, 1917), p. 235. Procksch (*Genesis*³, pp. 307-309) holds a similar view. They are followed by Skinner, *Genesis*², p. 325, and von Rad, *Genesis*, p. 231. Whether or not these detailed analyses are viable, the section 21:22-24 is clearly unitary and must be interpreted on its own, without reference to the dispute about the wells of vs. 25.

90. Gunkel interpreted Abimelech's action as a hedge

(ch. 20), Abimelech is understood to want to reassure himself of Abraham's loyalty to him. Glueck also interprets the *ḥesed* asked of Abraham as that of an inferior to his superior. He interprets the *gēr* relationship as a special type of host-guest relationship and argues that Abraham here swears to remain loyal to his protector.[91] Since Glueck was concerned only to demonstrate the presence of the "mutual relationship of rights and duties" it was of no concern for his thesis that this example stood alone in the (supposed) asking of *ḥesed* from the weaker party.

When this brief narrative is separated from the story of the well dispute and seen as the sequel to the Sarah incident of ch. 20,[92] it is quite possible to view Abraham as the party who is at this moment in the stronger position, as would be expected if there is consistency in the situation in which the word *ḥesed* is appropriate. The opening statement ("God is with you in all that you do. Therefore swear....") suggests that Abimelech did not feel safe near Abraham because his God was so powerful: he had seen God's action in the Sarah incident.

---

against the possibility that Abraham might become the stronger party in the future. (*Genesis*, p. 234). Speiser suggests that the presence of Phicol was designed "to strengthen his [Abimelech's] position as the stronger party, a claim which Abraham, as a newcomer, does not appear to dispute" (*Genesis*, p. 160). He regards the use of the verb *gwr* as a deliberate reference to Abraham's inferior status (p. 159). Von Rad is less explicit and takes notice of the significant prefatory remark that God is with Abraham; however, he still regards the action as a "concession" on Abimelech's part (*Genesis*, p. 231). S. R. Driver regards the entire passage as one story about Abraham under Abimelech's protection (*The Book of Genesis*[2] [WC; London: Methuen & Co., 1904], p. 214).

91. Glueck, pp. 10-11. Abimelech's *ḥesed*, according to Glueck, has been demonstrated by his return of Sarah to Abraham. "A protector could not take away the wife of a *gēr*. That would have been a breach of the...relationship existing between them" (p. 11).

92. So von Rad, *Genesis*, p. 231.

Because Abraham had lied about his wife, Abimelech had thought himself free to take Sarah into his harem. Despite his ignorance of the facts and lack of premeditation, Abimelech suddenly discovers he is objectively and publicly guilty of violating Abraham's marriage. In his dream he learns that he is in jeopardy of divine punishment on behalf of the aggrieved husband. He is convinced that God has the power to punish his guilt and yet the willingness to restore because of his error was inadvertent. It is finally through Abraham's intercession after the return of Sarah that Abimelech and his household are healed. Because of the breach of law and its consequences, Abraham with God's support is the stronger party. Abimelech asks that Abraham should refrain from causing him more trouble, even as Abimelech, when he had the upper hand, did not intentionally bring trouble upon Abraham.[93]

As Glueck recognized,[94] this tradition suggests that *ḥesed* may be used to summarize behavior which is appropriate to a covenant relationship. However, certain restrictions Glueck did not make should be noted. First the *ḥesed* is to be

---

93. The J parallel version of this oath, the coming of Phicol and Abimelech to Isaac (Gen. 26:26-33, cf. 26:12-17a), suggests that the tradition of the covenant between a patriarch and Abimelech may alternately (or additionally) have been consequent upon the increasing wealth and continuing good fortune which followed the patriarch after the wife-and-ruler incident. Isaac's material prosperity is specifically attributed to Yahweh's blessing (vss. 12-13) and becomes a source of friction (vss. 14, 27). A treaty *(bᵉrît)* is proposed by Abimelech and Phicol because "Yahweh is with you." The language used to describe the central content of the agreement is not that of *ḥesed* but instead the *ṭôb/rāʿâ* contrast (vs. 29). Isaac is not to do harm to the people of Abimelech because they have done good to him. If this tradition of material prosperity (rather than the Sarah incident) lies behind the Abraham and Abimelech pact of 21:22-24, the patriarch is again the stronger party. The particular reason varies, but the supportive help of his God as the basis for his more powerful status remains constant.

94. Glueck, p. 11.

understood as the responsibility of the more powerful party. Abimelech did *ḥesed* to Abraham when he was the more powerful, but now the tables are turned. Second, this is a special use of the term appropriate to political contexts. In immediate interpersonal relationships the word generally retains its association with specific and particular problems. But in the political context the word may take on the dual aspects of protection and refraining from false dealings (note the use of *šqr*). This happens because the person making the request is looking ahead to general future possibilities. He does not yet face a specific problem, but the treaty is a hedge against the future. Through the treaty he gains assurance that he will receive *ḥesed* when the need arises.[95] Glueck tends to generalize *ḥesed* to cover any action which is appropriate to the relationship between two persons or groups, so that the performance of any duty to another could be called *ḥesed*. Against this tendency it must be reiterated that *ḥesed* is regularly associated with specific actions in special situations. Only occasionally is it applied to what may be called an ongoing behavior or series of actions,[96] and even there *ḥesed* may be ongoing in that it is done whenever special circumstances call for it.

Hills, in his discussion of the relationship between *ḥesed* and *b^e^rît*, suggests that a *b^e^rît* where *ḥesed* is involved is "*a purely religious bond* and is motivated by *uncalculating concern on the part of the strong for the weak*." He cites Gen. 21:22-24 as a prime example. In contrast to this usage he proposes that a *b^e^rît* "can also denote *a relationship between equals*

---

95. Unfortunately, there are no detailed examples of this political usage, although II Sam. 10:2 may involve it and the David-Jonathan relationship appears to reflect it. Conceivably, this usage may lie beneath the surface of the Barzillai story also. The usage is quite important because it provides a clue to the covenantal aspect of the theological application of *ḥesed*.

96. Besides this tradition, other possible examples are the sons of Jerubbaal and Abner to Ishbaal. But in these cases there is still a degree of tie to specific action, as has been suggested in the discussion of them.

which, although sanctioned formally by religion, tends to become *more and more concerned with receiving rather than giving* and is enforced by *legal sanctions*, the threat of injury and the withholding of benefits."[97] From the discussion thus far it is possible to criticize Hills' analysis at several points. The distinction between "religious" and "secular" bonds is very misleading since these are all human relationships. A contrast of "moral" versus "legal" might better express Hills' intention, but even this cannot stand up to close scrutiny. In order to maintain the contrast, Hills must find *b^{e}rît* "implied" in sixteen of his nineteen examples of the *ḥesed* type. In some of these instances, especially political examples, the two parties involved may have concluded a *b^{e}rît* - we are not told. But it is not viable methodologically to label as *b^{e}rît* any relationship in which one party does one act of *ḥesed*. In the same way, it is quite possible to have the non-*ḥesed* type of action-within-relationship which Hills describes quite outside the context of a formal *b^{e}rît*. The bargain between Jacob and Esau for the birthright is an example.

B^{e}rît in secular usage most often appears in connection with political treaties or alliances or arrangements. In any such agreement there is normally giving and receiving by both parties, and this holds true even when the two parties are unequal in power. Such a political relationship between unequals may involve *ḥesed* on the part of the superior power, as in the case of Abraham and Abimelech. The variability is not so much in the term *b^{e}rît* as it is in the use of *ḥesed* itself. *Ḥesed* is aid to the inferior without coercion, as Hills notes. In a close personal relationship such an action may normally be completely "uncalculating." But the degree of calculation may be lesser or it may be greater. It is the flexibility in this aspect of the word[98] which allows it to be applied in political

---

97. "*Ḥesed* and *Berîth*," p. 2. He suggests nine possible examples for the latter type, nineteen for the former. These nineteen, however, are essentially the *ḥesed* passages discussed in this chapter, including even familial relationships.

98. Compare the extension of "love" and "hate" to political categories shown by Moran, "The Ancient Eastern Background

contexts such as Ahab with Ben-hadad or Abner with Ishbaal. It is also this flexibility which allows the word to be extended to the generalized covenant behavior of Genesis 21. Abraham cannot be coerced but it is not a necessary consequence that the pact is utterly one sided. It is based on the good treatment which he formerly received as the weaker party, but one should not assume that he would continue *ḥesed* behavior if the people of Gerar mistreated his retinue. This is the same point which is made explicitly in the Rahab story. Although she can offer the spies nothing, she can and is expected to keep the mission secret. Likewise, in the story of David and Hanun, the Ammonites lose David's *ḥesed* because they humiliate his official emissaries. The word *ḥesed* is applicable in these political situations primarily because coercion is not possible and the superior party gains no *essential* benefit from his action. The actor could withdraw his assistance at any time with little or no loss; yet the weaker party would lose essential help and would have no recourse even though a covenant (where one existed) had been broken.

II Samuel 10:1-2a // I Chronicles 19:1-2

> After some time the king of the Ammonites died and Hanun his son succeeded him as king. And David said, "I will do *ḥesed* with Hanun son of Nahash as his father did *ḥesed* with me." So David sent his servants to console him (Hanun) concerning his father.

Little can be said about this passage because nothing is known of the political or personal relationships between David and the Ammonites prior to this incident. According to the narrator, Hanun's advisers persuade him that David's real intent is to spy out their city in order to overthrow it. The emissaries are humiliated publicly and sent home; this action precipitates warfare.[99] The last reference to the Ammonites

---

of the Love of God in Deuteronomy," *CBQ* 25 (1963) 80-81. The imagery is preserved but the practical content inevitably becomes modified.

99. The relationship of the various sections of this war narrative to one another and to the materials of ch. 8 is much

before David's overture is the story of Saul's rout of Nahash when he was threatening Jabesh-Gilead (I Sam. 11), which according to the tradition took place before Saul was made king. If this tradition is correct, and if the placing of Nahash's death after David was settled in Jerusalem is also correct, then there is a gap of at least 27 years or more to be reckoned with.

In this long blank period it seems quite possible that Nahash could have regained strength. One may speculate that he was of some direct or indirect assistance to David in his lengthy dispute with the Saulides and north Israel. Of course there is no evidence for this supposition; but it is unrealistic to imagine that the struggle took place in a complete political vacuum, and the text certainly suggests a positive relationship between David and Nahash.

Although David's servants are described in the role of comforters, the importance attached to them by Hanun's advisers, as well as the use of *ḥesed* in the context, suggests that their mission was more than one of consolation and was in fact probably political in nature. The sending of an embassy appears to have been proper diplomacy whenever a treaty partner died and his successor was enthroned, and we may have here an example of this protocol.[100] If there was a treaty between equals, then David's intended *ḥesed* may still be understood in terms of assistance by a person in a more powerful position to a person who cannot control the other's action. Throughout the passages analyzed in this chapter, superiority has been regularly a matter of the immediate circumstances. In ancient royal succession it is well known that the successor often had to secure his throne internally and that there were often waiting predators on the borders. Clearly Hanun's advisers perceived David in this light, so that he was potentially Hanun's superior at the time of the embassy. David himself presumably wished to support Hanun's claim to the throne.

---

disputed, but neither the literary nor the historical aspect of the debate is germane to the understanding of *ḥesed* in the passage.

100. Moran, "Love of God," p. 80.

The *ḥesed* which David received may be only a formalized way of expressing the basis for David's action. Presumably there was a concrete political relationship with Nahash, and, as has been suggested, it is possible that Nahash even helped David to secure his own position.

It is worth observing that "to do *ḥesed*" here may be extended even further than in the story of Abraham and Abimelech. There, it was suggested, the phrase refers to continuing acts of *ḥesed* done in accordance with a pact or treaty. Here the usage may even be understood as "to make a treaty." The making of a treaty with Hanun would be the political concretizing of the kind of support for a new king which seems to be the essence of David's action.[101] Nevertheless, the making of the treaty is still a particular action in accordance with David's prior relationship to Nahash. Doing *ḥesed* and making a treaty are not to be generally equated even in political contexts.

I Samuel 15:6

> Then Saul said to the Kenites, "Come! Depart! Go down from Amalek so that I will not destroy you along with them; for (Heb. *w*) you yourselves did *ḥesed* with the Israelites when they came up from Egypt."

The English "destroy" probably best conveys the sense of the Hebrew *ʾōsīpkā* in this context. The Greek understands the consonants *ʾspk* as did the Masoretic punctators, but a meaning from the root *sph* is also possible. The Hebrew *kl* is probably secondary since none of the Greek manuscripts represents it.

---

101. This extension is possible in other contexts, though it seems most natural here. In the story of Ahab and Ben-hadad, *malkê ḥesed* could conceivably be extended to "kings who make (vassal-)treaties (on the basis of concessions)," since Ben-hadad is eventually released under such an arrangement. The recognition of the change of relative power positions is clear in Ben-hadad's statement: "you shall have bazaars in Damascus as my father had bazaars in Samaria." The usage of *ḥesed* in hendiadys with *bᵉrît* in theological language (see Chapter III) suggests that this tendency toward closer association with "covenant" was inherent in the term, even if not actualized.

This verse is the only case in which *ḥesed* appears as a word for the first action but not for the second in a related pair. Clearly Saul's action in warning the Kenites of his impending surprise attack has all the characteristics of *ḥesed* even though he simply performs it (without any comment from the narrator that he thought to himself or said to the Kenites, "I will do *ḥesed*..."). Saul warns the Kenites without any coercion and even at risk to his own plan, since word could leak to the Amalekites. From the subsequent rout of Amalek it appears that the Kenites would have had no chance of survival without the warning. And Saul obviously was motivated by what the Kenites had done for Israel.

The nature of the relationship the Kenites had with Israel in the wilderness period has long exercised historians' imagination and ingenuity. It seems agreed that the relationships were friendly, but the exact contribution to Israel's religion or life in the desert cannot be specified. Judges 1:16 preserves the tradition of Kenites accompanying the tribe of Judah into the Negeb and settling there. It is not impossible that these people assisted Judah in some of the military ventures mentioned there and that such a tradition could have lain behind Saul's action. Here again, as in the previous example, it is not unreasonable to assume some formal relationship between Israel and the Kenites which is not expressed but which is implied in the mention of *ḥesed*. A translation such as "you maintained a pact with..." would make sense - with the understanding that the Kenites had kept it even when they had been free not to, so that Saul now does the same.

3. Summary of Section B

In this section we have treated examples of *ḥesed* based on a prior action; this prior action may or may not be called *ḥesed*. We have seen that the examples are basically similar in character, whether or not the prior action is specified as *ḥesed*. Whenever a prior action is mentioned, the individuals or parties involved must be seen as discrete personal and/or political units; the relationships are sociologically "secondary" in type. The reference to a particular action as the basis or reason for *ḥesed* emphasizes this secondary character even where some previously existing relationship can be identified. Thus in the cases of David and Hanun or Saul and the Kenites or Abraham and Abimelech or Ahab and Ben-hadad the recognition of separate political entities is inherent in the wording of the texts. In some instances there is ambiguity as to whether *ḥesed* involves individual actions or a whole series of actions which fall together into an ongoing behavior which may be labelled "action appropriate to a treaty relationship even when one is free to do otherwise without fear of reprisal" (Abraham, the Kenites). By further extension, the making of a treaty or pact may itself be regarded as an act of *ḥesed* because the treaty was the free alternative to personal or national destruction or maltreatment (Ben-hadad, Hanun, the Kenites, Abimelech).

The three examples of *ḥesed* on a strictly individual level also involve discrete units or secondary relationships. Joseph and the Cup-bearer, Rahab and the spies, and the man caught by the spies at Luz are all cases in which specific actions form a connecting link between persons who otherwise have no relationship. Again it is problematic (and perhaps a matter of semantics) to attempt to define the "relationship" which is "created" in these situations. The point is that none of these relationships is of the same order as those in group A.[102]

In two examples of group B, Barzillai and Gideon, the "discrete" status of the parties is less clear. Gideon was of course an Israelite; but being an Israelite was not enough to establish a basis for doing *ḥesed*. The fact that he had led Israel against Midian might have been regarded as a base for a primary relationship. Cases like these are borderline (cf. Saul and the Jabesh-Gileadites in group A), as has been suggested above.

The role of Barzillai and Gilead prior to Absalom's revolt

---

102. Group A in review: Abraham,and Sarah, Jacob and Joseph, Abraham and Laban, David and Hushai, Abner and Ishbaal, the Jabesh Gileadites and Saul, Ruth and her dead husband. The "single unit" or "primary" nature of the human relationship in each of these examples, whether personal or political, is quite clear.

is not known; but if there was any substance to Ziba's accusation that Meribaal wanted to turn the Absalom revolt to Saulide advantage (II Sam. 16:3), it is possible that Gilead's support of David rather than a Saulide had not been a foregone conclusion and that in this respect Barzillai was independent of David[103] in a way that Hushai, for example, was not. It is the action performed which places a responsibility on the recipient that would not otherwise have been present. Even though the parties were not enemies or were not fully autonomous politically, they still did not have a positive personal relationship which could provide a basis for *ḥesed*. The action is the central feature, as in the other examples.

It has been suggested that *ḥesed* applies primarily to the second action, which is performed in fulfillment of the obligation created by the first action. The use of *ḥesed* in reference to the first action is then to be understood as an extended, dependent use of the term (Abimelech, Rahab, Hanun [Nahash], Barzillai, the Kenites) which serves to emphasize the reversal of relative positions of strength within a preexisting relationship. Such an extension, semantically speaking, could take place because the first act is similar in character to the second: (1) the individual cannot meet his own need; (2) the need involves essential rescue or support; (3) the deliverance or protection cannot be obtained elsewhere; and (4) the actor is thus free to do the *ḥesed* or to refuse. In short, the first act, like the second, could not be required or compelled.

However, the equally important feature of *ḥesed*, recognizable responsibility, is of a different character, for no intimate personal relationship exists and no still prior third action is solidly present. But some level of responsibility can be felt even though it is different from that which characterized the usual *ḥesed* action. Possible relationships can be perceived as the background of each of the prior acts called *ḥesed*. Although the reader never has specific information

---

103. The mention of Barzillai along with Shobi the Ammonite and Machir who had sheltered Meribaal further suggests his quasi-autonomous political status.

about the details of such relationships, it is clear that they are uniformly of the "secondary" or "discrete unit" type. Thus the narrator could understand the first *ḥesed* as prior action in accordance with a relationship. At the same time, the nature of the responsibility in the first act is qualitatively different: even though the relationship is of the secondary type, the person first in power has voluntarily acted on behalf of the other party. Thus within the relationship which is formally secondary there is a first act or series of acts of *ḥesed* which lacks a specific prior basis and in this respect is like the *ḥesed* of primary relationships in which prior acts have no important role. The parties may be equal in power when the relationship is established, so that at the outset the relationship is one of convenience in which each can be of some use to the other. Or a more powerful party may establish the relationship in his own self-interest or as a sheer act of good will. But when circumstances of need arise for one party, whether originally or only newly become the weaker party, the stronger has a responsibility to act because of the relationship to which he has voluntarily committed himself. The secondary relationship at this point stands close to the primary.

This analysis may seem more complicated that the evidence warrants, but it enables us to make two important distinctions. Against Glueck, it can be seen that the first acts of *ḥesed* in these instances do not involve a responsibility of the same magnitude as do either the second acts in group B (because of the prior act) or the acts in group A (because of the primary character of the relationship). Against Hills, on the other hand, it can be seen that *ḥesed* is never used for an action where it is impossible for the narrator to have imagined any sense of responsibility at all.[104]

---

104. Rahab is the most difficult. The writer doubts that Glueck's application of the law of hospitality is appropriate to harlot's quarters. One may suggest that Rahab's action was two-fold. She had first not sent the spies away when she learned of their mission and then followed through on her self-imposed relationship and responsibility by not giving them away when the real test came, when the soldiers came inquiring.

Ḥesed based on prior action has the same characteristics as *ḥesed* based implicitly on personal relationships. Prior actions are identified as the basis for *ḥesed* wherever no intimate personal relationship is apparent. *Ḥesed* is never performed randomly; a responsibility must always be implicit or explicit. But *ḥesed* is not just any responsible act. It is an act which fills an essential need which cannot be taken care of by the person in need and for which the person has no alternanate source for assistance.

The generalization of *ḥesed* from specific action to overall behavior is apparently a result of the association of the term with political arrangements. Parity treaties have no external basis for enforcement, nor is there any external control on the superior party of a suzerainty treaty. Whoever is permanently or temporarily in the position of advantage is free to do as he pleases. His self-restraint and general protection rather than exploitation of the weaker party may be understood as *ḥesed*, as well as any positive acts of deliverance which may be needed (Abraham and Abimelech, David and Hanun, the Kenites). It is clear that general protection and specific deliverance tend to overlap; the generalization to protection plays a significant role in the theological application of the word to be discussed in Chapter III.

C. *David and Jonathan*

A series of texts relate to David's request for *ḥesed* from Jonathan, Jonathan's request to David, and the fulfillment of their respective requests. The texts are here treated as a

---

Hence from the narrator's perspective it may have been the decision to keep the spies which established the relationship and the lie to the soldiers which constituted Rahab's *ḥesed* within the relationship. Since she had not sent the spies away at the outset, he could understand a level of responsibility even where it might not usually have been present. Alternately, one may simply suggest that Rahab is the single case in which the use of *ḥesed* is extended where there is no sense of responsibility and that the extension occurred because of the dominance of the other characteristics in this situation.

distinct unit because *ḥesed* is requested on the basis of a *b^e^rît* between the two men. In the group A examples, a pact or treaty would not have been expected in the nature of the relationships because they were essentially personal (sometimes political but still personal). In the examples of *ḥesed* based on specific actions, it has been suggested that the use of *ḥesed* may sometimes be closely connected to a formal covenant relationship. There are no examples in which it can be certainly demonstrated that a specific action called *ḥesed* is either the making of a treaty or based on an event called *ḥesed* which involved a treaty-making. Nevertheless, *ḥesed* may be understood as behavior commendable for a person in the situationally dominant position in a treaty relationship. In the story of David and Jonathan, this possibility is made explicit. Even here, however, the actions are always specific; it is not a matter of generalized behavior.

The problem of multiple traditions plagues every attempt to understand the actual political relationship between David and Jonathan. I Samuel especially consists of a mixture of folk-tale type material with theologically oriented narrative from various dates and perspectives. I Samuel 18:3, in which the *b^e^rît* between David and Jonathan is first established, exemplifies the difficulty. From Moran's study of the use of "to love" in political contexts it appears probable that a political relationship rather than a purely personal friendship may be the intention of the narrator here.[105] Yet the event is presented at the climax of David's victory over the Philistine, within one of the several versions of how David came to the court of Saul. The first meeting between the king's son and an unknown young warrior hardly seems a likely occasion for entering into such a political pact. Hence one suspects that an editor or compiler may have added verse 3 (and also 4) to provide a basis for 20:8 where the pact is presumed. It cannot be determined whether such an editor was the Deuteronomic historian or an earlier compiler.

The texts in which *ḥesed* appears are I Sam. 20:8; 20:14-15, and II Sam. 9:1,3,7. It seems possible that an editor's hand

---

105. Moran, "Love of God," p. 82, n.33.

can again be seen in I Sam. 20:14-15, since these verses appear to provide the basis for II Sam. 9:1-7. The texts are as follows:

I Samuel 20:8a

> And do *ḥesed* with (to) your servant because you have brought your servant into a covenant of Yahweh with you.

The MT reads *ʿl* as the preposition following *ḥsd*. Since there was regularly confusion between *ʿl* and *ʾl* in the late manuscript tradition, *ʾl* would be perfectly plausible. The Greek μετα suggests that *ʿm* was present in the tradition originally, in accordance with the more usual idiom.[106]

The phrase *bryt yhwh* is used uniquely here in that it refers to a pact between two men. (In all other instances Yahweh is understood as party to a covenant with Israel.)[107] Presumably David is stressing the seriousness of the relationship sworn to before Yahweh.[108] This expression may be refracted in the phrases "*ḥesed yhwh*" (II Sam. 20:14) and *ḥesed ʾĕlōhîm* (II Sam. 9:3) which are likewise unique as references to human *ḥesed* action.

David's expression "your servant" makes clear that he is the subordinate party in the relationship *de jure* as well as *de facto*. Because the narrative is disjointed, it is not clear exactly what David desired of Jonathan. As the narrative opens (20:1-4), David appears certain that he is marked for death and would thus want Jonathan to make an excuse for his disappearance. But in the remainder of the chapter his concern is to have Jonathan find out what in fact is Saul's attitude toward him. Despite the conflation of tradition, it is clear that although Jonathan would be humanly free to ignore David's request, he is considered obligated by their *b^e^rît*.

---

106. Cf. Driver, *Notes on Samuel*, p. 128.

107. So Dt. 4:23; 29:11,24; Jos. 23:16; Jer. 22:9. Also *b^e^rît ʾĕlōhîm* in Ps. 78:10; II Chr. 34:32. Elsewhere the phrase appears linked with *ʾărôn* as the abbreviated name of the ark.

108. Cf. an alternate version of their covenant "before Yahweh" in I Sam. 23:18; also 20:42.

I Samuel 20:14-15

These two verses are part of a pericope (vss. 12-18) which is fraught with extreme textual difficulties and for which no translation is given here. The text is so defective that any translation must involve some degree of conjecture.

Of the various modern attempts in English Bibles and commentaries, that of the New American Bible[109] is the most critical and accords best with what can be reconstructed from the surviving Hebrew and Greek traditions. Nevertheless, it is clear upon close examination of the Hebrew (and Greek) that the original text of this pericope is lost beyond recovery. The reconstruction of a Hebrew text which would be both grammatically correct and orderly in its thought progression would involve broad conjectures without textual basis. One imaginative guess might be as good as another - the evidence is wholly inadequate. Nevertheless, the major sources of difficulty in the surviving text can be identified and used as clues to the direction in which the solution must lie.

The problems may be summarized as follows: (1) Jonathan makes two oaths, one in vs. 12 (emending by adding *ḥy*) and the second immediately following in vs. 13. The general content of the two oaths seems to be parallel, and the verb *šlḥ* and phrase *wglyty ʾt ʾznk* appear in both.

(2) In vs. 17 the Hebrew as vocalized by the Masoretes clearly reads "and Jonathan made David swear again," while the Greek reads "and Jonathan again swore to David." With the final phrase "because he loved him as himself,"[110] the Greek

109. *The New American Bible, Translated from the Original Languages with Critical Use of All the Ancient Sources*, by Members of the Catholic Biblical Association of America, sponsored by the Bishop's Committee of the Confraternity of Christian Doctrine (Paterson, N.J.: St. Anthony Guild Press, 1970). F.M. Cross, Jr., and Patrick Skehan were chief collaborators on the Samuel text. Their emendations in these verses are essentially the same as those proposed by J. Wellhausen, *Der Text der Bücher Samuelis* (Göttingen: Vandenhoeck und Ruprecht's Verlag, 1871), pp. 116-117.

110. The intervening *bʾhbtw ʾtw* is not in the Greek and

reading appears superior; yet the presence of the more difficult Hebrew cannot be disregarded. In the larger context, David has not sworn anything as the text now stands; yet there is no content given for Jonathan's third swearing and it seems to be neither an appropriate conclusion to his plea to David nor a suitable connecting link to his subsequent explanation of a specific plan for informing David.

(3) The word *wlʾ* appears six times in the pericope, five of these in vss. 14-15 alone. Of the six, only the last in vs. 14 and the first in vs. 15 are readily readable as the Hebrew text now stands. When the Greek readings are accounted for, even the last in vs. 14 becomes awkward. The problem can be reduced as in the New American translation by repunctuating one (moving the *ʾathnaḥ* in vs. 12), relocating one (from 15b to 16a), and repointing three as *wᵉlū(ʾ)*. But *lū* is rare enough (particularly with the imperfect) that this solution must be considered *ad hoc*.

(4) The implication of vs. 13b is that Jonathan regards David as the future king. With no more introduction than *kʾšr hyh ʿm ʾby*, Jonathan in vss. 14-16 is suddenly looking to the future and asking for *ḥesed* for himself if he is alive or for his offspring if he is no longer alive. The abruptness with which this line of thought is introduced suggests the hand of an editor anticipating the story of Meribaal. Whether this is the work of the Deuteronomic historian himself or of an earlier hand cannot be determined, but it is unlikely that either would deliberately compose such a rough text.

When these four major problem areas are considered together, it appears likely that the root of the trouble is in major and irrecoverable haplographies. One may conjecture that Jonathan's second oath (vs. 13) might have been introduced by "and Jonathan swore again to David...." Verse 14 might have been prefixed by some more explicit comment about David's future rule, plus "and Jonathan made David swear...." If this last were in fact the case, the proliferation of *wlʾ* would have

---

ought probably to be dropped as a secondary expansion from the influence of I Sam. 18:3 (against the fuller New American Bible reading).

a reasonable explanation; the reading *wlʾ tʿśh ʿmdy ḥsd* would be original as a positive construction in an oath context - "you shall indeed do *ḥesed* with me."[111] With the loss of the oath request, the proper placement of *wlʾ* would become problematic at once and would be still further compounded by any subsequent haplographies. Scribal attempts at correction would easily generate the confusion now found in the MT. Given these conjectures, the MT tradition in vs. 17 of David's swearing again could be understood. It could even be regarded as misplaced material already accounted for in the haplographic material (as a combination of "Jonathan swore again" and "Jonathan made David swear"). It is further conceivable that both the not cutting off of Jonathan's name and also the cutting of a covenant with David were originally present behind vss. 16-17. There is of course no way to demonstrate this possibility directly, though the repeated occurrence of *krt* in the passage would occasion haplographies. The best "evidence" is from the related passages in which David's kingship is expressly anticipated, namely I Sam. 24:21-23 (cf. note 111) and I Sam. 23:16-18 (cf. 18:3; 20:42). In ch. 24 Saul recognizes David's future reign and asks him to swear that his seed *(zrʿ)* not be cut off (*krt*, hi.) and his name *(šm)* not be destroyed (*šmd*, hi.). In ch. 23 Jonathan in another context recognizes David's coming kingship and the two of them make a covenant *(wykrtw šnyhm bryt)*. If both themes were not present originally in 20:16-17, then it is likely that scribal knowledge of the absent theme (covenant) has aided in the corruption process.

It must be reemphasized that the preceding suggestions are

---

111. Although this special usage of *lʾ* to express the positive in an oath context is not usually found with the second person, there is an analogous usage in II Sam. 24:21-23 where, following *šbʿ*, *ʾm* is twice used with the second person in the sense "you shall not." It should be observed that these verses also concern the preserving of Saul's line when David is king and could conceivably come from the same author. Cf. also the examples of *ʾm* for the negative with the second person in oath contexts in Gen. 21:23 // Gen. 26:29.

only conjectures so that no specific text can or should be reconstructed. Nevertheless, these proposals are reasonable extrapolation from the evidence at hand. They are individually and as a group consonant with the surviving text and appropriate to our best understanding of what is actually going on in the text.

In review, vss. 14-15 are Jonathan's request that David do *ḥesed* with him by preserving his lineage whether he be alive or dead when David comes to power. An oath by David is possible and is appropriate for the circumstances, especially since the action may take place after Jonathan's death (cf. above, pp. 38-39). Although David is *de jure* the subordinate party in the existing relationship, the *ḥesed* is clearly related to a *de facto* situation in which the actual roles will be reversed. David's action will be the free act of a superior to an inferior performed in compliance with a specific political (and humanly personal) obligation.

As Hills has pointed out, Jonathan swears to fulfill David's request before he makes his own request of David. This appears to confirm the suggestion that *ḥesed* is not a matter of even exchange.[112] Because the text is defective and parts of vss. 12-18 may be editorial additions in anticipation of II Sam. 9, this conclusion is not certain. Practically speaking, there is no need for Jonathan's request unless he accedes to David's: if David is killed then Jonathan and his family will never be in danger. Nevertheless, the passage as a whole is consistent with the theme of individual salvatory action done as the need arises rather than as a "bribe" to get something in return. The possibility for a return action is certain only in the editor's historical retrospect.

II Sam. 9:1,3,7

> And David said, "Is there still someone surviving of the house of Saul, that I may do *ḥesed* with him for Jonathan's sake?" ...And David said [to Ziba] "Is there not still a man of the house of Saul, that I may do the *ḥesed* of God with him?" ...And David said to him [Meribaal], "Do not fear

---

112. Hills, "*Ḥesed* of Man," p. 2.

> because I will certainly do *ḥesed* with you for the sake of Jonathan your father: (and) I will restore to you all the land of Saul your father, and you yourself shall always eat bread at my table."

This passage records the "fulfillment" of I Sam. 20:12-18, and of I Sam. 24:21-22 as well, although at least the material in ch. 20 appears to have been inserted in anticipation of II Sam. 9. The historical position of the events of ch. 9 in relation to the tradition of II Sam. 21:1-14 can no longer be determined. Ch. 21, which now stands as an appendix to Samuel, records the death of seven of Saul's descendants at the hands of the Gibeonites as an expiation. The comment that Meribaal is saved "because of the oath of Yahweh" between David and Jonathan (21:7) is probably a later addition,[113] which seemed appropriate when this small section was appended to the Court History in which Meribaal plays a prominent role.

In ch. 9, in any case, David is pictured as not knowing the whereabouts of any of Saul's family. This is probably a dramatic device, although it is possible that Meribaal had actually concealed himself at Lo-debar.[114] Judging from David's opening comment to Meribaal that he need not be afraid, Meribaal was probably brought to David under duress (cf. 19:28). The double-edged significance of eating at the king's table has been discussed in connection with Barzillai (see above, pp. 60-63). Here David protects Meribaal from any zealous persons who might desire to dispose of any descendants of Saul. This is in agreement with the general picture which the narrative paints of David's sorrow at the death of Saul, Jonathan, and Ishbaal, even when others expected him to rejoice. At the same time, David protects himself to some degree by placing Saul's

---

113. Hertzberg, *I & II Samuel*, p. 383.

114. Machir son of Ammiel, in whose house Meribaal is located, appears again in 17:27 among those who bring provisions when David is fleeing in Absalom's revolt. One may speculate that Machir may have been a supporter of Saul's line in the original struggle for kingship who was eventually won over, possibly by David's *ḥesed* to Meribaal.

grandson where he can be watched. In his use of *ḥesed*, the narrator focuses on the former aspect of David's decree. David was free to have Meribaal executed, but because of his relationship with Jonathan he had a responsibility to protect Jonathan's son. Jonathan, already dead many years, had no recourse, but David still fulfilled his responsibility.

The restoration of Saul's land to Meribaal at first glance appears to be special blessing and thus not in accord with the usual usage of *ḥesed*. But the limits of minimal responsibility are not easy to assess historically. In light of the later story of Naboth's vineyard (I Ki. 21) which could not be transferred even for money, it seems quite possible that the return of the land was not regarded as a special gift.[115] In the strictly practical realm, the return of the land should have made Meribaal more content and less likely to cause trouble. But the author intends David's action to be understood as just doing what was right for Jonathan's son. The use of *ḥesed* pushes the practical political considerations into the background. Such motivations can be reconstructed by the historian but they are not the point which the narrator wishes to emphasize. His point is that the easy solution would have been to kill Meribaal,[116] but that David instead honored his obligation to Jonathan by saving Meribaal alive and making him a part of the court.

Summary of Section C

In the series of texts concerning Jonathan's *ḥesed* to David and David's to Jonathan the essential features of responsibility, special need, special ability to fulfill the need,

---

115. In II Sam. 19:24-30 David is apparently unsure whether to believe Ziba or Meribaal concerning Meribaal's loyalty during the Absalom revolt. In 16:4 David assigned the Saulide land to Ziba when he heard (from Ziba) that Meribaal saw the revolt as an occasion for a Saulide resurgence. Now Meribaal says Ziba tricked him and David settles the issue by dividing the land between them.

116. Conceivably the fickle Ziba even expected this result when he told of Meribaal's whereabouts.

and freedom of decision are present as expected. The passages are distinctive because it is made explicit that the *b^{e}rît* relationship is the basis for the obligation to do *ḥesed*. Yet it is apparent that David's responsibility to preserve Jonathan's name lies not solely in the fact that they were personal friends, but also in the fact that Jonathan did *ḥesed* for David in accordance with the responsibility voluntarily taken on in a formal pact. Thus, as was suggested from the texts in group B, *ḥesed* in a political context can be action appropriate to a pact or treaty relationship. But the responsibility could be nullified if one party failed to perform *ḥesed* when the occasion arose: this would be tantamount to breaking the covenant. It is for this reason that the basis for *ḥesed* in political contexts is so often stated in terms of a specific action. The underlying formal relationship is "secondary" and hence relatively fragile. While *ḥesed* is not exchanged *quid pro quo*, it is rooted in responsibility, and the reference to a prior action concretizes that responsibility. This aspect of the term is constantly stretched in theological application, to which we now turn, because Israel never fully maintained her part of the relationship which Yahweh established with her. Israel could only offer obedience, but she did not even do that consistently.

CHAPTER III
THE *ḤESED* OF GOD IN PRE-EXILIC PROSE

The texts for this chapter have been grouped into four sets based on usage. The first set concerns the relationship between Yahweh and various individuals in a context of specific aid to the person. These are the most closely comparable to the group A texts (intimate personal relationships) of the previous chapter. The second set consists of blessing/benediction formulae directed to specific individuals. Liturgical phrases or formulae from the context of the Sinai covenant comprise the third set; the ongoing use of these phrases in exilic and post-exilic materials is introduced with the earlier texts. The fourth set is the Deuteronomic historian's application of *ḥesed* to the establishment of the Davidic dynasty.

A. *Yahweh's* Ḥesed *to Individuals*

There are four examples in clearly pre-exilic narrative in which Yahweh does *ḥesed* to individuals,[1] all in the J portions of Genesis. In addition, one text from Ruth shows affinity with the Genesis usage.[2] The absence of such usage from the Elohistic material cannot be evaluated, since it may be simply a matter of circumstance in the combining of the J and E traditions, during which much of E was presumably omitted. In general, the *ḥesed* shown in the following texts corresponds close closely to that which has been described for human personal relationships. God responds to a specific personal need of the individual which might not otherwise be met. In each case the recipient is a worshipper of Yahweh; all the J texts involve prominent patriarchal figures.

Genesis 32:10-12

And Jacob said, "O, God of my father Abraham and

---

1. Excluding Yahweh's *ḥesed* to David, which is treated separately under Part D of this Chapter.

2. As in the previous chapter, the thorny problem of the date of Ruth is set aside and the texts are introduced where they belong typologically, with the pre-exilic materials.

> God of my father Isaac, Yahweh, who has said to me, 'return to your land and to your kindred and I will do good with you *('ytybh 'mk)*,' I am unworthy of all the *ḥesed* which you have done so reliably with *('t)* your servant; for with (only) my staff I passed over this Jordan and now I have become two companies. Deliver me from the hand of my brother, from Esau's hand, for I am afraid of him...."

The phrase *wmkl h'mt* has been rendered "so reliably."[3] The reading of a singular form of *ḥesed* follows the unanimous Greek witness. The plural uses of the word are otherwise confined to exilic and post-exilic sources and Psalms. The present MT reading *hsdym* may be explained as a dittography *wm* of the beginning of the following word *wmkl*, which was reinterpreted by the next scribe as the plural ending *-ym*.

As Jacob returns to the land at God's command he takes all reasonable precautions to insure a successful return. He sends messengers ahead to Esau calling himself "servant" and mentioning his acquired wealth (vss. 4-5), presumably to suggest the possibility of gifts (which is made explicit in the doublet or elaboration of the story, vss. 13-21). Jacob also divides his family and property into two companies so that at least one may survive. Having done what is humanly possible to prepare for the encounter, he calls on Yahweh for assistance. The force of the prayer is a request for an additional act of *ḥesed*. The same features noted for human acts of *ḥesed* are present, except that there is no human source of assistance. Jacob's need is essential - it involves the preservation of his own life and the lives of his family and retinue. Yahweh is the obvious and presumably sole source of deliverance. From a theological perspective, it is of interest that the survival of the heirs to the promises are at stake, so that the listener/reader understands the importance of Jacob's deliverance in a wider context.

Although the primary focus of the prayer is on the *ḥesed* which Jacob hopes to receive in his immediate crisis, it is possible to look back from the J narrator's viewpoint to

---

3. Cf. discussion of *ḥesed we'ĕmet* in Chapter II, pp. 32-4.

identify other actions of Yahweh for Jacob which may also be subsumed under the phrase "all the *ḥesed* which you have done." As Jacob says, God has caused him to prosper and gain in wealth. The giving of prosperity or special blessing, as we have seen, is not normally a part of a *ḥesed* action. But the point here is that in each step of Jacob's way, God has overcome the obstacles which Jacob could not handle. This is probably a stylized aspect of the prayer form which the Yahwist is using,[4] since the Yahwist generally presents Jacob as the crafty man who wins out by his own patience and cleverness.

The nature of Yahweh's responsibility for Jacob is a matter of central importance, for it is the J writer's emphasis on this feature which sets the text apart from supplicatory prayer in general. In words of his own composition, the J writer has associated the request for *ḥesed* with the tradition of the patriarchal "god of the fathers," upon which he elaborates throughout his narrative to suggest the "inner" relationship between Abraham, Isaac, and Jacob.[5] The address to the "God of my father Abraham and God of my father Isaac, Yahweh" is to be associated with the J theophany to Isaac (Gen. 26:24) and to Jacob himself (Gen. 28:13), all of which Alt correctly treats as the composition of the J writer.[6] Nevertheless, other

---

4. See Gunkel, *Genesis*, p. 358.

5. The classic statement of the god of the fathers tradition is that of Albrecht Alt, "Der Gott der Väter," *Beiträge zur Wissenschaft vom Alten und Neuen Testament* III, 12 (1929). Republished in A. Alt, *Kleine Schriften zur Geschichte des Volkes Israel* I (Munich: C. H. Beck, 1953), pp. 1-78, and translated in A. Alt, "The God of the Fathers," *Essays on Old Testament History and Religion*, tr. by R. A. Wilson (Oxford: Basil Blackwell, 1966), pp. 3-77. Cappadocian parallels were adduced by J. Lewy, "Les textes paléo-assyriens et l'Ancien Testament," *Revue de l'histoire des religions* 110 (1934) 29-65. A recent critique and presentation of new evidence is that of F. M. Cross, "Yahweh and the God of the Patriarchs," *HTR* 55 (1962) 225-259. See also L. Bailey, "Israelite *ʾEl Šadday* and Amorite *Bêl Sadê*," *JBL* 87 (1968) 434-438.

6. "The God of the Fathers," pp. 16, 19.

passages suggest clearly that the god of the father was not an invention of the J and E narrators but was an authentic pre-Mosaic tradition which survived and was amplified.[7] It is extremely difficult to assess the degree of memory or consciousness of the old tradition which the Genesis narrators may have had three or four centuries after the emergence of Yahwism. Presumably they were not aware of the old family or clan significance of the fragmentary phrases they preserved, or they would have handled them more precisely.

Since *ḥesed* does not appear in connection with any texts which are regarded as "surviving fragments" of this tradition, there is no concrete evidence that the term may have been especially associated with the action of the deities in this tradition. Nevertheless, the word would be appropriate for the protective care of such a god as the "...patron of the clan, the social group...who enters into a kinship or covenantal relationship with a clan and who guides the social group in its peregrinations, its wars...."[8] One may speculate that this aspect of the patriarchal religion, which thought of man's relationship to the deity in terms of kinship,[9] would be a likely context for the first use of the word *ḥesed* as a theological term. But there is no evidence for establishing such a starting point. The word is thoroughly entrenched in the theological language of the Mosaic covenant tradition before the time of our earliest written sources (cf. Ex. 15:13; Ex. 34 discussed below).

Even though the J writer probably was not specifically aware of the tutelary deity tradition, we may presume that his use of *ḥesed* in a prayer such as Jacob's was appropriately based in the personal relationship which God himself established in the theophany to Jacob, in which God assumed responsibility for Jacob's welfare. Jacob's faithfulness within the relationship is reinforced by the immediate fact (which Jacob

---

7. *Ibid.*, pp. 19-21. Prominent among the surviving clues are Gen. 31:53a; 46:1, 3; 49:25.

8. Cross, "Yahweh and the God of the Patriarchs," p. 228.

9. Cross notes the importance of kinship elements in second millennium Amorite names and early Hebrew onomastica. *Ibid.*, p. 228, n.7. See also his *Canaanite Myth*, pp. 270-273.

mentions) that Yahweh himself has commanded Jacob to go to the land where he will meet Esau and that Jacob is complying with the command. The relationship between God and man is such that God should protect and deliver the man simply because he is his God. Yet there is the notion that the man's obedience is somehow at stake in the god's answer to the supplication (even though the man may never fully measure up - "I am not worthy....."). This tension between an act based only in the fact of the relationship and one which has in some way to be "deserved" even within the relationship, is inherent in the human relationships where *ḥesed* appears and is heightened in the relationship between an individual and God. Both of these aspects of God's responsibility to do *ḥesed* are present to some degree in each situation involving an individual, with the emphasis varying from one occasion to another.[10] The other central features of *ḥesed*, circumstantial dominance in a situation of need, freedom not to fulfill the need, and lack of other source of help for the suppliant, are all inherent in a human request for divine help.

Genesis 19:19

> 19 Even though your servant has found favor before you and you have already done great *ḥesed* for me in preserving my life, [literally; you have made great your *ḥesed* which you have done for me] I am nevertheless not able to escape to the hills lest disaster overtake me and I die.
> 20 This town here is near enough that I could flee to it - and it is a little one - so please let me escape to it (is it not a small thing [*ḥesed*]?) that I may survive.

Two minor text questions emerge from the verses translated. The first is the LXX addition of ἕνεκεν σου at the end of verse 20. The plus appears to be distributed randomly in the Greek manuscripts,[11] and it is impossible to be sure which

---

10. In the Psalms, *ḥesed* is sometimes deliverance deserved because of faithfulness, sometimes deliverance asked despite unfaithfulness. See Chapter VI.

11. The phrase is omitted in Dehlmoqs(txt)tuvc_2 B̸E̸L̸

of a variety of Hebrew prepositions may be represented. If the addition was generated from a Hebrew manuscript, one might suggest *biglālěkā* as the *Vorlage* reading because of the affinity in vocabulary and circumstance between the present text and the shortly preceding usage of Gen. 12:13.[12]

A more important question concerns the double usage of *whwʾ mṣʿr* and *hlʾ mṣʿr hwʾ*, each following *šmh*. It has been suggested that the first phrase may be a gloss.[13] Since the Greek and versions are practically unanimous in attesting both readings, such a gloss would have to be quite early. The function of the phrases as an aetiology for Zoar (vs. 22) makes the double reading plausible and the writer has elected to retain it. Part of the reason for regarding one phrase as a gloss or possibly a dittography must be that the context of the remark itself has been regarded as duplication: both phrases have been understood as referring to the town which Lot is pointing out. The Masoretes' feminine punctuation of *hwʾ* in each instance supports this interpretation. Yet it seems possible, as is suggested in the translation given above, that the writer had two different points to make. The first is the small size of the town; the second is the smallness of the additional act needed to save Lot in contrast with the greatness (cf. use of *gdl*) of the earlier act which has saved his life thus far, namely the rescue from the men of Sodom (vss. 10-11) during the preceding night. It is not that saving Lot is insignificant, but that the new request should not be difficult in light of what has been done already.

The introduction of Lot's request in vs. 18 presents additional difficulties. The narrative up to this point has concerned Lot's encounter with two messengers but the address in vs. 19ff. uses the singular form of "you." There is difficulty

---

Phil-arm Just Chr Cyr Thdt T-A. With the exception of the very small Byzantine group Ay, none of the Genesis textual families (as identified by F. M. Cross, private communication) systematically includes or omits the reading.

12. *ʿl, lmʿn, bʿbwr, b, l* are other prepositional possibilities.

13. So, e.g., Kittel, notes on Genesis, *BH*, *ad loc.*

in the shift in vs. 18, both in the Hebrew and Greek versions. The difficulty is occasioned by the incorporation and integration of vss. 17-22, once perhaps an independent aetiological tradition, into the story of Sodom's destruction.[14] In the preceding verses the messengers have explained that they have been sent by Yahweh to destroy the city and at the same time comment that the Lord is about to destroy it. In the following section we hear no more of the messengers; Yahweh himself is the only actor in the destruction of the city. The Masoretic pointing *ʾădōnāy* in vs. 18 may well indicate that the punctators understood Lot's request to be directed to Yahweh. The consonantal text could, of course, also be read "my lords" (presumably identical pointing in pausal position) or "my lord" (with change of pointing), addressing one or both of the messengers; the *wayyōmer* of vs. 21 is ambiguous: "and he said" or "and one said." All three interpretations have been adopted by various translators and commentators.[15] The writer follows von Rad's interpretation that the content of the petition and response involved a decision which lay properly in God's hands.[16] In the narrative of the messengers' visit with Abraham and Yahweh's announcement of the destruction of the city (ch. 18) there is a similar tension between Yahweh and the messengers which is alleviated by the specific mention of Yahweh. Of interest for the argument here is the fact that in his petitions for the deliverance of the city Abraham always addresses "*ʾădōnāy*." *Yhwh* is never used in the actual words of address.

The similarity of the general form of this petition to that of Jacob's request for deliverance from Esau further suggests that we are dealing here with a theological rather than a secular use of *ḥesed*. Past *ḥesed* is acknowledged as a way of

---

14. Von Rad, *Genesis*, p. 215.

15. "My lords": RSV; "my lord": Speiser, *Genesis*, p. 137; "my Lord": BDB; von Rad, *Genesis*, p. 215.

16. Von Rad, *Genesis*, p. 215. Gunkel's contention that the phrase "I am not able" (vs. 22) would be inappropriate words for Yahweh (*Genesis*, p. 212) must be rejected. The speaker is merely explaining why Lot must hurry; no comment on God's power is involved even indirectly.

introducing a petition for another action which is understood by implication to be a new act of *ḥesed*. Lot is grateful that his life has been preserved thus far. Here there is of course a point of contact with "human" action: it is the messengers who rescued Lot from the men of Sodom who tried to tear down his house and who also warned him to leave and hurried him along when he lingered. Yet it is clear that both aspects of the rescue thus far involve supernatural intervention. The Sodomites were struck by a "blinding light"[17] and knowledge of God's plan was prerequisite for the warning. In both instances, Lot had no other source of assistance in a time of essential need; in both instances, the divine helpers were free not to act. These same features apply likewise to Lot's new request.

Yahweh's immediate responsibility for Lot is similar to the responsibility for Jacob. There is an appeal to God's own recognition of some responsibility implied in the use of the term *ḥesed*: "You, yourself, God, have taken responsibility for my welfare in your past assistance, for which I am grateful. But what was the use of all that past deliverance if you do not rescue me now?" Although Lot receives no special theophany and although he is a side figure in the patriarchal tradition and even is regarded as progenitor of the Ammonites and Moabites, in this narrative Lot as the nephew of Abraham is distinguished from the Sodomites as the recipient of God's deliverance. His position as a relative of the recipient of the promise is in the foreground. Lot may also be understood as a "righteous man" in the narrative: since there were not ten, the city was not saved, but the one, Lot, proved himself by protecting the messengers against the Sodomites.

The arguments for this text as a theological use of *ḥesed* are set over against Glueck, who assumes that Lot addresses a single person and that the text is a purely secular use of *ḥesed*. In interpreting the passage, Glueck argues for a "reciprocal protective relationship" between host and guest, so that Lot's granting of protection to the messengers "put them

---

17. Speiser's translation. See E. A. Speiser, "The 'Elative' in West-semitic and Akkadian," *Journal of Cuneiform Studies* 6 (1952) 89, n.52.

under an obligation to be loyal to him, to render assistance and to show him *ḥesed*."[18] Although it is generally agreed that a host is required by customary law to protect his guests at all costs,[19] the reciprocal responsibility of the protected person appears to be Glueck's own inference.[20]

In addition to the internal difficulty of Glueck's interpretation, it should be observed that as a human act of *ḥesed* this example cannot readily be accommodated to either of the major categories of *ḥesed* suggested for the previous chapter. In all cases where there was not an intimate and ongoing personal relationship between the parties, separate actions of the two parties were always directly involved. In this text, the relationship of host and guest, although legally binding, is neither intimately personal nor of indefinite duration. Yet Lot appeals not to his own action in offering his daughter to the men of Sodom, which we might expect him to do if his request were for human *ḥesed*, but instead he appeals to the previous *ḥesed* of Yahweh/the messengers. While such a break in the pattern is not conclusive evidence that we are here dealing with theological usage, it provides strong reinforcement when coupled with the similarity to Jacob's petition, the use of *ʾădōnāy* in address to the deity in ch. 18, and the contrast between Lot and the Sodomites.

---

18. Glueck, p. 9.

19. So deVaux, *Ancient Israel*, p. 10; Johannes Pedersen, *Israel: Its Life and Culture* I-II (London: Oxford University Press, 1926), p. 357. W. R. Smith, *Kinship*, p. 48. The present passage and the story of the man of Gibeah in Jd. 19 are the classic examples. It should be observed that the analogies cited for the custom are generally from the nomadic context, while these two cases represent an urban adaptation.

20. Glueck (p. 8, n.5, 6 and p. 9, n.1) cites W. R. Smith, *Kinship*, pp. 41 and 14. (Glueck refers to the 1885 edition; corresponding pages in the 1903 edition are pp. 48 and 15.) But there are difficulties in combining the tribal referent of p. 14 with the individual referent of p. 41. It is not at all clear that "brotherhood" could be extended to any situation in which the law of hospitality prevailed.

Genesis 39:21-22b

> And Yahweh was with Joseph and extended *(nṭh)* *ḥesed* to him, and gave him favor before the chief jailer; and the chief jailer gave Joseph charge over all the prisoners who were in the prison.

Yahweh has been with Joseph all along; and now that Joseph is again in dire straits God sets in motion the mechanism for his deliverance. The narrator attributes to God's doing the favorable notice which Joseph receives from the jailer. It is Joseph's supervisory position which provides the occasion for the interpreting of his fellow-prisoners' dreams in ch. 40 and for his request for the human *ḥesed* through which he is eventually released from prison.[21] Here Yahweh does for Joseph what Joseph presumably could not be sure to accomplish, humanly speaking. God is as always (by definition) free to do as he wills in the situation - he can do nothing or he can bring Joseph to the attention of the jailer. That God has freely assumed responsibility for Joseph is presupposed in the theological setting of the story. A son of Jacob is in a foreign land because of God's still hidden purpose. There is an undercurrent of a personal relationship of Yahweh to Joseph; Yahweh is with him and blesses him throughout his stay in Potiphar's house. Now, although free to do nothing for Joseph in his time of need, God helps him, acting in accordance with his responsibility for Joseph, extending *ḥesed* to him. Further, Joseph is faultless in the matter of Potiphar's wife for which he is imprisoned. The action of Yahweh in initiating his deliverance is thus "deserved" at the same time that it is freely given.

Genesis 24:12, 14, 27

> 12 And he (Abraham's servant) said, "O Yahweh, God of my master Abraham, grant me good fortune today, and so do *ḥesed* with my master Abraham.
> 14 "Let the maiden to whom I shall say..., and she shall say... - let her be the one whom thou has appointed for thy servant Isaac. And by this I shall know that you have done *ḥesed* with my master."

---

21. See discussion of 40:14 in Chapter II, pp. 46-48.

27 And he said, "Blessed be Yahweh God of my master Abraham who has not abandoned (*ʿāzab*) his *ḥesed* and his *ʾĕmet* from with (*mēʿīm*) my master."

In the *ʾăšer* clause of vs. 27, which may be a semi-fixed formulaic construction,[22] the construction *ʿzb X mʿm N* seems awkward, at least from the English viewpoint. Taking *ḥesed* as the subject of the verb does not ease the syntax and would be anomalous as a prose usage (although if the clause has a formulaic background an alternate usage might be possible). *ʿzb* normally takes only a single, direct object. It seems possible that the *mʿm* is an attempt to convey a double-object idea. The use of *mʿm* may be associated with other constructions in which *ḥesed* is "cut off (*krt*) *mʿm*" or "removed (*swr*) *mʿm*" a person (cf. II Sam. 7:15; I Sam. 20:15). Possibly *mʿm* here may also be influenced by the frequent use of *ʿm N* for the doing of *ḥesed*. The meaning in any case is clear: God has not abandoned Abraham; God has not failed to do *ḥesed*.

The background of the pericope has been given in some detail in connection with the secular use of *ḥesed* in 24:49.[23] Abraham's servant is sent to find a wife for Isaac from Abraham's kindred and to return with her to Canaan. If he cannot bring her back then he will be free from his oath to Abraham. In these verses of supplication and thanksgiving, just as in the secular use of vs. 49, the J narrator makes specifically clear that the *ḥesed* is for Abraham, not for his servant. The person in need is Abraham - the continuity of his line (and of God's promise to his descendants) is at stake in this mission.

The twice-repeated address to "Yahweh, God of my master Abraham" further reinforces the point that Abraham's need is at stake. At the same time, this mode of address directs the reader's attention to the personal relationship between Yahweh and Abraham whom he called and with whom he entered into covenant. Yahweh's responsibility for Abraham, which he assumed in establishing that relationship, is counted upon by the servant

---

22. Cf. Ruth 2:20a, discussed immediately below.

23. Chapter II, pp. 34-36. Narratives such as this point up the artificiality of absolute distinctions among "secular," "theological," and "religious" usage in any word study.

and also by Abraham, who has assured the servant that the Lord who swore to give Abraham's descendants the land will indeed bring the mission to fruition (24:7). The idea of the tutelary deity may again be projected behind the usage, as with the prayer for the survival of Jacob's wives and children, although here also we are dealing with a narrative artfully constructed by the Yahwist. Beyond the basic fact of Abraham's ongoing relationship to his God, it is clear here as in the previous examples that Abraham is doing what is right in the specific situation. By not taking a Canaanite wife for Isaac, by trusting Yahweh to provide for the maintaining of the purity of his line, Abraham does his part to keep the relationship to Yahweh in good repair. Thus the basis for Yahweh's assumption of responsibility for Abraham is reinforced.

The servant asks for and receives a particular sign by which he may identify the girl of Yahweh's choosing. This is the specific act of *ḥesed* by which he is assured that God is acting reliably *(= 'ĕmet)* on Abraham's behalf. The identification of the chosen girl is an act which could not be accomplished by human means alone. There was no recourse aside from Yahweh's action. In this instance as with Joseph in prison the initial step in the sequence of human actions which leads to deliverance from the dilemma is Yahweh's action of *ḥesed*.

Ruth 2:20

> And Naomi said to her daughter-in-law, "Blessed be he by Yahweh who has not abandoned *(ʿzb)* his *ḥesed* with *('t)* the living or with *('t)* the dead."

The MT *'ăšer* clause is ambiguous in two respects: (1) the place of *ḥesed* as subject or object is unclear, and (2) the personal referent may be either he (Boaz) or Yahweh.

With respect to the first problem, the simplest grammatical solution would seem to be to take *ḥesed* as subject and read the *'t*'s as object markers: "whose *ḥesed* has not forsaken the living or the dead."[24] But two considerations suggest that this simpler interpretation may be incorrect. First of all, the Greek tradition unanimously translates each *'t* by μετά, clearly reading prepositionally. And in the manuscripts which generally use a masculine (rather than neuter) declension for

24. The RSV adopts this translation.

ἔλεος, so that a case distinction appear, the reading is the accusative ἔλεον. Hence, the Greek translators understood a personal subject for *ʿzb* in this clause. The second consideration is the comparison of this clause to that of the similar clause in Gen. 24:27. There the use of the preposition *mēʿīm* (where *ʾt* is used here) indicated that *ḥesed* should properly be understood as object of the verb *ʿzb*.[25] Although *ʿm* is the preposition most often associated with the doing of *ḥesed*, prepositional *ʾt* is also attested,[26] so that its appearance here with *lʾ ʿzb* would not be surprising. For these reasons the more awkward translation (from the English viewpoint) has been adopted.

The text is equally ambiguous on the second question, whether Yahweh or Boaz has done *ḥesed* to Naomi and Ruth. Although the *ʾăšer* clause may normally refer to its immediate antecedent, the fixed phrase "blessed ~~by~~ be N by YHWH" would not comfortably allow for insertion of a long clause. Glueck argues that blessing is invoked for Boaz because he did *ḥesed* for Ruth and thus regards this text as an example of human *ḥesed*. His arguments are two: first, that only here would *ḥesed* of God be applied to the dead;[27] second, that there is a grammatical parallel in II Sam. 2:5. Against Glueck's first point it may be said that the absence of other examples of God's *ḥesed* to the dead is perhaps a matter of circumstance. The repetition of key words and phrases found in Ruth[28] should be observed in the occurrences of "the dead" in 1:8 and 2:20. Stylistic considerations may have precipitated the use of the expression here. More important, Glueck himself recognizes that *ḥesed* can be done for the dead by living persons;[29] it

---

25. See argument immediately above, p. 103.

26. E.g., Gen. 32:11; 24:49; (II Sam. 16:17).

27. The dead "generally are described as having absolutely no relationship with God" (Glueck, p. 7).

28. See summary of examples in unpublished paper on Ruth (read before the Biblical Colloquium meeting in Washington, D.C., November 8, 1969) by Edward F. Campbell, pp. 20-24.

29. So especially Ruth 1:8. Also II Sam. 2:5 (burial of Saul); Gen. 47:29 (anticipation of burial of Jacob). And for

does not seem necessary to suppose that the use of *ḥesed* could not be extended theologically in this context as well, or to say that the living have a relationship to the dead which Yahweh does not. Finally, Glueck does not comment on the specific nature of Boaz' *ḥesed*; it is scarcely obvious that allowing the girl to glean and to receive a few extra stalks of grain can be regarded as *ḥesed* to the dead husbands, or even to Ruth herself.

Glueck's second argument, the analogy of II Sam. 2:5,[30] is attractive and cannot be disclaimed on grammatical grounds; the second person usage makes clear that there the men of Jabesh Gilead are blessed because they have done *(ʿśh) ḥesed*. However, the text of Gen. 24:27 provides an analogy in the other direction. There we find the only other example of *lʾ ʿzb* with *ḥesed*, in a far more common construction in which the speaker blesses Yahweh himself and an *ʾăšer* clause describing Yahweh's action follows. No definitive decision is possible from analogies of grammar and vocabulary alone. Perhaps the writer is deliberately ambiguous.

On the grounds of meaning, however, it is probable that God's *ḥesed* is the primary focus of attention at this point in the story. Boaz' actions thus far cannot readily be described as *ḥesed* in terms of the characteristics established in Chapter II for the meaning of the term in secular usage. He has only the most generalized responsibility for Ruth as a poor person, although since he has learned of her background he may regard her as a relative (vs. 11) even though he does not mention it to her. Furthermore, his action, even in arranging for the generous extra leavings, cannot really be described as supplying an essential need which Ruth could not have fulfilled otherwise. And there would be recourse - presumably legal action could be taken if he refused to permit her to glean (cf. Lev. 19:9-10).

God's action, however, is analogous to that called *ḥesed* in Gen. 24 and in Gen. 39:21. The import of the conversation

---

the living in behalf of the dead, cf. II Sam. 9 (David to Meribaal for Jonathan's sake).

30. *brwkym ʾtm lyhwh ʾšr ʿśytm hḥsd hzh*. See above, Chapter II, pp. 40-42.

between Ruth and Naomi in 2:19-21 is surely that it is Yahweh who has caused Ruth to "happen to come to the part of the field belonging to Boaz" (2:3). Despite the many difficulties in the narrative sequence of the story, it appears that here again God had initiated the sequence of events by which the problem of progeny for the dead will eventually be resolved. He has provided for initial contact with Boaz and a favorable response. This Ruth could not accomplish for herself; and as it turns out, Boaz is her only source of help since the closer-of-kin rejects her. The narrator is looking ahead as well as back. God's responsibility for Ruth, Naomi, and the dead was general in terms of their role as worshippers of Yahweh. But here as in the other examples of this group, God's *ḥesed* is again preceded by an action which suggests that the recipient was deserving. Ruth has forsaken her own country in order to follow her mother-in-law. She has done even more than what is right.

Summary

In all five examples Yahweh is asked for or does *ḥesed* for a person who worships him and who is clearly acting in obedience to God's specific command or else doing what is humanly right against difficult odds. Thus because the person is acting faithfully within a relationship initiated by God there is a clear sense that God should exercise responsible care for that person. At the same time, it is presupposed that God is free not to act on the person's behalf; he alone is powerful, so there is no recourse if he does not act. The action requested or received is one which the person could not accomplish for himself or by available human means. The specific *ḥesed* action of God, just as in human relationships, fulfills an essential need; it does not bestow extra blessings or privilege.

B. *Blessing/Benedictory Use of* Ḥesed

The three examples of this usage (II Sam. 2:6; 15:20; Ruth 1:8) suggest that it was peculiarly appropriate to situations of parting under adverse circumstances. When a recipient of human *ḥesed* would not ever again be in a position to do *ḥesed* for his benefactor, it was appropriate to ask God to do *ḥesed* for the benefactor. It will be suggested that permanent separation (or death) and the transfer to God of one's potential responsibility for doing *ḥesed* were correlated: this usage appears to have served as a technical way of bringing a relationship to an end.

II Samuel 15:20

> Only yesterday you came: today should I make you go wandering with us, when I am going whatever way I may go? Return, and take your brothers with you, and may Yahweh be sure to do *ḥesed* with you.

The MT omits *wyhwh y‘ś ‘mk*, which is read throughout the Greek. This is clearly a haplography; the immediately preceding phrase ends with *‘mk*. For the translation of *w’mt* as "be sure to," see the discussion of Chapter II, pp. 32-34.

As David flees Jerusalem during Absalom's revolt, Ittai and the Gittites are among those who set out with him. David urges him to return to "stay with the king." The implication seems to be that this display of allegiance is extraordinary on the part of these "exiles," and that David is freeing Ittai to end his relationship to David and establish one with Absalom instead. Ittai refuses to leave, swearing instead that he will be with the king in life or death. For all the differences in circumstance, the scene itself brings to mind the departure of Naomi in Ruth 1 (see below).

David can no longer protect or provide for the men who have served him briefly and now wish to follow him. He invokes God's *ḥesed* on their behalf. The concrete content of *ḥesed* cannot be stated for an expression such as this, but "protective care" is certainly appropriate to the context and consonant with the more specific usage. We are not told whether Ittai's action in following David is to be regarded as *ḥesed*. One has the impression that Ittai was doing *ḥesed*, but David felt that the relationship present was not strong enough to allow him to accept it in good conscience. Ittai's protest prevailed, and the Gittites accompanied David after all.

Ruth 1:8

> And Naomi said to her (two) daughters-in-law, "Go now, return, each to her own mother's household.

May Yahweh do *ḥesed* with you, as *(k'šr)* you did with the dead and with me."

The two daughters-in-law have started out with Naomi on her return to Bethlehem. At some point along the way she urges them to return home rather than accompany her. Here Yahweh's *ḥesed* is invoked in accordance with the human *ḥesed* which Naomi and her dead sons have received but now are unable to return. The human *ḥesed* of Ruth and Orpah might be understood to be their starting out on the journey with Naomi - it cannot here be limited to Ruth's actual return alone, since the blessing is clearly addressed to both Ruth and Orpah. It is also possible that *ḥesed* here constitutes the ongoing behavior of the daughters-in-law which was appropriate to their family status. But their journey with Naomi climaxes their active demonstration of willingness to stay with the foreigner's family even in death. Naomi is in need, and they have freely met their responsibility for her.

As in the previous example, God's *ḥesed* cannot be defined more than to say that deliverance from adverse circumstances would be an appropriate content. Since Naomi cannot now do anything for the girls and sees no prospect of ever being again in a position to do so, she must turn this future responsibility over to God. Her inability to do *ḥesed* is further emphasized by the separation which she urges. If the girls come into trouble she will no longer be with them; hence she must commit them to God's keeping.

Naomi's urging that Ruth and Orpah return to their own families does more than commit them to God's keeping; it declares her intent to free them from their responsibility - which circumstantially they had been free to disregard in any case. The invocation of God's *ḥesed* here, as in the political parallel of David and Ittai, may be understood as a formal way of ending the voluntary relationship within which the parties have accepted responsibility for one another. David tells Ittai he should serve the new king; Naomi tells the two girls they should go home and remarry. These texts are not simply a matter of "good-bye for now, and God take care of your needs while we are apart." Each case involves a final decision concerning change of primary personal relationships. This interpretation is also appropriate for the third example of this usage.

II Samuel 2:6

> Now, therefore, may Yahweh be sure to do *ḥesed* with you. And I, for my part, will make a treaty of friendship with you because you have done this thing.

The translation "make a treaty of friendship" *ʿśh hṭwbh hzʾt* is based on the study of Delbert Hillers.[31] This verse is the middle section of David's message to the Jabesh Gileadites after he hears that they have buried Saul. In vs. 5 he has invoked Yahweh's blessing upon them because of that act of *ḥesed*.[32] Now, in a sentence which at first glance seems almost redundant, he adds "May Yahweh be sure to do *ḥesed* with you." Since Saul is dead, he will not be able to do *ḥesed* again for the men of Jabesh Gilead. On the human political plane David is at this time formally in the enemy camp, since he fled to the Philistines and only by the chance of their warlords' decision was not at the Battle of Gilboa. At the same time the narrator has pictured David as one who has never lost his respect for Saul as the Lord's anointed. Hence there is one narrative level at which David is not in a proper position to do *ḥesed* for the men of Jabesh Gilead: he is the enemy, with no positive relationship and no responsibility. On a second level, which the narrator alone may recognize, David would wish to do *ḥesed* for the Jabesh Gileadites should the occasion arise. The tension is neatly solved by David's invoking Yahweh's *ḥesed* upon them.

But there is more at stake than David's personal feelings. He immediately continues with an offer to establish a formal relationship with Jabesh Gilead, commenting that Saul is dead

---

31. "A Note on Some Treaty Terminology in the Old Testament," 46-47. Hillers extends to this text the work of W. L. Moran on *ṭb* and *rʿm* in political contexts in Aramaic and Akkadian in his (Moran's) "A Note on the Treaty Terminology of the Sefîre Stelas," 173-176.

32. See discussion of this secular use of *ḥesed* in Chapter II, pp. 40-42.

and Judah has already recognized him as king. It is of interest that he begins *w^e gam 'ānōkî*, clearly setting his action over against Yahweh's doing *ḥesed*. This emphasis, coupled with the references to Saul's death and his own anointing, suggest that "may Yahweh do *ḥesed*..." implies "now your relationship to Saul's household may be, or can be, ended." To the extent that this verse reflects a historical background, we know that the message was sent when Saul's sons and Abner still survived. David in using the phrase "may Yahweh do *ḥesed*" is apparently suggesting that the Jabesh Gileadites' political relationship was to Saul and that with his death that relationship is now ended. They are now free to establish a new formal relationship with David (rather than with Saul's descendants), which David offers and suggests that they do. The outcome is not told us, since the story moves immediately to Abner and Ishbaal. Perhaps the political loyalty of the region was not finally settled until even as late as Abner's revolt.[33]

Summary

In these "blessing/benedictory" passages, the exact content of God's *ḥesed* cannot be specified since the reference is to indefinite future circumstances. In each of the three examples the expression "may Yahweh do *ḥesed* with you" is associated with the ending of human relationships, personal or political, and the ending of responsibilities, however freely performed, which are assumed in such relationships. This repeated context suggests the possibility of a technical usage for the phrase under these circumstances.

C. *Liturgical Formulae*

The liturgical formulae using *ḥesed* which appear in preexilic narrative fall into three general types. Each will be discussed in turn, along with a brief presentation of the texts from prophecy and Psalms which reflect the respective types.

---

33. See Chapter II, pp. 60-64 for discussion of the role of Barzillai from Rogelim in Gilead.

Type One: Exodus 34:6-7[34]

And Yahweh crossed before him and called out: "Yahweh Yahweh:

'l rḥwm wḥnwn	6	'El merciful and gracious
'rk 'pym wrb ḥsd (w'mt)	7	patient and great of *ḥesed*
nṣr ḥsd l'lpym	7	keeper of *ḥesed* for thousands
nś' ‘wn wpś‘ (wḥṭ'h)	6	forgiver of iniquity and transgression
(w) nqh l' ynqh	6	(but) he will by no means declare innocent (the guilty)
pqd ‘wn 'bwt ‘l bnym (w‘l bny bnym)	9	requiter of iniquity of the fathers upon the sons
‘l šlšym w‘l rb‘ym	9	unto the third and unto the fourth generations"

This arrangement of the text suggests what the writer considers to be the likely metrical pattern underlying the text of this liturgical statement. The words in parentheses are not included in the syllable counts and are regarded as probable secondary elaborations on a more basic form of the text. Of the four items in parentheses, only the *waw* preceding *nqh* appears in any of the other occurrences of these liturgical phrases.

From the earliest stages of literary-critical analysis, these verses have been regarded as the secondary addition of some redactor, such as R^{JE} or some subsequent editor, and this interpretation has persisted among more recent commentators.[35]

---

34. Actually, only the first, second, fourth, and fifth lines of the proposed metric rendering belong to what is here discussed as Type One. Line three belongs with lines six and seven which together constitute a modified form of Type Two (see pp. 129-133). The conflate Exodus tradition is used as the starting point because it is presumably the earliest written form of the Type One usage. Arguments that Ex. 34:6-7 represents the combining of at least two ancient formulae appear in the course of the discussion.

35. A long catalogue of those holding this position is provided in R. C. Dentan, "The Literary Affinities of Exodus xxxiv 6f," *VT* 13 (1963), 36, notes 2-9. The commentators cited

Others have suggested that the verses are out of place at this point. McNeile, for example, suggests that the formula should precede 33:14-16, although his reason for this location is not clear.[36] Rylaarsdam apparently moves vss. 5b-9 to follow 33:23,[37] which would seem to be a preferable placement if one is going to engage in this sort of hypothetical rearrangement. Obviously some joins and dislocations have been made necessary in the joining of the J and E Sinai traditions; no reconstruction can be definitive in all details. But the primary question here is whether these verses must be regarded as secondary to J. Can their function (or lack of function) in the context be established?

The early view that the verses were secondary grew out of the developmental theory of Israel's religion which posited a very primitive stage as late as the end of the second millennium B.C. "Such aggregates of predicates are supposed to belong to a more advanced devotional vocabulary than can be traced with certainty in writers of the eighth century."[38] A slightly more credible, if still very subjective, basis for excluding the material as secondary is that its lack of

---

include Holzinger, Kautzsch, Baentsch, Rudolph, Carpenter and Harford-Battersby, Beer and Galling, and Bennett. Most recently, Martin Noth (*Exodus: A Commentary*, tr. by J. S. Bowden from the 1959 German ed. [OTL; Philadelphia: Westminster Press, 1962]) regarded vss. 6abβ, 7, as "an addition which is made up of customary, stereotyped phrases" (p. 261). He does not attempt to determine a particular date or occasion for the addition.

36. A. H. McNeile, *The Book of Exodus* (WC; New York: Edwin S. Gorham, 1908), p. 217.

37. J. Coert Rylaarsdam, *The Book of Exodus* (IB: New York: Abingdon Press, 1952), p. 1075.

38. The position is so summarized by J. E. Carpenter and G. Harford-Battersby, who record this reasoning but do not fully commit themselves to it. *The Hexateuch according to the Revised Version* (London: Longmans, Green, and Co., 1900), II, 134. Note that J is now probably to be attributed to the tenth century rather than to the eighth.

concreteness is not typical of J's style.[39] But who can be sure that J would so restrict himself in such a manner that he could not draw upon materials with which he might have been familiar?

R. C. Dentan begins with the supposition that the verses are secondary and therefore examines them in isolation in an effort to identify some theological "party" which might have inserted these phrases. He studies the words individually (with the exception of *ḥesed weʾĕmet* which he keeps together even though the *ʾĕmet* may possibly be secondary here) and concludes that the primary affinities of the vocabulary are late and are not Deuteronomic but are with the Wisdom literature.[40] The writer disagrees with Dentan's analysis in many points of detail, but only a few general observations are required here. First, the general affinities of vocabulary are tendencies at best; the distribution depends to a large extent on the type of materials preserved from any particular period, and the circumstances which evoked them. It is not surprising, for example, that most of the references to God's mercy *(rḥm)* are late, since mercy would be a national concern in the exile and later. This term was not appropriate to the emphases of the theological thrust of pre-exilic prophecy or of the Deuteronomist. But one may not infer that the word was not available or was never used of God in any of the earlier public worship or personal prayer in Israel. Of all the words treated, only *nṣr* cannot be shown to occur in some pre-Isaianic context outside the formula

---

39. So Bruno Baentsch, *Exodus-Leviticus-Numbers* (HkzAT I,2; Göttingen: Vandenhoeck and Ruprecht, 1903), p. 281.

40. Dentan's conclusions (p. 48) in brief: (1) "...it is inconceivable that the credo is an original part of the J document or even a stray formula which has survived from early times." (2) Dt. 7:9 is "obviously dependent" on Ex. 34:6f but has Deuteronomic features added. There is no Deuteronomic "vocabulary or style" in Ex. 34:6f, which to Dentan apparently means there are no covenantal associations either. (3) "...one can assert with confidence that the entire formula is a product of the School of the Wise Men."

and its derivative and related texts.[41] Even all the "affinities" taken together cannot make an early date "inconceivable."

Second, it is scarcely surprising that the phrases of the Ex. 34 "formula" which have no counterpart in the Dt. 5 = Ex. 20 formulations (see below) are not found to be Deuteronomic in character. The two words "*ḥesed* to thousands" and the final phrase "requiter of the iniquities..." are the only items used in common, and Dentan does not accurately assess the implications of the affinities of these phrases.[42] In any case, there is no reason to assume that anything covenantal must be Deuteronomic and hence that anything without Deuteronomic affinities in vocabulary cannot have covenantal associations. Surely the Sinai covenant had not been forgotten by the time of the United Monarchy (J). E preserves the tradition; and Jeremiah (who most often speaks of Yahweh as *pōqēd*) presumably came from a tradition (related to the Deuteronomic school) familiar with the Sinai covenant theme. This is not to argue that the material of Ex 34:6-7 and elsewhere is therefore necessarily to be associated solely with the Sinai covenant; but Dentan cannot disprove a covenant association by divorcing the materials from Deuteronomy.

---

41. The term *nṣr* appears in Dt. 33:9; but this verse is generally regarded as a late addition to the poem. (F. M. Cross, Jr., *Ancient Yahwistic Poetry* [Baltimore: Johns Hopkins, 1950], p. 220).

42. *Ḥesed* he treats only in connection with *ʾĕmet*, although it occurs alone in the phrase "*ḥesed* to thousands." He claims that *ḥesed* contains only "the most general moral sense" (p. 44). Although this may be true in certain late texts, it cannot be generalized to all occurrences of the word. Further, Dentan does not recognize that the Hebrew phrases *ḥsd lʾlpym* and *pqd ʿwn*... are found together only and precisely in the formulae of Ex. 34 and Dt. 5 = Ex. 20. Dt. 7:9 cannot be related to Ex. 34:6f without consideration of its relationship to Dt. 5. The absence of *pqd ʿwn* in Dt. 7:9 does not prove the writer's lack of familiarity with the phrase or his unwillingness to use it; rather, he has paraphrased and spelled out the meaning more graphically.

Finally, although there are many occurrences of some of these "abstract" words in the wisdom literature, as Dentan shows, one expects to find a higher concentration of abstracts in such literature. All the words occur elsewhere, in prophecy, other poetry, narrative, and one cannot suppose that just because so many of them are gathered in one series of liturgical phrases in one place that only wisdom-oriented persons could have used them in this way. These words were part of the Hebrew vocabulary, not of the "wisdom" vocabulary. It is equally likely that the frequency of these words in the sayings of Proverbs came from the development of many sayings using words well known to the sages from their liturgical life. Since these phrases do deal with traits of character and traits of character are a major concern of the wisdom literature, it is again not surprising that "affinities" appear to exist. But "character traits" is too general a topic to be restricted to a single school of thought.

Against this scholarly tradition regarding Ex. 34:6-7 as a late secondary addition, the writer would argue that there are important grounds for understanding this liturgical material as (1) essential to the purpose of the J narrator at this point and hence included by J himself, not added by some later redactor, and (2) very ancient, pre-J, in its ultimate origin.

To assess the possible role of the liturgical phrases within the J narrative, it is necessary first to decide what is the central thrust of the passage. Although Ex. 34:10ff. deals with J's version of the Sinai covenant, J's primary concern in chs. 33-34 appears rather to be God's revelation to Moses. The covenant is stated only in the briefest possible way,[43] in

---

43. The covenant appears to be stated as a promise: "'I will do marvels....'" Vss. 11-16 provide a homiletical warning in a "proto-Deuteronomic" style into which has been worked the primitive first commandment against worship of other gods. On the problem of the authorship of these verses, see F. Langlamet, "Israël et 'l'habitant du pays' (à suivre)," *RB* 76 (1969), 321-350. After the statement of the second commandment, there follows a summary of materials from the Book of the Covenant (G. E. Wright, private communication, May 1970) and a concluding

contrast to the essentially E form of chs. 19-24. God's proclamation of his own name, however, the giving of content to his name through liturgical phrases in 34:5b-7, provides the appropriate conclusion and climax to his announcement in 33:19 that he will proclaim his name to Moses. This revelation of the name in the J narrative ought probably to be compared to God's revelation of his name to Moses in the E (Ex. 3) and P (Ex. 6) traditions. Since the J writer has been using "Yahweh" from the start, this name is not the focus of attention as in E or P, but the "character" of God is summarized by the use of excerpted phrases from liturgical "titles" or names.[44] Thus these verses do have an actual function within the J tradition and it is not necessary to suppose that they can only have been a later addition.[45]

---

comment that Moses wrote the ten words of the covenant on the tablets.

44. The writer is grateful for this interpretation suggested by G. E. Wright, private communication, May 1970. It may be added that the apparent promise of 34:10 and 11 provides strong corroborative evidence for Wright's interpretation. The E tradition of the revelation of God's name is associated with similar assurance of wondrous works and gift of the land.

45. Thorir Thordarson, following Wright's suggestion, also asserts that these verses involve proclamation of the Name. But he goes on to argue that the *Sitz im Leben* of the formula (which he apparently regards as an original unit) is in the "Covenant festival" as a proclamation of forgiveness. He reaches this conclusion by associating divine *ḥesed* with Psalms of lamentation on a statistical basis, then tying Psalms of lamentation to the day of Atonement and this to the "New Year festival." ("The Form-Historical Problem of Ex. 34:6-7[[unpublished Ph.D. dissertation, University of Chicago Divinity School, 1959]) This line of argument is tenuous at best, since each link in the chain is weak. (Also, there is no discussion of fall vs. spring new year festivals.) Thordarson presumes the meanings of the words of the formula(e) and thus deals only with *Sitz im Leben* and possible historicity as an event originally involving Moses.

The metric structure into which these lines can so readily be analyzed suggests that J was relying upon liturgical traditions already well established. The poetic lines were probably fixed before the monarchy and may have been carried in the *Grundlage* of J and E as well as in hymnic use for praise of Yahweh. Liturgical titles composed with *ʾēl*, as are the opening lines here, are generally of ancient origin; there are no certain examples of the devising of new *ʾēl* titles during later times.[46] Hence it is probable not only that these lines are originally part of J but also that they were taken by J from even older tradition.

It is impossible to determine with certainty whether the Ex. 34 tradition in its present form was originally a single formula or whether two or more independent formulae have been incorporated into vss. 6-7.[47] The double appearance of *ḥesed* and the separation of "*ḥesed* to thousands" from the final contrasting lines about requiting iniquities with which it elsewhere appears suggest that two formulae may have been combined. Whereas the theme of the opening formula is the greatness of God's *ḥesed* even to the point of forgiveness, the theme of the last is God's reserving of *ḥesed* for those who are faithful and his requital of the disobedient. Lines 4 and 5 serve to tie

46. F. M. Cross, Jr., private communication, June 1970.

47. For a schematic presentation of the other appearances of all elements of this and related formulaic expressions, see Josef Scharbert, "Formgeschichte und Exegese von Ex. 34,6f und seiner Parallelen," *Biblica* 38 (1957) 130-137. Scharbert's conclusions concerning the original confessional formulae used in different periods (p. 137) are debatable at several points. Principally, "Yahweh 'Ēl Qannā'" may be a liturgical title but is surely too brief to be classified as a "confessional formula" *(Bekenntnisformeln)*. Second, the phrase *nōṣēr ḥesed* should not be included without the comment that this combination is found nowhere in formulae except in Ex. 34:7. Third, his "post-exilic" form is also pre-exilic (I Ki. 8:23 is ascribed to Dtr[1] under Josiah, see Cross, "The Structure of the Deuteronomic History," esp. p. 19) and also should not be divorced from his second Deuteronomic form based on Dt. 7:9f.

the two principal themes together, but one would expect line 3 to follow rather than to precede them.

Thematically and in accordance with the witness of Type Two (see below), we may speculate that this second formula originally began with *ʾēl qannāʾ*.[48] Several metrical forms of such a formula can be reconstructed. Simply prefacing line 3 of the Ex. 34 version with *ʾēl qannāʾ* and retaining lines 6 and 7 intact would yield good sense and a 10/9/9 tricolon. But since none of the examples of Type Two can be scanned metrically in their surviving form, further speculation is fruitless. All that we know of oral transmission of poetic material suggests that variability and fluidity were always present, and these factors surely played their part in the tradition culminating in J's fixing of a particular variant in writing.

The meaning of *ḥesed* in these liturgical formulae is difficult to determine positively, just as in the "blessing/benedictory" expressions. In the present combination of phrases, the placement of the first use of *ḥesed (rb ḥsd)* alongside of "slow to anger" and parallel to "merciful and gracious" suggests a meaning such as "so great in faithfulness that he is willing even to forgive breach of relationship." It is this aspect of God's *ḥesed* (as his mercy) which takes on greater importance in exilic and post-exilic writings. The increased use of the word with this connotation in the later period probably led to the regular Greek translation ἔλεος, "merciful." But although this usage is an extension beyond the normal range of meaning for human *ḥesed*, there is no reason to suppose that it cannot have existed much earlier than the Exile. The possibility of God's *ḥesed* encompassing even forgiveness must always have been latent in the theological use of *ḥesed*. Since in the Mosaic tradition the possession of land was dependent upon Israel's obedience, it followed that disobedience, sin, would result in destruction of the people and the land, this presumably through some historical agent or natural catastrophe at God's bidding. Hence forgiveness did not involve

48. Note also that in Jos. 24:19 God as *ʾēl qannôʾ* is specifically described as "he who does *not* forgive iniquities and sins."

merely being freed from some inner mental anxiety rooted in feelings of guilt; forgiveness could also result in, could be equated with, could be signified by, *deliverance* from some actual physical threat to the people. While punishment for sin could and did occur, forgiveness involved preservation of the covenant community from destruction. And such deliverance conforms to the circumstances and conditions under which we have seen that concrete action is called *ḥesed*. Israel is by definition unable to deliver herself when God's punishment is upon her. Nor is anyone else able to rescue her. Since Yahweh himself is bringing the destruction, he alone can set it aside, give deliverance, give forgiveness. He is in control and he is free to act or not to act.

In terms of Yahweh's responsibility for Israel, the use of *ḥesed* becomes "stretched" in its theological application: in cases where deliverance is coextensive with forgiveness, the people's sin should have ended the relationship, thus relieving God of any responsibility for them. The greatness of his *ḥesed* consists in his refusal, even in the face of rejection, to give up on his people, to set aside the responsibility which he took upon himself in choosing them as his people. It is not surprising that this usage came to full fruition in the exile and later, with the amazing theological "discovery" that God did not utterly cut off his people, even in his final judgment on their apostasy, the exile and the destruction of Jerusalem and the nation state.

The meaning of *ḥesed* here cannot be understood apart from Israel's covenant traditions. Whether Yahweh's assuming of responsibility was explicit in terms of a promise while Israel's obedience was only implicit (as in Gen. 15 or the Davidic covenant) or whether his responsibility was implicit (future benevolence and protection to be assumed based on past action) while Israel's duty was explicit in terms of commandments (Ex. 19-24), the covenant understanding had to cope with the problem of sin.[49] The Mosaic tradition assumed that sin would result in

---

49. See Mendenhall, *Law and Covenant*, p. 36; D. N. Freedman, "Divine Commitment and Human Obligation," *Interpretation* 18 (1964), 420-421.

the ending of the relationship. The preservation of the community despite repeated disobedience is understood in terms of God's *surprising* (rather than deserved) *ḥesed*. So also, the Abrahamic and Davidic traditions understand the preservation of the covenant relationship in terms of God's promised (rather than deserved) *ḥesed*. The very act of preservation of the covenant community itself (as a concrete expression of *ḥesed*) was so closely intertwined with the decision to preserve (forgiveness) that the word *ḥesed* could be broadened to include God's patient willingness to forgive in order to maintain the relationship.[50]

The second use of *ḥesed* in the Ex. 34 formula *(nṣr ḥsd lʾlpym)* apparently applies to thousands of generations, if the paraphrase of Dt. 7:9 *(ʾlp dr)* is to be generalized. As Freedman points out, the implication would seem to be that God here is unconditionally committed to his people,[51] although it is conceivable that the contrast of E and D between the thousands who love and the fathers...who hate is intended even here. The rearrangement of the lines in the combining of the two basic formula types suggests, however, that God's willingness not to retaliate for sin (even while not ignoring it) is primarily at issue,[52] so that forgiveness becomes the basis for constancy in the God-man relationship. God's *ḥesed* here is understood as

---

50. The interpreting of this theological use of *ḥesed* in terms of Israel's covenantal self-understanding is not necessarily to tie it exclusively to covenant renewal. From this verse it cannot be demonstrated that *ḥesed* is a "covenantal word" (*pace* Dentan, p. 48). Yet Israel's theological vocabulary cannot be compartmentalized (national vs. individual) and cannot be evaluated completely apart from the pervasive covenant thought-framework.

51. D. N. Freedman, "God Compassionate and Gracious," *Western Watch* 6/1 (1955) 17. See this article for a compact exegetical interpretation of all the phrases in Ex. 34:6-7. On *nśʾ ʿwn* see also Freedman, "A Limited Study of the Root *nśʾ*," (typescript of address delivered before the Biblical Colloquium, Pittsburgh, November 29, 1952), pp. 38-47.

52. Freedman, "*nśʾ*," p. 40.

persistent behavior more than as a series of discrete acts; this nuance is carried effectively in the unusual verb *nṣr*.

The combined form of the formulaic tradition, with its double use of *ḥesed*, thus highlights God's surprising *ḥesed* offered even to the undeserving and hints also at his promised *ḥesed*. In this context *ḥesed* expresses succinctly the grounding of Israel's relationship to Yahweh in his divine freedom and persistent faithfulness.

The passages most closely related to Ex. 34:6-7 and particularly to the first couplet will be presented with brief comments in the next paragraphs. Aside from Num. 14:18 these involve only the first two lines of the phrases combined here. A single passage relating to the second occurrence of *ḥesed* (line 3) will be dealt with in connection with the Type Two formula.

Numbers 14:18 (and 19)

(yhwh) ’rk ’pym wrb ḥsd	6	Yahweh is patient and great of *ḥesed*
nś’ ‘wn wpš‘	6	forgiver of iniquity and transgressions
(w) nqh l’ ynqh	6	(but) he will by no means declare innocent (the guilty)
pqd ‘wn ’bwt ‘l bnym	9	requiter of iniquity of the fathers upon the sons
‘l šlšym w‘l rb‘ym	9	unto the third and unto the fourth generations

The context clearly indicates that this passage is intended to refer to Ex. 34:6-7. Moses is interceding for the people and prays "as Thou hast said...." The quotation is incomplete: the first line of the first standard liturgical couplet is missing; the line with the second occurrence of *ḥesed* (which elsewhere is associated with the final two lines) is also missing. It is of interest that the three major extrametrical plusses are also absent here, possibly indicating that they are later expansions in the Ex. 34 text.

The entire section in which the passage is embedded, vss. 11-24 (Noth: 11b-23a) is generally regarded as an addition to J,[53] but the date or source cannot be determined with any

53. So George Gray, *A Critical and Exegetical Commentary*

certainty. If an early date be allowed for the materials in Ex. 34, then this passage might also be regarded as "proto-Deuteronomistic" in style.

In vs. 18, Moses prays, "Forgive then the iniquity of this people according to the greatness *(gdl)* of thy *ḥesed* and according as thou has forgiven this people from Egypt even unto this place." So *ḥesed* seems to mean faithfulness to be given expression in willingness to forgive, ability to forgive, as known from God's forgiving action thus far. It is important to recognize that in this entire address to Yahweh, Moses' concern is for Yahweh's power. He introduces the formulaic material by saying, "And now let the power *(kōaḥ)* of the Lord become great *(ygdl)*" (vs. 17). And his first argument is that the people should not be killed lest the nations should assume that Yahweh was unable to fulfill his promise to bring them into the land. So forgiveness, i.e. not destroying the people utterly because they rejected the good report of Caleb and Joshua, is a manifestation of God's power: before the nations because they would misinterpret his punishment as failure, and before Israel because only the truly powerful can afford to forgive rebellion. Again the analogy is from the political realm. The suzerain maintains power over his vassals by marching against them to destroy them whenever they rebel. Only when his power is not seriously threatened by the rebellious act can he afford to take less stringent measures. Yahweh's sovereignty is not threatened by Israel's rebellion; he is powerful enough to be able to forgive (deliver) if he wills to do so.

Here, because it is a question of deliverance despite disobedience, it is God's willingness to forgive (not his ability to do so) which is in question for Israel herself;[54] hence "let

---

on Numbers (ICC; Edinburgh: T. & T. Clark, 1903), p. 155, and earlier commentators cited therein; Baentsch, *Numbers*, pp. 525-528; John Marsh, *The Book of Numbers: Introduction and Exegesis* (IB; New York: Abingdon Press, 1953), pp. 211-212; Martin Noth, *Numbers: A Commentary* (tr. by J. D. Martin from the 1966 German ed.; OTL; London: SCM Press Ltd., 1968), pp. 108-110.

54. While for the nations it is a question of God's ability. The idea of God's *ḥesed* as his strength, might, ability

the power of the Lord become great" is set alongside of "according to the greatness of thy *ḥesed*." God's forgiveness of Israel's repeated lack of trust has already been experienced. He has shown willingness to maintain the covenant relationship even when Israel's actions ought to have freed him from any responsibility for the people. Once he established the relationship he has maintained it. His *ḥesed* is "great" *(gdl, rb)* by contrast to human *ḥesed* which always depends upon a relationship in good repair so that the deliverance or rescue is deserved. God is able and willing (when the people repent) to deliver even when his help is undeserved, and this deliverance of the penitent, as well as the "deserved" deliverance of the upright, is called *ḥesed*. The tradition of Num. 14 thus illustrates even more sharply than the usage in Ex. 34 the theological use of *ḥesed* for acts of forgiveness and for the ongoing attitude which leads to forgiveness.

It should also be observed that in the received form of the text the formula in Num. 14 has been incorporated into the priestly version of the story of the spies. In this priestly context, with its emphasis on the permanence of God's promises to the people, we find that the promised *ḥesed* of God is in the foreground, despite the judgment upon the rebellious individuals of the wilderness generation. The earlier tradition,[55] which P incorporated in part, carried the more Mosaic emphasis on the surprising *ḥesed* of God, embodied in the forgiveness which forestalled the deserved destruction of the covenant community.

Thus the levels of tradition in Num. 14 show diachronically

---

to deliver, is clear in poetic usage, which will be dealt with in Chapter VI. See, e.g., Ps. 59:10-11; 62:12-13; Ex. 15:13, and on this meaning L. J. Kuyper, "The Meaning of *ḥsdw* [in] Isa. XL 6," *VT* 13 (1963) 489-492. The nuances of ability to deliver, willingness to deliver, and deliverance/protection as the act itself can all be applied to God's *ḥesed*.

55. Basically 14:1b, 4, 11-25; possibly also 14:3, 30-33. While the "possible" material is taken by some as P or post-P, there is wide consensus that the basic verses listed are pre-P material. See above, pp. 122-23, n.53.

the dual emphases which are expressed synchronically in the Ex. 34 passage. *Ḥesed* as act and attitude basic to God's relationship to Israel could be understood as either surprising or promised. What was clear in either case was that the very existence of the relationship depended upon the divine willingness to forgive. This concern will be further developed in the treatment of God's *ḥesed* to the Davidic line and in the study of the divine *ḥesed* in the prophetic literature.

Psalm 86:15

(w)'th 'dny 'l rḥwm wḥnwn	11 (12)	And Thou, O Lord, art God merciful and gracious
'rk 'pym wrb ḥsd w'mt	10	patient, and great of constant *ḥesed*

In this poetic variant the meter requires the longer form with *w'mt* in the final phrase.

The formula is set in the context of a prayer for deliverance from personal enemies who, unlike the petitioner, are not god-fearing. The nuance of *ḥesed* as forgiveness appears to be present in the psalm, for in vs. 5 *rab ḥesed* is set in parallel to *tōb w*^{e}*sallāḥ*. Yet the overall theme emphasizes the suppliant's trust in God[56] and thanksgiving for past deliverance from Sheol (God's *ḥesed* to him, vs. 13). The general tenor of the prayer is reminiscent of the patriarch Jacob's appeal for *ḥesed* (Gen. 32:10-12; see above, pp. 93-97). The primary focus is on deliverance which God is willing to give because he is merciful and gracious. The psalmist thus identifies himself as one in relationship to Yahweh and yet recognizes implicitly his own unworthiness and God's freely given care.

---

56. As one who trusts *(bṭḥ)* in God, the petitioner describes himself as *ḥāsîd*. See Appendix; also Ps. 18:26a = II Sam. 22:26a, "with the *ḥāsîd* thou wilt show thyself as [a God of] *ḥesed*." From the extant materials it appears that *ḥāsîd* could early be used for a man in proper relation to God. This stative form provided one basis from which the prophets, especially Hosea (see Chapter V), could turn the one-way action of *ḥesed* itself upside down.

Psalm 103:8

rḥwm wḥnwn yhwh	7	merciful and gracious is Yahweh
'rk 'pym wrb ḥsd	7	patient and great of *ḥesed*

The following verses show clearly that the formula is intended as an assurance of God's forgiveness. The first half of the psalm focuses on praise to God for his forgiveness. But even here forgiveness is set alongside of health, life itself, the good things which make life worth living, justice and vindication. These are not equated with forgiveness, but it is clear that *ḥesed* is extended to cover God's acts of deliverance and benevolence as well (vs. 4). Almost in the same breath, the psalmist speaks of God's *ḥesed* as belonging to those who fear God (v. 11). This theme is repeated in the metrically awkward vss. 17-18, where the reference to covenant-keeping underscores the idea that God's *ḥesed* is not a gift to be taken lightly. Despite the initial impression in these lines of restriction of *ḥesed* to the faithful, the juxtaposition of vs. 11 with the preceding lines suggests that the psalmist's intention is to emphasize the forgiveness of God to those who repent.

Psalm 145:8

ḥnwn wrḥwm yhwh	7	Gracious and merciful is Yahweh
'rk 'pym wgdl ḥsd	7	Patient and great of *ḥesed*

Here the *rḥwm wḥnwn* of the first line appears in reverse order, as in the three examples still to be listed. Since the two words are identical in structure and meter, free variation was possible. In this case the order was determined by the location within the psalm: this is the *ḥ* line of an acrostic hymn of praise. The context is not unified in theme so no particular nuance for *ḥesed* can be determined.

Joel 2:13

(w) šwbw 'l yhwh 'lhykm	9(10)	and return to Yahweh your God
ky ḥnwn wrḥwm hw'	7	for fracious and merciful is he
'rk 'pym wrb ḥsd	7	patient and great of *ḥesed*
wnḥm ʿl hrʿh	7	and relenting of evil

Here the formula is filled out with the specification that God's act of cataclysmic judgment may yet be revoked if the people will repent. *Ḥesed* as forgiveness is at the same time deliverance. The pericope as a whole (vss. 12-17) is a call to national repentance in which the formula is used as an assurance of God's willingness to respond favorably.

Jonah 4:2b

> For I know that you are God gracious and merciful,
> patient and great of *ḥesed* and relenting of evil.

Jonah complains bitterly because God has seen the repentance of Nineveh and has decided not to destroy the city. He claims he tried to flee to Tarshish because he knew all along that God would forgive Nineveh and Jonah would look like a prophet whose words of doom did not come to pass. In this setting, *ḥesed* must again have the double connotation of forgiveness and deliverance from destruction. Under Jonah's personal objection lies the deeper issue of the relationship between God and post-exilic Judaism and the non-Jewish world in which the Jews found themselves. If the parabolic interpretation is correct,[57] then the use of the formula is the more remarkable, for it is extended beyond Israel herself. Judaism is confronted with its own exclusivism by the use of its own central affirmation. That assurance of patient faithfulness for which God is always praised is here used by Jonah as a rebuke to God, and the writer's ironic point is brought home forcefully by the use of traditional language.

Nehemiah 9:17b

> For you are a God ready to forgive *(s^{e}līḥôt)*, gracious and merciful, patient and great of *ḥesed*;
> and you did not abandon them.

Ezra's long prayer draws upon the entire tradition of Israel recorded in Exodus and subsequent historical books. In this verse the reference to the choice of a new leader to return the people to Egypt suggests dependence upon the Numbers 14 text where in vs. 4 there is reference to such a plan. The next event Ezra mentions, though, is the molten calf; and the Ex. 34 use of the formula is connected (in the received text tradition which Ezra would have known) with forgiveness for the apostasy of the calf. Since the formula is well established in

---

57. See James D. Smart, *The Book of Jonah: Introduction and Exegesis* (IB; New York: Abingdon Press, 1956), pp. 872-873.

the form Ezra uses, since the Numbers form is missing a part while the Exodus form is expanded, and since the Ezra tradition apparently reverses the JE tradition of the order of events, it is best not to draw specific lines of dependence. It is probable, nonetheless, that knowledge of the traditional association of the formula with those two events led to its inclusion here. God's protective and providing presence is associated with his forgiveness; again *ḥesed* is a two-edged expression of God's faithfulness.[58] *Ḥesed* means God's deliverance and care; but more than that it means his attitude which results in deliverance and care even when it is not deserved, an attitude which takes form in forgiveness. The theological use of *ḥesed* (contrary to secular usage) centers on this attitude of persistent faithfulness, faithfulness which is patient and forgiving despite the murmuring and unresponsiveness and ungratefulness and even open rebellion of the weaker party within the covenant relationship.

In review of these passages related to Ex. 34:6-7, it should be noted that all the definitely datable examples (Nehemiah, Jonah, Joel)[59] come from the post-exilic literature. The Psalm occurrences also are generally considered late, insofar as relative dates may be assigned.[60] This clustering has probably been one source of the tendency to regard the Exodus and Numbers passages as late additions. But, as has already been suggested, there is no reason to suppose that the broadening of

---

58. Note that here *lʾ ʿzb* is used with the people as object and God as subject as a succinct expression of God's *ḥesed*. Compare the complex use of *ʿzb* with *ḥesed* as object; above, pp. 103-105.

59. On the arguments for Joel as post-exilic, see John A. Thompson, *The Book of Joel: Introduction and Exegesis* (IB; New York: Abingdon Press, 1956), pp. 732-733; on the arguments for Jonah as post-exilic, see Smart, *Jonah*, p. 873.

60. See, e.g., Hans-Joachim Kraus, *Psalmen* (BK XV; Neukirchen Kreis Moers: Neukirchener Verlag der Buchhandlung des Erziehungsverein, 1960), pp. 597, 702, 948. It should be realized that the assigning of dates may be dependent in part upon the appearance of the formula in late datable sources.

ḥesed to include the nuance of forgiveness as a corollary of deliverance could not have occurred early; we have relatively little literature extant in which such a usage would be appropriate. At the same time, the emphasis on forgiveness would be expected to come to the fore with the problem of what becomes of the covenant in the exile. Thus a shift in relative emphasis of the word may well have occurred.

Type Two: Exodus 20:5b-6 = Deuteronomy 5:9b-10

> For I Yahweh am (a) jealous God *(ʾēl qannāʾ)*, He who charges fathers' iniquities unto sons, unto the third and fourth generations, to those who hate me; but doer of *ḥesed* to thousands, to those who love me and keep my commandments.

In both the surviving versions of the decalogue[61] this predication is placed upon the prohibition, "You shall not bow down to them nor serve them," which properly refers to the other gods whose worship is prohibited in the first commandment, "You shall have no other gods besides me."[62] The prohibition against bowing down has apparently been shifted in the tradition as idol worship and worship of other gods have come to be identified as a single concept over against the aniconic worship of Yahweh.

The association between the zealous/jealous character of Yahweh and his demand for exclusive worship is clear throughout

---

61. These two versions are usually regarded as E (Ex. 20) and D (Dt. 5). Both, however, in their present form have been reworked by P, as is seen for example in the reference to "the heavens above and the earth beneath" in the prohibition of images. There has also been substantial mutual influence and conflation of variant traditions in the process of transmission, as is witnessed by the Septuagint traditions, the Nash Papyrus, and more recently by texts from Qumran (F. M. Cross, Jr., private communication, June 1970).

62. Walther Zimmerli, *Gottes Offenbarung; gesammelte Aufsätze zum Alten Testament* (Munich: Chr. Kaiser Verlag, 1960), pp. 237-246, who shows that "bow down and serve" is used only of foreign deities forbidden to Israel, not of Yahweh and not of images.

the tradition. The link is direct in the Ex. 34 version of the first commandment: "You shall not bow down to another God, for Yahweh's name is zealous, (a) zealous god is he." And in Jos. 24:19-20, Joshua says, "he is (a) zealous God: he will not forgive *(nś')* your transgressions and your sins. If you abandon Yahweh and serve foreign gods, he will turn and do ill to you and consume you...."[63] Nevertheless, the formula cannot be regarded as original to the primitive decalogue, where a series of short second-person prohibitions presumably stood in sequence.[64]

The time at which these changes and additions took place cannot be determined with certainty, nor can it be demonstrated that either of the two identical texts is necessarily literarily dependent upon the other. This modified tradition could well have emerged early enough that E would have access to it[65] and have been maintained long enough by the same circles that the writer responsible for the central core of Deuteronomy would have known the tradition apart from the written form of an E or Old Epic (JE) document as such. The slight variations of wording in several of the commandments themselves (as well as in the obvious expansions), beginning with the Sabbath commandment, may indicate the overall presence of independent traditions. If D were deliberately copying from E, one might expect him to be more consistent. If a later hand were at work in the single identical insertion here, one might expect it to

---

63. On the arguments for a pre-Deuteronomic date for this section of Jos. 24, see Bernard Renaud, *Je suis un dieu jaloux* (Paris: Les Editions du Cerf, 1963), pp. 36-38.

64. Albrecht Alt, "The Origins of Israelite Law," *Essays in Old Testament History and Religion* (Oxford: Basil Blackwell, 1966), tr. by R. A. Wilson, pp. 116-119. Cf. J. Stamm with M. Andrew, *The Ten Commandments in Recent Research* (London: SCM Press Ltd., 1967), pp. 18-20. Even if the primitive forms of the commandments were somewhat varied, it is improbable that such a long commentary would have been included.

65. Probably taking written form in the late tenth century B.C. See Jenks, "The Elohist and North Israelite Traditions," pp. 253-266.

be very late[66] so that both texts could be supplemented at one time. Yet there is evidence that D himself develops a variation of this formula (Dt. 7:9) which is then used by Dtr; and Jeremiah 32:18 also appears to build upon this formulaic usage. Further, Moran suggests that Dt. 6:4-18 is comment on the first part of the decalogue of ch. 5, with 6:5 presupposing 5:10 and 6:15 presupposing 5:9.[67] Hence the formula could not be some later addition at least in D.

The use of *ḥesed* in this version of the formula is certainly conditional: *ḥesed* is reserved for those who are "deserving" because they are fulfilling the requirements of their relationship to Yahweh. The nuance of forgiveness is not present; the emphasis is more closely analogous to the secular usage in which the good behavior of the recipient is important. The vocabulary of loving and hating here suggests an explicit covenantal context for the use of *ḥesed*.[68] God does not formally bind himself, but he makes a declaration of intention: those who are loyal (loving) will receive *ḥesed* while those who are disloyal (hating) will be punished. Loyalty is further defined as obedience to the commandments. The use of *ʾēl qannāʾ* and the setting in the context of the opening section of the decalogue suggests that exclusive worship of Yahweh is particularly in view. God's *ḥesed* for the obedient may be understood in terms of the help and support, perhaps especially the protection, which the suzerain provided for the loyal vassal in the human political context known from ancient Near Eastern suzerainty treaties.[69] Protection of the vassals can almost be

---

66. To be sure, we have no sure knowledge of the history of D and E as manuscript traditions through the centuries. But Noth's tetrateuchal hypothesis suggests that they may have maintained a relatively independent existence till late exilic or post-exilic times.

67. "The Love of God in Deuteronomy," p. 85 and n.46.

68. *Ibid.*, *passim.*

69. See Mendenhall, *Law and Covenant*, p. 30. Dennis McCarthy (*Treaty and Covenant* [Rome: Pontifical Biblical Institute, 1963], pp. 33-34) cites several examples of advantages accruing to vassals in Hittite treaties. These most often are

assumed as a key responsibility of a suzerain. Regularly vassals had to promise to supply troops when the need arose; presumably these would be dispatched to protect some other vassal territory which formed a part of the suzerain's domain. Nevertheless, a vassal in need could never compel his suzerain to fulfill this responsibility for protection. He could request assistance, but it was up to the suzerain to send help voluntarily.

Within the theological covenant analogy,[70] *ḥesed* provided a concise way of expressing the action of Yahweh as suzerain on behalf of his vassal Israel. Depending on the context, the usage could emphasize either the suzerain's concern for the vassal's responsibility (as here) or the suzerain's surprising commitment beyond the usual limits (as in forgiveness). In either case, the term highlighted the helplessness of the vassal, the provision of essential needs but not special favors,[71] the freedom of the suzerain to ignore his responsibility for the vassal's welfare (with no recourse available to the vassal), all perspectives which were inherent in the covenant relationship between Yahweh and Israel. The word *ḥesed* held together the voluntarily assumed responsibility and the complete freedom of God the Suzerain as two sides of a single coin.

Only one passage contains formulaic usage related to this second type. Most others in this tradition conform more closely to the modification of this type described below as Type Three.

Jeremiah 32:17b-18 (LXX ch. 39)

> Nothing is too difficult for thee, doer of *ḥesed*
> to thousands, he who recompenses *(mᵉšallēm)* fathers'
> iniquity to their son's bosom after them....

This modified use of the formula appears in an extensive addition to a prayer by Jeremiah which probably was originally

---

associated with succession rights (cf. use of *ḥesed* for David).

70. How early the word was adapted to the Sinai covenantal vocabulary cannot be determined, but there is no reason to suppose that it cannot have been used in the period of the League. *Ḥesed* appears in Ex. 15:13, but the (probable) covenantal association can only be inferred.

71. Although the word could easily slide into connotations of God's goodness generally, as is seen in some Psalms.

only vss. 16-17aα and vss. 24-25.[72] The original prayer was associated with the purchase of the field in Anathoth dated by 32:1 to 588/7 B.C.,[73] but the date of the additions may be much later.

The example here is very much a mixed form and hence difficult to classify. Several features should be noted. The order of phrases with *ḥesed* first and the fate of the iniquitous second is like that found in Ex. 34, and also like that of the tradition of Dt. 7:9-10 and the uses more closely related to it (cf. below). In the use of "to thousands" without any modifiers this variant is again like Ex. 34. But the use of the root *šlm* instead of *pqd* is related to the usage of Dt. 7:10.[74] The use of "do *(ʿśh) ḥesed*" is found elsewhere in formulaic expressions only in Ex. 20:6 = Dt. 5:10, where of course the order of the two main phrases is reversed.

The formula variant is probably intended to extol God's protective care and his justice, but nothing more can be said since the entire context is only a collection of such traditional themes and phrases.

Type Three: Deuteronomy 7:9-10b (cf. 7:12)

> And you know that Yahweh your God is the God, the faithful God, keeper of covenant and *ḥesed (šmr bryt wḥsd)* to those who love him and to those who keep his commandments, to a thousand generations; but giver of recompense *(mšlm)* to those who hate him to his face by destroying them.

The relation of this type to Type Two is apparent, although the order of lovers and haters is reversed. Nevertheless, it

---

72. F. Giesebrecht, *Das Buch Jeremia* (HkzAT; Göttingen: Vandenhoeck & Ruprecht, 1907), pp. 178-179; Wilhelm Rudolph, *Jeremia*[2] (HAT I, 12; Tübingen: J. C. B. Mohr, 1958), p. 193; John Bright, *Jeremiah* (AB; Garden City, N. Y.: Doubleday & Company, Inc., 1965), p. 297.

73. Bright, *Jeremiah*, p. 238.

74. In Isa. 65:6-7 this threat tradition also appears with *šlm ḥyq* and *ʿwn ʾbwt*, but the form is so different that the Isaiah passage must be regarded as an independent reflection of the same tradition.

is classified as a separate type because here the Deuteronomist introduces an important new usage, combining *b^{e}rît* and *ḥesed* in what appears to be hendiadys and using the verb *šmr* which is appropriate to *b^{e}rît* but does not so obviously appear appropriate to *ḥesed*. Whether the Deuteronomist coined the usage himself or only recorded a phrase already in use we cannot know; but its importance and persistence is clear, since the Deuteronomic historian made use of it and post-exilic prayer traditions also include it.

The implication of the usage is that doing of *ḥesed* is the keeping of the covenant by the powerful party. Here the series of discrete acts is fully merged with the continuing mode of behavior, so that the connotation of special help in a specific situation of need is forced into the background. God is continuing to act in accordance with the covenant because of his love and his choice, not because of any special merit on Israel's part (vss. 6-8). The keeping of covenant and *ḥesed* is the fulfilling of the oath which God swore to the fathers (vs. 8). As in the closely related Type Two formula, the expression here highlights the importance of Israel's obedience within the relationship.

The theme is reiterated in vs. 12: "and so long as *(ʿqb)* you keep these ordinances and are careful to do them, Yahweh you God will keep *(šmr)* for you the covenant and the *ḥesed* which he swore to your fathers." The following verses then expand and restate the traditional promises of blessing, increase and the gift of the land, but clearly the promises are here conditioned upon obedience. The Deuteronomist has linked up the patriarchal promise tradition with the requirements placed upon the people by the Sinai covenant. The fulfillment of the promises is seen as God's keeping of covenant. God as suzerain is the powerful party to the covenant, always free to do as he pleases and yet responsible for the people he has chosen so long as they are loyal to him, giving to Israel what she could not achieve by her own action or her own inherent qualities. As the continued giving of blessing and prosperity, *ḥesed* is not exactly what we have seen before, rescue in dire circumstances. Yet, God is still doing for Israel what she could not herself accomplish. Even though *ḥesed* here appears to involve giving Israel everything instead of nothing, it is understood that without Yahweh's covenant *ḥesed* she would have had nothing at all. In this sense, even her blessing cannot be divorced from essential assistance. And without this fulfillment, without the establishment of a great people in its own land, the covenant relationship (now linked to the traditional promises) would have been rendered meaningless. In this sense also, God's *ḥesed* here remains that action which is essential to the maintaining of the covenant relationship with his people.

Nehemiah 1:5

> And he said, "Alas, O Yahweh, God of the heavens, the great and awesome God, keeper of the covenant and the[75] *ḥesed* to those who love him and to those who keep his commandments...."

This invocation is the opening to Nehemiah's prayer when he hears of Jerusalem's troubles and disrepair. It is interesting to see that despite the strong conditional note in Deuteronomy, this address is used now in an intercessory prayer for forgiveness. This possibility is opened up by the assurance that those who repent will be forgiven; and repentance ("returning") is understood as "keeping commandments and doing them" (vs. 9), a verbal restatement of the basis for *ḥesed* in the formula. *Ḥesed* here, however, is not simply forgiveness, as in Neh. 9:17, nor is it the blessing anticipated in Dt. 7. Insofar as there is particular content (rather than "thoughtless" use of a stereotyped form), *ḥesed* once again is associated with deliverance from distress. The association is only indirect; because of the formula, the immediate tie is to covenant-keeping in general. But in this prayer God's maintaining of the covenant must involve his rescue of Jerusalem from her distress.[76]

---

75. Reading definite article with LXX and Syriac.

76. Israel's understanding of covenant must have been modified with the dissolution of kingship and the end of the nation as an independent state. Neither the old political analogy of Sinai nor the theological interpretation of the rule of the Davidic line could withstand these pressures. But this liturgical use of *ḥesed* persisted for centuries. The new

Nehemiah 9:32

> And now, O our God, the great God, the warrior, and the awesome one, keeper of the covenant and the *ḥesed*, let not all the disasters which have befallen us be a small matter before thee....

This abbreviated form of the invocation adds *gibbôr*, which is not in Neh. 1:5 or Dan. 9:4; it does not specify for whom covenant and *ḥesed* are kept. Although the formula is not complete, the remainder was probably in the minds of the speaker, hearers, or readers, especially since the first part of the formula never stands alone elsewhere in the extant texts, and since the usage outside of Dt. 7 is always in a prayer invocation. The explicit recognition of God's justice in his dealings with the people (vs. 34ff.) further confirms this understanding that God keeps covenant and *ḥesed* for those who love him and keep his commandments.

Ezra, praying on behalf of the people, has already catalogued the long tradition of God's patience in the face of the people's disobedience, culminating with the fact (vs. 31) that even in exile he did not completely destroy them because he is *ʾēl ḥannûn wᵉraḥḥûm*, again using just the first phrase of the longer (Type One) formula. The juxtaposition of the two formulae of forgiveness and of conditional covenant keeping again points up the exilic transformation in which *ḥesed* becomes more prominently associated with forgiveness. The New American Bible translation of this verse, "you who in your mercy preserve the covenant," conveys one nuance of the phrase in post-exilic usage. Yet the nuance of deliverance from distress, which is appropriately received by the covenant people, is also present here, just as in Neh. 9:17. The request for deliverance from distress is plain in this portion of the prayer. If the prayer is to be read in connection with the putting away of foreign wives,[77] then deliverance is concretely associated with

---

emphasis on obedience to the law as the basis of the community may have found its source in liturgical traditions such as this; and the persistence of the formula may in turn have been associated with the increased emphasis on law.

77. So Wilhelm Rudolph, *Esra und Nehemiah* (HAT; Tübingen:

an act of repentance.

Daniel 9:4

> And I prayed to Yahweh my God and I confessed and said, "Alas my Lord (or Yhwh), the great and awesome God, keeper of the covenant and the *ḥesed* to those who love him and to those who keep his commandments...."

In this the latest of the Old Testament books, Daniel opens a prayer of confession with an invocation identical to that of Nehemiah 1:5. Although it is possible that the usage is simply modeled on the Nehemiah passage, it is equally likely that this introduction to a confession had become a traditional fixed form. The formula does not appear to have any concrete ties to the content of the prayer which follows. Repentance is implied in the act of intercessory confession, but God is called upon to act because of his great mercy (*rḥm*, vs. 18) and for the sake of his own reputation (vs. 19). Although the cry for rescue from distress is present,[78] there is no impression that it is tied in any specific way to the opening liturgical appellations. The invocation merely sets the stage for the repeated declaration of the people's unworthiness because of their sin and disobedience.

I Kings 8:23 = II Chronicles 6:14

> And he said, "Yahweh, God of Israel, there is no god like you in heaven above or on the earth beneath, keeper of the covenant and the *ḥesed* for your servants who walk before you with all their heart...."

The translation follows the MT of Kings and Chronicles with the Greek of Chronicles, over against the Greek of Kings which unanimously reads the singular "your servant who walks

---

J. C. B. Mohr, 1949), p. 154; Jacob M. Myers, *Ezra, Nehemiah* (AB; Garden City, N.Y.: Doubleday and Company, Inc., 1965), p. 165.

78. The rule of Antiochus IV during which the book is probably to be dated was certainly a time of persecution for faithful Jews. (See, e.g., Bright, *History of Israel*^{2}, pp. 420, 428, esp. p. 426.)

before you with all his heart." The Greek of Kings is apparently adjusted to the singular reference to "your servant David my father" of vss. 24 and 25; manuscripts Zboc$_2$e$_2$ insert the specification "David my father" here and omit the singular reference to "your servant" in vs. 24. Probably the plural was original in vs. 23.[79] The introduction of David by anticipation of vss. 23,24 would lead to the change to singular forms; in later correction the reference to David would be omitted.

In his composition of Solomon's prayer at the dedication of the temple, the Deuteronomic historian used a favorite phrase, "to walk with a whole heart,"[80] to ring the changes on the formula of Deut. 7:9-10b.[81] Following this invocation, the prayer continues with a petition for the establishment of the promise of the Davidic line and a series of petitions for justice and forgiveness to the people who repent. The prayer looks ahead to future difficulties and anticipates the historian's view of the people's life on the land. In Solomon's charge to the people which follows his prayer, the concluding exhortation to "walk in his statutes and keep his commandments" (8:61) completes the use of the theme of Deut. 7:9-11.

In applying the formula to all Israel, the historian is consistent with his theological use of *b^{e}rît* for the people as a whole, not for David or the king alone.[82] This problem will

---

79. "Thy servants" is used later in the prayer for the people of Israel, vss. 32, 36.

80. I Ki. 2:4; 14:8; II Ki. 10:31; 23:3; cf. use with other verbs, I Ki. 8:48; II Ki. 23:25. The Deuteronomist used "with a whole heart" most often with the verb *'hb* (Dt. 6:5; 10:12; 11:13; 13:4; 30:6).

81. It is of interest that the historian's only use of this phrase is in this invocation, where its exact meaning for him is not apparent. One cannot know whether the phrase was already in use in such prayer contexts or whether his composition set the stage for the post-exilic usage which in the extant texts is likewise restricted to invocations.

82. Theological uses: II Ki. 11:17; 17:15, 35, 38; II Ki. 23:3. In I Ki. 11:11 Solomon is to be punished for breaking the covenant, but his sin of going after other gods relates the

be discussed in connection with II Sam. 7:15 in section D of this chapter. Here it may just be observed that even though Solomon's thanksgiving and petition for the fulfillment of the promises made to David follow immediately upon the use of the generalized formula, no connection between the formula with *b^e^rît* and the promises to David is explicitly required by the text. The *ʾšr šmrt* which opens vs. 24 can be understood either as "because you have kept" or as "you who have kept..." continuing the invocation address, but with the presence of the direct object *ʾt ʾšr* it cannot refer to *hbryt whḥsd*.[83]

D. *The Deuteronomic Historian's Conception of God's* Ḥesed *to the Davidic Line*

II Samuel 7:15 // I Chronicles 17:13

> And my *ḥesed* I will not remove from him as I removed (it) from the one who was before you, from Saul, whom I removed from before me.

The translation represents the probable full text from which all extant traditions appear to have suffered haplographies. The multiple appearance of *kʾšr, mʾšr, ʾšr* together with *lpny, mlpnyk* must have led to the confusion.[84]

Although it is likely that there is a historical kernel in at least the first part of Nathan's oracle, the material has been reworked by the Deuteronomic historian. At least by vs. 14 (with the references to the permanent throne reemphasized in vs. 15, along with the language of sonship to express the king's

---

covenant to the central demand placed upon all the people.

83. The LXX^B "ἅ...καὶ γὰρ..." appears to be based on a wrongly corrected version of the now conflate MT of vs. 24. The Lucianic Greek probably represents the original text *ʾt ʾšr dbrt bpyk* (omitting *lw wtdbr*). The ἅ at the beginning of vs. 24 in LXX^L then becomes optional and is based in the understanding that the servant of vs. 23 is singular (David).

84. It is possible that the reference to Saul is a late addition, since it appears only in the MT of Samuel, the Samuel Coptic, and the Targum of Chronicles. So far as the content is concerned, it is clearly Saul who is meant, whether or not he was originally mentioned by name.

relationship to Yahweh) we must have material from the period of the fully developed Judahite kingship ideology and possibly from the hand of the Deuteronomic historian himself, making use of available liturgical materials.[85] The materials here have their closest biblical affinities with Psalm 89, especially vss. 19-37.[86]

In II Sam. 7:15 God's *ḥesed* is that which maintains the king on his throne. It is the basis for the promise of a permanent, "unconditional" dynasty. The writer makes clear that the kings will not have free rein no matter what - they will be punished with *human* rod and stripes. Yet the *divine* punishment of the withdrawal of *ḥesed* and the concomitant cutting off of the dynasty will not come upon them. Cross has suggested that the historian here seems surprisingly to accept the theology of an unconditional Davidic dynasty which must have been prevalent in his time.[87] The phrase "for the sake of David" appears to Cross to confirm this interpretation further. Yet it must be kept in mind that the Deuteronomic historian was working with a historical "given": the Davidic dynasty had in

---

85. It is likely that the shift comes as early as vs. 13 with the anticipation of the building of the temple *(byt)*; if this is accepted as addition to the oracle, then the historian's expansion may begin as early as vs. 11b, where the idea of David's dynasty *(byt)* to be established is first introduced. For the very extensive bibliography on this problem, consult H. Gese, "Der Davidsbund und die Zionserwählung," *ZTK* 61 (1964), 10-26. See also Cross, "The Structure of the Deuteronomic History," p. 14.

86. There is extensive debate in the literature over the unity or appropriate sectioning of Psalm 89, as well as over the precise relationship between the Psalm and II Sam. 7. For bibliography, see J. M. Ward, "The Literary Form and Liturgical Background of Psalm LXXXIX," *VT* 11 (1961) 321-339; N. M. Sarna, "Psalm 89: A Study in Inner-Biblical Exegesis," *Biblical and Other Studies* (Lown Institute Studies I), ed. by A. Altmann (Cambridge: Harvard University Press, 1963), pp. 29-46.

87. Cross, "Structure of the Deuteronomic History," p. 14; Cross, *Canaanite Myth*, pp. 281-285.

point of fact endured up until his time, even though (according to the teaching of Deuteronomy and especially in light of the example of Saul in I Sam. 15 which is here alluded to) the apostasy of many of Judah's kings might have been expected to lead to a change of dynasty. Thus the expression "for the sake of David" may have been his way of accounting theologically for the historical reality that the dynasty had survived despite its wicked kings.

That there was a form of the promise to David (probably early) which was conditional is evident from Ps. 132:11-12, and perhaps from II Sam. 23:5[88] and the beginning of Ps. 89 (vss. 3-5). Elsewhere in his work, the historian makes use of this tradition (though studiously avoiding the use of the word *b^erît*), for on three occasions on which the promise to David is cited (I Ki. 2:4, David to Solomon; I Ki. 8:25, Solomon to God; I Ki. 9:4, God to Solomon) it is unquestionably stated in conditional terms.[89] It is significant that all these statements, whether general or particular, take place in connection with Solomon. The turning point for the historian comes with God's decision not to tear the entire kingdom away from Solomon despite his cardinal sin of apostasy (I Ki. 11). Twice this theme is repeated, first in a direct statement by God to Solomon and then in Ahijah's prophecy. In each case, change of dynasty is stated as the basic fact, with "Yet, because of David" as a secondary, mitigating statement; and it is because of David's perfect obedience to Yahweh, not merely because of

---

88. See. M. Tsevat, "The Steadfast House: What Was David Promised in II Sam. 7:11b-16?" *HUCA* 34 (1963) 75-76, for the argument that this passage is conditional. Ps. 89:3-5 should follow by analogy. The writer does not accept Tsevat's conclusions for II Sam. 7, however.

89. Cross has suggested (*Canaanite Myth*, p. 287) that the conditional clauses in each of these passages may have been inserted by the exilic editor of the work. However, the condition provides the theological background for the splitting off of the northern kingdom from Jerusalem and hence is not easily excised. While there are surely exilic additions to the work of Dtr[1], the writer is not convinced that these are among them.

Yahweh's own promise, that he preserves a tribe for Solomon's son.[90] In short, although the II Sam. 7 passage seems to be a clear statement of the unconditional dynasty theology, the historian himself takes a modified view by regarding the promise as conditional and the survival of the dynasty as God's concession to human weakness for David's sake. It must then be assumed that dependence on liturgical materials rather than the writer's own theology dominates the expression of II Sam. 7.

Yet there is one respect in which the usage in II Sam. 7 seems to have been affected by the historian's own viewpoint: This is in the conspicuous omission of the word *b*^{e}*rît* in vs. 15, where judging from the use of *ḥesed* and knowing of the writer's dependence on Deuteronomy (cf. 7:9) in general and here on traditions like those of Ps. 89 in particular,[91] one might expect him to use the word "covenant." It is possible that he is simply using "remove *ḥesed*" as an alternate way to speak of covenant violation, but in light of the parallelism of Ps. 89:29, 34-35, the historian's omission of *b*^{e}*rît* may well be deliberate.

---

90. In II Ki. 8:19 the promise is cited as the primary reason. Yet David's obedience is the basis for God's maintaining of the promise despite the behavior of the successors to the throne.

91. The affinity in thought between II Sam. 7:14a *(bn, ʾb)* and Ps. 89:27-28 *(ʾb, bkwr)* and between the thought progression of II Sam. 7:14b-16 and Ps. 89:31-38 (with the identical use of *šbt* and *ngʿ* for the punishments short of removal of *ḥesed*) are to be noted. There is difficulty with the incorrect verb form *ʾăpîr* used with *ḥesed* in Ps. 89:34a. The correct hiphil of *prr* requires a *ṣere* written defectively. The verb is never used with *ḥesed* except here; although it is used regularly with *berît*, the correct preposition on such an analogy should be *ʾt*, not *mʿm* (cf. e.g., Jd. 2:1; Lev. 26:44; Jer. 14:21). For these reasons, it has often been suggested that the reading should be *ʾsyr* (so *BDB*) as in II Sam. 7 and following the traditions of Jerome and the Syriac. An alternate solution may be to interpret the MT as "*prr*, hi. to banish," as Mitchell Dahood suggests in *Psalms II* (AB: Garden City, N.Y.: Doubleday & Company, Inc., 1968), pp. 318, 287.

It has already been pointed out that the historian restricts his theological use of *b^e^rît* in the period of the monarchy to occasions which include all the people. He also associates the national covenant-making with religious purification. Jehoiada's covenant that the people should be the Lord's is followed immediately by the destruction of Baal's house, its priest and accoutrements (II Ki. 11:17-18).[92] In II Ki. 23:3ff. Josiah's covenant "before" the Lord, in which the people participate, is followed immediately by the purification of the temple. This action is extended to include the destruction of other places of worship for foreign deities set up by Solomon (23:13). The establishment of these altars is described in I Ki. 11. There Yahweh indicts Solomon for not keeping "covenant" in his going after other gods. The usage in II Ki. 17:15, in peroration on the fall of Samaria, ties (north) Israel's rejection of the covenant "made with the fathers" to following false gods and particularly to making of the molten calves.[93]

The historian sets the stage for this theme in his overall introduction to his work. In Dt. 4:13 and 33 the covenant is made at Horeb, with its essential "ten words," and the prohibition of images receives special stress. Although the historian knows of the possible close association between *b^e^rît* and *ḥesed*, and even uses the Deuteronomic combined formula (I Ki. 8:23), he prefers to reserve *b^e^rît* for a relationship involving all the people in obedience to Yahweh, while he uses *ḥesed* for God's maintenance of the Davidic line, the keeping of a promise because of David's perfect obedience. The tradition of a covenant which insists that the people will lose the land for

---

92. This passage may be part of the source material rather than the historian's own composition (cf. Martin Noth, *Überlieferungsgeschichtliche Studien* [Halle: Max Niemeyer Verlag, 1943], pp. 77, 84). It is impossible to determine the extent to which it may be his own wording. Certainly he felt free to select and to reuse materials as he saw fit.

93. God's covenant with the people, epitomized in the command for exclusive worship, also appears in II Ki. 17:35, 38, but the pericope seems loosely related to the context and may well be a late supplement in Deuteronomic style.

apostasy is held in tension with the historical and theological fact that the dynasty has survived despite its mixture of relatively good and bad kings. *Ḥesed* to David, "for the sake of David,"[94] is the historian's explanation not just for the survival of the dynasty but for the survival of the wayward covenant people itself.[95]

The actual content of the *ḥesed* here in II Sam. 7:15 is the supportive power by which God maintains the family line on the throne.[96] The odd application of *ḥesed* to David's son (rather than to David himself) in the comparison with Saul is perhaps related to a change from traditional plurals (see Ps. 89) to the singular, occasioned here by the reference to the building of the temple.[97] God's choice of David provides the basis for the relationship. From the whole narrative which unfolds, it is seen that *ḥesed* continues to be done in accordance with David's obedience in the relationship. Theologically speaking, the choice of the king is always in God's hands; it is not within the king's own power to maintain his line on the throne, nor is there any other than Yahweh who can provide this support. Although maintenance of kingship may seem to be special privilege, it should be recognized that the removal of the dynasty would be the equivalent of severing the relationship

---

94. Although the word *ḥesed* never appears with this phrase, the action is always the preservation of the dynasty, which is the intent of *ḥesed* here (as can be seen more clearly from I Ki. 3:6). The parallel with the human usage should be noted: David does *ḥesed* to Meribaal "for the sake of Jonathan" (II Sam. 9:1).

95. Gese suggests that the Davidic promise was incorporated within the Israel covenant ("Davidsbund," p. 26). A more conservative interpretation of the evidence is that with the avoidance of the term *b^{e}rît* it was possible for the historian to hold the two traditions in balanced tension.

96. This is the focus in Ps. 89; the tradition of Ps. 89 may also be that from which the aphorism of Prv. 20:28 is drawn.

97. The historian's anticipation that Solomon will lose most but not all of the kingdom may also be a source for the application to Solomon.

itself. The act of *ḥesed* is simply the provision for the continuance of the relationship; it is faithful protection rather than particular deliverance.

I Kings 3:6 // II Chr. 1:8

> And Solomon said, "You have done great *ḥesed* with your servant David my father, according as he walked before you in faithfulness and in righteousness and in uprightness of heart with you; you have kept *(šmr)* for him *(lô)* this great *ḥesed*: you have given to him a son sitting on his throne, as at this day." (I Ki. 3:6)

In the last phrase, the Greek reads "in putting his son on his throne," reading an infinitive and omitting *yšb* (except in hexaplaric texts). This may represent an ancient variant, possibly occasioned by syntactic difficulty after *šmr*; the sense is not substantially affected.

The Chronicles parallel shortens this entire pericope substantially. II Chr. 1:8 combines the material of I Ki. 3:6 and 7a, reading, "And Solomon said to God, 'You have done great *ḥesed* with David my father: you have made me king in his stead.'" Despite the abbreviation, the content of God's *ḥesed* remains the same.

This verse opens Solomon's prayer for wisdom in connection with Yahweh's appearance to him at Gibeon. It provides important confirmation of the Deuteronomic historian's understanding of *ḥesed* in God's relationship to the Davidic line which has been suggested for II Sam. 7:15. Here even with the verb *šmr* the word *b^{e}rît* is not used; here David's upright behavior (required for the maintenance of relationship with Yahweh) is cited as David's action in accordance with which God has performed *ḥesed* (also the action required for the maintenance of the relationship). The verse makes clearer what was implied in the oracle of II Sam. 7: the *ḥesed* done for David is carried out through the preservation of the dynastic line in a specific event of succession, so that it becomes an action which will be done for each descendant in turn, always "for the sake of David."

Summary

It is remarkable that, after the pregnant use of *ḥesed* in II Sam. 7 and the additional exploitation of the theme in I Ki. 3, the Deuteronomic historian makes no more use of the word *ḥesed*.[98] He seems to set the stage for the use of the word whenever he comments "for David's sake"; yet he only states the specific action, Yahweh's allowing the dynasty to continue. It should be noted, however, that five of the nine occurrences of "for David's sake" are in I Ki. 11 concerning the loss of the northern kingdom.[99] It will be recalled that II Sam. 7:15 as it stands concerns the non-removal of *ḥesed* from Solomon (although he is not named). It seems possible, therefore, that the historian found his understanding of the continuation of the dynasty to his own time precisely in the fact that God did not tear all the kingdom away from Solomon's hand. This affirmation of the dynastic promise provided a basis for understanding the persistence of the Davidic line despite its wicked kings. Yet the historian still was not convinced that God would continue the dynasty no matter what. The book found in the temple and used as a base for his work made clear that faithfulness was requisite for life in the land. National life on the land and dynastic survival could not be independent variables.

If the tradition of Ps. 89 was prevalent in Josiah's time, then *ḥesed* and dynastic preservation were probably popularly regarded as an automatic and deserved gift of Yahweh. The historian, by contrast, saw the *ḥesed* based in God's free and patient response to David's faithfulness and regarded it as good fortune that Yahweh had not given up on the dynasty already. By using the word *ḥesed*, he might only reinforce the popular notions of an inviolable kingship in which uprightness was not important. Hence, it seems, he used the word briefly

---

98. Except for the formulaic usage in I Ki. 8, discussed above.

99. Of the other four, one each refers to the Abijam-Asa and Jehoram-Ahaziah successions. The other two refer to the preservation of Jerusalem (rather than the dynasty) after a wicked king.

to make a basic theological point, then let it go.

E. *Theological Use of* Ḥesed: *A Summarizing Statement*

The evidence of the many particular texts examined in this chapter suggests that the theological meaning of the word *ḥesed* developed within the framework of various polarities: the individual-communal, the deserved-undeserved, the surprising-promised, and the varying covenant traditions of the patriarchs, Moses, and David. Obviously these aspects of usage are intertwined in many ways: promises were made to the patriarchs individually but had all-Israel implications; *ḥesed* was promised to those in the Davidic line despite sin, while it was offered to those in the Mosaic tradition as surprising and undeserved forgiveness of sin. This variety of concerns can perhaps be reduced to two central polarities: the term *ḥesed* was used to express God's free care both for individual suppliants and for his people as a whole; the term was used to express the central character of God's action both in conditional and in unconditional types of covenant theologies.

Within the preserved narrative contexts concerning God's *ḥesed* to individuals, the upright character of the recipient is generally stressed, either directly or by implication. When one turns to the use of *ḥesed* in individual psalms of petition, however, there can be concern either for the uprightness of the suppliant or for the patient and forgiving nature of God in the face of the petitioner's unfaithfulness. In both cases, *ḥesed* involves the sovereign God's free willingness to hear and rescue the one who trusts in him, who is in dire straits, who has no other help but God. The former case is more closely analogous to the secular usage, in which it is always evident that the relationship between the parties is in good repair. The latter type of usage, in which *ḥesed* is associated with forgiveness, goes beyond the secular usage in that deliverance is given even when it is not deserved. The association of destruction by natural or historical enemies with divine punishment for sin may have encouraged a reverse association of divine deliverance from destruction with divine forgiveness of sin; in the end it is clear that the preservation of the relationship between God and the petitioner is based essentially on God's willingness to maintain the relationship and to preserve the one who depends upon him. This understanding is summarized succinctly in the appeal to the *ḥesed* of God.

The communal side of the usage, God's concern for his people as a whole, took shape in two principal forms: conditional (suzerainty) and unconditional (patron) covenant theological traditions. The conditional tradition of course centered around the Mosaic covenant, while the unconditional focused on the promise to David (with refractory reference to the promises to Abraham). Within both these traditions, the term *ḥesed* played a central role as a way of expressing God's sovereignty and power on the one hand and his enduring commitment to Israel on the other. So long as *ḥesed* is understood as protection and deliverance which is "deserved" because of the uprightness of the community, these covenant traditions can stand close together. But it is over the question of sin that the traditions part company. The understanding of *ḥesed* as attitude which yields forgiveness and even as act of forgiveness provides a connecting link which enables these two theological emphases to stand in tension.

The conditional (Mosaic or Sinaitic) tradition emphasizes the importance of human obedience. That perspective has no inherent way to provide for continuation of the relationship once it is broken by sin. God's *ḥesed*, stretched to encompass deliverance recognized as forgiveness (he alone is *rab ḥesed*), provides the ever surprising basis upon which the covenant is maintained.

The unconditional (Davidic, Abrahamic) tradition, by contrast, handles the problem of sin by describing God's relationship to the people as one based on the divine promise alone, not subject to collapse because of human failure. Here *ḥesed* as the basis for the preservation of the covenant is understood as promised rather than unexpected. Yet this tradition too found it necessary to take the question of sin very seriously. The priestly editor of the Tetrateuch and prophets such as Isaiah of Jerusalem struggle with the question of how God can be present in the midst of a sinful people. His commitment to the Davidic line is a source of puzzlement as well as of assurance. It is the association of promised faithfulness with undeserved deliverance and protection in the term *ḥesed* which provides theological language for expressing the tension.

The liturgical formulae of Ex. 34, Ex. 20, and Dt. 7 thus take on varied nuancing depending on their setting. The emphasis on the importance of human obedience as prerequisite for *ḥesed* is present. Yet the overtone of *ḥesed* as forgiveness - understood as preservation of relationship - is also present and is highlighted in both individual and communal contexts.

Psalm 89 gives classic expression to the fully developed theology of God's *ḥesed* as promised faithfulness to the Davidic line, epitomized in vs. 28: "My *ḥesed* I will keep for him forever and my covenant will stand for him." Here *ḥesed* clearly means preservation of the line on the throne, commitment to that central promise, in a way which allows for particular chastisement within the larger framework. God is related to his people indirectly, through his anointed.

The Deuteronomic historian, as we have seen, appears to pick up this Davidic perspective in his use of *ḥesed* in II Sam. 7. And yet, overall, he is surprisingly careful and reticent in his use of this particular word. He restricts *b^erît* to contexts involving the people as well as the king, and he uses *ḥesed* again only in I Ki. 3[100] where the importance of David's uprightness is made explicit. The historian, in contrast to the popular view of his own time that God's *ḥesed* is irrevocable and therefore to be taken lightly, emphasizes by implication that faithfulness like that of David is required and that the Mosaic concern for obedience is ignored at great peril.

Thus we may say that *ḥesed* was a particularly useful word for speaking of God's relationship to his people, collectively and individually, because it held together in a single expression an emphasis on divine freedom on the one hand and divine commitment on the other, an emphasis on divine power on the one hand and divine care on the other, an emphasis on human need and weakness on the one hand and human responsibility to trust in God alone on the other. By a stretching of the secular usage for delivering and protective action and concern to

---

100. Outside of the formulaic use in I Ki. 8, which we have suggested refers to the people as a whole.

embrace even forgiveness, the term came to express the uniqueness of God's *ḥesed* as the basis for a relationship stronger than any human bond. This perspective, apparent in the usage in pre-exilic narrative, finds confirmation and elaboration in the occurrences in late prose, prophecy, and psalms which are investigated in the remaining chapters.

CHAPTER IV

HUMAN *ḤESED* AND DIVINE *ḤESED* IN POST-EXILIC NARRATIVE

Because of the relatively smaller number of texts to be examined, the post-exilic counterparts of Chapters II and III are treated here as Parts A and B in a single chapter. Although the theological usage exhibits a considerable degree of continuity with some of the earlier examples, there is a substantial shift in usage with a human subject. The main sources are Chronicles-Ezra-Nehemiah; in addition, there are two examples from Esther and one from Daniel. The Chronicler's parallels to Kings and the liturgical materials dependent upon earlier traditions have been dealt with in Chapters II and III and will not be included here.

A. Ḥesed *with Human Subject*

There are two different meanings for human *ḥesed* in narratives composed in the post-exilic period. The first, "pious acts," is found in Chronicles and Nehemiah and may be described as a "religious" usage; the second, "favor" or "beauty," occurs only in Esther.

1. Religious Usage

Nehemiah 13:14

> Remember me, O my God, on account of this, and do not blot out my *ḥesed*s which I have done for (lit. *b*, "in") the house of my God (and for [*b*] its functionaries).

The Greek translators took *ḥsdy* as a singular, which is possible from the consonantal text. However, the plural of the Masoretic pointing ought to be read, since it corresponds to the related usages in II Chr. 32:32 and 35:26 where the consonantal *ḥsdyw* requires the plural. The mention of the functionaries is not found in many Greek manuscripts and may be an expansionistic gloss based on the immediately preceding context.

Neh. 13:7-30 summarizes the initial or principal reforms enacted by Nehemiah during his second administration. Three major topics are covered - temple purification and maintenance, sabbath observance, and foreign marriages - and at the conclusion of each section (vss. 14, 22, 31) Nehemiah asks God to "remember" him favorably for that action. Although all three actions involve purification, only the one specifically involving temple use and rites is described as Nehemiah's "*ḥeseds*." The action involved the eviction of one Tobiah, who had taken up housekeeping in a storeroom formerly used for the Levites' portions. This reuse of the storeroom had evidently been associated with stopping of the Levites' allotment and of the people's offerings, for Nehemiah has to gather the Levites back from the countryside and arrange for the collection and distribution of their allotted grain, wine and oil. These actions he summarizes as his *ḥeseds*.

It is immediately obvious that this use of *ḥesed* is completely different from anything found in pre-exilic narrative. The plural form is new, of course. But beyond that, the sense of "pious acts" suggests a great shift in emphasis. The action may be understood as a responsibility, but it is responsibility to God, not for another man, so that this is the first narrative example of "religious" usage. The whole notion of freedom of action is severely clouded by this shift. In the earlier secular usage, freedom of decision existed with respect to the other party involved; there was always the possibility that God as ultimate judge would require the failure to do *ḥesed*. But here the *ḥesed* is done with respect to God and it is assumed that lack of action would lead to punishment. As if this were not enough, pious acts with respect to the temple involve the action of the weaker party (Nehemiah) on behalf of the cause of the stronger (God). Someone else certainly could have exercised this power; Nehemiah's *ḥesed* consisted in taking the initiative and accomplishing the task.

How may this transformation have come about? In the first place, it must be recognized that approximately two hundred years have passed since the writing of the latest texts examined in Chapter II. Although the texts in Chapter II covered a much longer time span, they represented the comparatively stable and cohesive period of the monarchy, whereas this two hundred years has seen the exile and return and the corresponding efforts to create a viable "national" existence in a situation where nationhood has been erased.

More important, it is apparent from texts not yet discussed that the seeds which were to bear fruit in Nehemiah's use of the term had been planted much earlier, for in prophecy as early as Hosea we find the "religious" use of the singular "*ḥesed*."[1] The development of the plural usage involves the movement from pious behavior in general to the reference to particular pious acts. But the ritual- and temple-related content here is a new focus of concern consonant with the interests of the writers of these materials.[2] It is possible that this plural usage with human subject was restricted to pious acts related to the temple and its ritual, since all the extant examples fit this category. This distribution may be a chance circumstance of the preserved texts, however, and no special weight should be placed upon it.

II Chronicles 32:32

> And the rest of the acts of Hezekiah, and his *ḥeseds*, behold they are written in the vision of Isaiah, son of Amoz, the prophet, in the Book of the Kings of Judah and Israel.

The Greek reads the singular τὸ ἔλεος, although the Hebrew *ḥsdyw* must be plural. Probably the vision of Isaiah refers to materials in the history book named rather than in another book such as our prophet Isaiah.[3] The Greek καὶ suggesting two separate books is probably incorrect.

---

1. See Chapter V, where it will be suggested that the use of *ḥāsîd* (see Appendix) and perhaps traditions of poetic parallelism with words such as *ʾĕmet* (which could properly be used of men in relation to God) may have provided the background for a new use of *ḥesed* to describe the covenant community's relationship to God.

2. The prophetic examples are tied instead to the piety of right relations among men in the social sphere. They apply predominantly to the people as a whole rather than to particular individuals.

3. Werner Lemke, "Synoptic Studies in the Chronicler's History" (unpublished Th.D. dissertation, Harvard Divinity School, 1963), p. 218.

The II Ki. 20:20-21 summary of Hezekiah's reign mentions his "might" and the building of the water tunnel. The Chronicler has dealt with the water tunnel in his narrative of Hezekiah's reign. But he has given the central emphasis to the cleansing of the temple and celebration of the Passover and to the role of the Levites in these activities.[4] Since his use of *ḥesed*s is found in summary statements about kings who performed such actions on behalf of the temple and right worship, it is more than likely that the word refers particularly to these activities.[5]

II Chronicles 35:26

> And the rest of the acts of Josiah, and his *ḥesed*s in accordance with [what is] written in the law of God, and his acts first and last, behold they are written in the Book of the Kings of Israel and and Judah.

The Paraleipomenon Greek text reads ἐλπὶς for *ḥesed*s. There is no apparent rationale for such a translation; perhaps this is an inner Greek corruption from ἔλεος. The preposition *k* before *ktwb* seems not to be represented. The Esdras A text (in which this Hebrew verse = 1:31b) either is uncharacteristically expansionist and/or periphrastic or else represents a variant Hebrew tradition. In the phrase under scrutiny it reads, "and (of) his glory (δόξης) and his wisdom (συνέσεως) in the law of the Lord." It is possible that "glory and wisdom" represent the translator's idea of the meaning of *ḥesed*s. However, the absence of any representation for *kktwb* suggests that the Esdras A text may represent a different *Vorlage*, perhaps *ḥmd(y)w wḥkmtw btwrt yhwh*. The confusion of *ḥmd/ḥsd* is

---

4. The encounter with the Assyrians recorded in Kings is told much more briefly here.

5. Kuyper's suggestion ("The Meaning of *ḥsdy* [in] Isa. XL 6," p. 491) that *ḥesed* here stands as the equivalent of the g^{e}*bûrâ* in Kings cannot be sustained. Despite the inclusion of "strength" in the nuances of *ḥesed*, the two are never simple equivalents. See discussion in Chapter V, p. 190, and Chapter VI, p. 222.

plausible,[6] and either might have been the original reading. It is not inconceivable that the presence of *ktwbym* in both the preceding and following verses could have precipitated a misreading of *w wḥkmtw btwrt* as *w kktwb btwrt*. The clear difference between *k* and either *ḥ* or *m* in every script stage from 400 B.C. on of course militates against the possibility of such a misreading, so the suggestion is conjectural at best. The *ḥkmtw* of the Esdras text would then have to be regarded as correct, with the error coming into the MT tradition. While we have no reference to the wisdom of any Israelite king other than Solomon, there is no reason that the Chronicler could not have introduced this in his summary.[7]

If *ḥesed* did belong to the original text tradition, Josiah's *ḥesed*s were most probably understood as his acts of piety in the restoration of the temple, the provision for its proper service, and his observance of the Passover. Although the Chronicler is not unaware of the political events of Josiah's reign, and even gives information not found in Kings, his chief focus here and elsewhere is on cult and temple activities. The restriction of "*ḥesed*s" to the deeds of Hezekiah and Josiah (and perhaps additionally to David, see below) suggests that the cult observance and conceivably especially the role of the Levites is the special focus of the word here.[8]

---

6. See discussion of Isa. 40:6, Chapter V, p. 191. The *m/s* confusion could easily take place. It must be admitted, however, that there are no certain examples of such a scribal error.

7. It may also be observed that the usage of *kktwb* in the MT seems awkward here. Normally, this participle is used adjectivally rather than substantively. The closest parallels are I Ki. 23:21; and II Chr. 31:3. But even these examples fall within the usual usage referring to named items recorded in a particular book. It is highly unlikely that the Chronicler would have claimed that Josiah's good deeds were recorded in the Torah itself. On the other hand, good deed - even law fulfillment - "according as it is written in the law" is an anomalous usage in the sense of "required by law."

8. Note that the Chronicler attributes to David the

II Chronicles 6:42

> O Lord God, do not reject the plea (lit.: turn aside the face) of your anointed; remember the *ḥesed*s of David your servant.

Vaticanus and a few minuscules read "your face," omitting "anointed"; Alexandrinus and most minuscules follow MT, except reading the singular of "anointed" as in the translation given above. Possibly an earlier form of the text read *pnyk mmšyḥk*. The Vaticanus tradition could then be explained as simple haplography following the first *k*; the MT and Alexandrinus text tradition would represent a harmonization to Ps. 132:10b, since II Chr. 6:41-42 is throughout a paraphrase of Ps. 132:1,8-10.

The grammatical construction of the verb *zkr* with preposition *l* for the object *(rei)* is anomalous. The only other instance is in Jer. 31:34, where the usage is probably under the influence of the parallel *slḥ l* which regularly takes *l* + *rei*. Elsewhere *zkr* normally is followed by *l* + person; hence a reading *ly ḥsdy* has been proposed.[9] There is no textual evidence, however, and the Greek simply ignores the *l*, apparently feeling no difficulty. In any case, it seems clear from the context that it is on Solomon's behalf that God is asked to remember David's *ḥesed*s.

The *ḥesed*s of David are not mentioned in Ps. 132; there the plea is made *b ʿbwr* David. In fact, the only other occurrence of the phrase is in Isa. 55:3,[10] where it is generally

---

establishment of the orders of temple officials, as well as all the plans and provisions for the temple itself. Although the concern of other kings for temple affairs receives attention throughout the narrative, these three kings are the only ones who engage in major cult and temple activities and who also receive a completely positive treatment from the Chronicler. Several start out well and end up faithless (Rehoboam, Asa, Joash). Jehoshaphat did well except in not tearing down the high places and in building ships with Ahaziah. Only Jotham appears perfect - but his only mentioned activity is the building of a temple gate; no major cultic reform (beyond avoiding the desecrations done by his father) is recorded.

9. J. Begrich, apparatus for Chronicles, *BH*, *ad loc.*

10. This text will be discussed in Chapter V, pp. 201-205.

taken to refer to God's *ḥesed*s to David. The difficulty there, and even more so here, is that everywhere else, in singular or plural, the second member of the construct or the pronominal suffix must clearly refer to the actor, not the recipient. The usage in Nehemiah and in the Hezekiah and Josiah summaries of the Chronicler would suggest that David may here have been understood as the actor, the one who made all the plans and arrangements for the building of the temple and for its service. In this sense, the text belongs with this series of examples of human *ḥesed*.

At the same time, it is probable that the construct could have been earlier, and even in the Chronicler's time, understood as a dative - "the *ḥesed*s of David."[11] Since the setting here is the conclusion of Solomon's prayer at the dedication of the temple, the theological nuance of the usage should hark back to the body of the prayer (taken from Kings) in which God's promises to David concerning temple and dynasty are cited: the fulfillment of the first is proclaimed and the fulfillment of the second is petitioned for. The establishment of the temple and the continuance of the dynasty are tied together as God's *ḥesed*s to David, as his promises, as what he swore to David.

As Gese observes, there is a level at which Ps. 132 seems to make the dynastic promise consequent upon David's establishment of the ark in Zion.[12] Since the Chronicler gives David a much larger role in the temple planning, it is reasonable to

---

11. Dahood has pointed out a number of examples in which the personal suffix of the noun is "dative" in the sense of *y* being the recipient of the action: e.g. Ps. 16:4; 20:3; 25:5; 50:5 (although here his third person interpretation of the suffix is debatable) (*Psalms I* [AB; Garden City, N.Y.: Doubleday & Company, 1966], pp. 88, 127, 156, 307). See also Paul Joüon, *Grammaire de l'Hébreu Biblique*² (Rome: Pontifical Biblical Institute, 1947), Par. 129h, p. 389. It should be noted that in these examples the recipient becomes the possessor; it may be this coalescence which leads to the suffixal rather than prepositional usage.

12. "Davidsbund," pp. 13, 16.

suppose that he has deliberately used "*ḥesed*s of David" with the Ps. 132 tradition to convey the ambiguous (dual) human and/or theological sense of the phrase: David's piety and God's promises.

2. Old Secular Usage: Deliverance

II Chronicles 24:22

> For Joash (the king) did not remember the *ḥesed* which Jehoiada his [Zechariah's] father had done with him [Joash]; and he killed him [Zechariah]. And as he died he said, "may Yahweh see and seek (avenge)."

There has been a history of debate among commentators concerning the origin of the Chronicler's extensive materials (beyond Kings) for the reign of Joash.[13] In his dissertation on the Chronicler's use of Kings and possible theological slant, Werner Lemke is inclined to regard the entire account as from some independent source. He notes that the materials which are parallel in content to Kings are worded differently from Kings. The "changes" cannot be attributed to text traditions or to any slant of the Chronicler; hence a separate source is the probable explanation.[14]

The theory of a separate source (rather than free composition) accords well with the fact that the usage of *ḥesed* in this pericope resembles the pre-exilic secular examples and is unlike any occurrences from texts written in the post-exilic

---

13. Among those attributing this material to an unpreserved source are I. Benzinger, *Die Bücher der Chronik* (KHCzAT; Tübingen: J.C.B. Mohr, 1901), p. 113, and Wilhelm Rudolph, *Chronikbücher* (HAT; Tübingen: J.C.B. Mohr, 1955), p. 273. Those regarding it as free composition by the Chronicler include Kurt Galling, *Die Bücher der Chronik, Esra, Nehemiah* (ATD; Göttingen: Vandenhoeck & Ruprecht, 1954), p. 138. Rudolph Kittel (*Die Bücher Chronik* [HAT; Göttingen, 1902], p. 49) and Jacob Myers (*II Chronicles* [AB; Garden City, N.Y.: Doubleday & Company, Inc., 1965], p. 136) allow for either possibility.

14. "Synoptic Studies in the Chronicler's History," pp. 187-192.

period. All the Chronicler's human examples aside from quotations of Kings are plural forms for acts of religious piety, in the category of "religious" rather than "secular" usage. Besides II Chr. 24:22, the only post-exilic secular examples are from Esther, where the meaning is "favor" or "beauty" (see below). The absence of the old usage from late texts could be a matter of chance, but it seems plausible to assume that this text has survived from an earlier period.

The classic features described in Chapter II are present, with the situation bearing the closest resemblance to Judges 8:35. Joash is accused of Zechariah's murder because he did not stop the people who rose up to stone him. The implication is that he did not do *ḥesed* in accordance with the *ḥesed* Jehoiada had done for him. The transfer of responsibility to the next generation is clear here as in the story of Jerubbaal and also in the David-Jonathan narrative. Jehoiada's *ḥesed* to Joash was of course in secretly preserving him and crowning him - from a position of freedom with respect to the infant, yet from a position of responsibility ensuing from his personal and political relationship to the Davidic line - providing for survival at a time when all others had turned away. The action Joash failed to do has the same characteristics: rescue to be provided by one especially able to determine the outcome, responsibility because of what Zechariah's father had done for him, and the freedom (wrongly used) not to act at all. Zechariah's dying prayer sums up the focus of this usage. There is no human recourse for Zechariah himself and no formal action possible within the legal system. It is God who must punish the failure to do *ḥesed*.[15]

3. Late Secular Usage: "Favor" or "Beauty"

Esther 2:9, 17a

> (9) And the lass was good in his eyes and she bore *(nś')* *ḥesed* before him...
>
> (17a) And the king loved Esther more than all the

---

15. Though the punishment comes through human agency, in this instance in the form of a murder conspiracy against Joash by his own servants (vs. 25).

> [other] women and she bore *(nśʾ)* more *ḥēn* and *ḥesed* than all the virgins.

Although the details of the Greek traditions vary in these verses, it is clear that the phrases in question are translated by χάρις with the verb εὑρίσκω.[16] The double *ḥn wḥsd* is translated by a single χάρις. Hebrew *nśʾ ḥn* is translated by the same Greek phrase in 2:15, as is also *mṣʾ ḥn* in 5:8; 7:3; 8:5. It is clear first that *ḥesed* and *ḥēn* have fallen together in this late writing, and second that the Greek translators felt no distinction between the traditional idiom *mṣʾ ḥn* and the usage (found only here) *nśʾ ḥn/ḥsd*. If the Greek usage is a correct guide, then the idiom simply means to obtain favor in a situation where the more powerful party has no responsibility at all for the weaker.[17]

The possibility that there is some distinction between the idioms based on the choice of verb ought also to be considered. In the first place, it should be observed that all three occurrences with *mṣʾ* are part of a request form in direct address, whereas all four[18] of the *nśʾ* forms are statements of fact about Esther. The idiom with *nśʾ* is used in comparing Esther to the other virgins (2:17), in describing the reaction of people who "see" her (2:15), in describing the response of the head of the harem (2:9). In each of these cases, one would expect her physical appearance to be the primary object of attention. Only the response of the king upon seeing his queen unbidden (5:2) might be ambiguous, but even here it is possible that her beauty caused the king to grant clemency. Hence for the idiom *nśʾ ḥn/ḥsd* a translation such as "appeared beautiful" may be preferable.

---

16. On the problem of the varying traditions in Esther, see Lewis B. Paton, *Esther: A Critical and Exegetical Commentary* (ICC; New York: Charles Scribner's Sons, 1908), pp. 29-47; Sidney Jellicoe, *The Septuagint and Modern Study* (Oxford: Clarendon Press, 1968), pp. 167, 294-295.

17. Freedman, "*nśʾ*," p. 5, follows this interpretation of *nśʾ ḥsd*, comparing the usage to *nśʾ pnym*.

18. Adding 5:2, which is translated by a circumlocution in Greek.

In either case, it is clear that the meaning of *ḥesed* in Esther has little if any relation to the old tradition. Even if "obtain favor" is the correct interpretation, *ḥesed* in this usage involves special favor rather than essential need and appears in a situation where the actor has no responsibility for the recipient.

B. Ḥesed *with God as Subject*

1. *Ḥesed* for Specific Individuals or Groups

Ezra 7:28a

> (Blessed be Yahweh...) who extended *ḥesed* to me before the king and his counselors and before all the mighty officers of the king.

Ezra 9:9

> For we are bondsmen, but in our bondage our God has not abandoned us but extended *ḥesed* to us before the kings of Persia to give us reviving to erect the house of our God...

The Hebrew idiom used in Ezra 7:28a is *nṭh* (hi.) *ḥsd ʿl* N_1 *lpny* N_2, although the Greek tradition here reads *bʿny* instead of *lpny*. The identical expression is found also in Ezra 9:9, where the Greek does read *lpny*, and the two examples may be discussed together.

BDB suggests that the force of the preposition *ʿl* here may be "from above."[19] However, the example of Pr. 21:1 suggests that this variation from the more usual *l*, *ʾl* should not be given undue weight. The idiom as a whole should be carefully noted, however, because it provides an insight into the transition stage by which *ḥesed* and *ḥēn* fell together.

The shift can be seen when this Ezra usage is set alongside the old usage of Gen. 39:21: "But Yahweh was with Joseph and extended *ḥesed* to him (*nṭh*[qal] + *ʾl*) and gave him *ḥēn* in the eyes of the jail-keeper." Here *ḥēn* is appropriately used for that in Joseph which evokes a response in the jailer; and from the human viewpoint the jailer's response (also implied in the use of *ḥēn*) in putting Joseph in charge of the prisoners is a special favor which he had no responsibility to perform. But

---

19. BDB, p. 641a.

ḥesed, as shown in Chapter II, is God's essential and responsible assistance to Joseph which also takes its concrete form in the jailer's recognition of Joseph. Here *ḥesed* and *ḥēn* have in common the factors of (1) a circumstantially superior party acting on behalf of another and hence (2) a freely given benefit. But, to repeat, the perspective is different - from the *ḥesed* perspective the benefit is essential assistance and responsible action within a relationship; from the *ḥēn* perspective the benefit is special favor and no relationship or responsibility is involved.[20]

In looking at the Ezra usage, it is evident that the late idiom combines the two stages or viewpoints of the Genesis statement, thus "short-circuiting" the distinction between *ḥēn* and *ḥesed* which was present in the earlier text. In the doxology of 7:27-28a[21] God is blessed because "the king granted him

---

20. W. F. Lofthouse, following Glueck's analysis of *ḥesed*, suggested that *ḥēn* is used "chiefly of men between whom there is or can be no specific bond or covenant." He concluded that this factor made *ḥesed* and *ḥēn* "opposite" to each other ("*Ḥēn* and *Ḥesed* in the Old Testament," pp. 31, 33). Although it is certainly true that in some cases of *ḥēn* there is no bond between the parties (as in the Joseph incident, and also in the early part of the Ruth-Boaz relationship where a parallel distinction between *ḥesed* and *ḥēn* can be perceived), Lofthouse's own list of examples suggests that this cannot be the sole distinction. The relationships between Jacob and Esau, Joseph and his brothers, David and Joab are cases in point. The complicating factors include the status of the relationship (is it in disrepair by some act of enmity?), the nature of the request or action (is it in fact a special favor and hence morally optional for the actor?), and the presence of idiomatic usage (is it a simple statement of "please" or "thank you"?). If Lofthouse had accounted for these factors, his analysis could have been more acute, but in following Glueck he would still have overlooked the importance of the common factor - action of a superior toward an inferior - which eventually allows the two terms to fall together.

21. The blessing serves to tie the third person materials

[Ezra] all that he asked, for the hand of the Lord was upon him" (7:6). But the formula *nṭh ḥsd lpny* does not maintain the distinction between God's action to Ezra and the king's response to Ezra. In terms of historical results, the two are of course identical, so it is easy to see how the distinction could be lost. The same tension applies to the usage in 9:9, where it is further compounded by the infinitival "to give us reviving," the subject of which may be either God or the kings. The usage allows *ḥesed* to be interpreted both as essential assistance within a relationship (God to Ezra, the people) and also as the granting of a special request outside of a relationship of responsibility (the king to Ezra, the people). We cannot be certain whether the traditional or the new nuancing of a word, or even both, was present in the writer's mind. But it is easy to see how the shift could take place, once such an idiom developed.

Daniel 1:9

> And the (true) God made Daniel the object of *ḥesed* and mercy *(rḥmym)* before the head of the eunuchs.

The awkward English translation is intended to convey the Hebrew idiom literally: *ntn* N_1 *lḥsd wlrḥmym lpny* N_2. This text, like the previous ones, exhibits the collapse of the responsibility aspect of *ḥesed*. But here in the usage with *rḥmym* the essential assistance (over against special favor) aspect of *ḥesed* may be retained. The identical idiom using only *rḥmym* appears in three other Hebrew texts: an exilic addition to Solomon's dedicatory prayer (I Ki. 8:50),[22] of the people before their captors; in Neh. 1:11, of Nehemiah before "this man" (the king); and in Ps. 106:46, again of the people before their captors.[23] The usage makes clear that while the action is

---

and letter of ch. 7 to the first person materials which follow.

22. Dtr^2. Cf. Cross, "The Structure of the Deuteronomic History," p. 11, n.16; Cross, *Canaanite Myth*, p. 287.

23. Probably exilic or later. The usage here concludes a section on God's remembrance of covenant and relenting in accordance with his great *ḥesed*. These three examples have already been cited by J. A. Montgomery, who adds from the

God's, the *ḥesed* and mercy are performed by the head of the eunuchs. The case is borderline between divine and human *ḥesed*, falling off on the human side; but it has been placed here because the development can be better understood in the light of the preceding examples from Ezra. The *ḥesed* which Daniel receives is the freedom not to defile himself by eating the king's diet. The substitution of other foods was, religiously speaking, a matter of essential assistance freely granted by the one in charge of the matter. Yet the head of the eunuchs had no responsibility for Daniel in this matter - in this respect *ḥesed* has fallen together with *rḥmym*, and in this respect it was important for the narrator to comment on God's role in the matter.

Nehemiah 13:22b

> Remember this also in my favor (lit.: to me), O my God, and look with compassion upon me in accordance with the greatness of your *ḥesed*.

This brief prayer by Nehemiah concludes the section on his restoration of proper sabbath observance during his second administration.[24] The verb here is *ḥws*, which with God (or his eye) as subject is occasionally used to refer to the sparing of repenting people.[25] More often, however (primarily in Ezekiel), this verb is used with the negative to express God's refusal to have compassion on those who have gone against his will.[26] The Nehemiah text is the only instance of the verb used of God's relationship to an individual, but it appears that Nehemiah is emphasizing on the personal level the opposite of Ezekiel's theme. Because he has been zealous for the right worship of God, he should be remembered favorably, shown compassion.

Apocrypha the examples of Test. Jos. 2:3 like these and also Judith 10:8 which uses χάρις alone (i.e., representing only *ḥsd*). (*A Critical and Exegetical Commentary on Daniel* [ICC; New York: Charles Scribner's Sons, 1927], p. 133.)

24. See above, under section on Neh. 13:14, p. 152.

25. Joel 2:17; Jonah 4:11. Also once, in Ezek. 20:17, of not making a full end of the people in the wilderness, despite their disobedience.

26. Jer. 13:14; Ezek. 5:11; 7:4,9; 8:18; 24:14.

Whether this means that God should forgive him his personal shortcomings because of this act of piety, or whether he is asking to be excused from the general punishment of the people for their impiety is not clear. The former seems more likely, since at Nehemiah's behest the people have at least outwardly reformed.

The addition of *k^{e}rōb ḥesed* may be just a part of a stylized expression, but it is interesting to see here once again a tension between what is from the human viewpoint God's self-imposed responsibility and what is not, namely forgiveness. On the one hand, Nehemiah is claiming something which he feels he "deserves": he hopes that God will (and feels that God should) take some responsibility for him because of his (Nehemiah's) pious work. At the same time, he appears to be requesting to be spared (delivered, forgiven) as the content of what he "deserves." The greatness of God's *ḥesed* consists in his willingness to forgive, yet the notion of human action as requisite for God's ongoing assuming of responsibility persists here in Nehemiah. Theoretically, any sin should result in a broken relationship; hopefully, God's *ḥesed* is great enough to forgive any sin. Yet, humanly considered, Nehemiah implies that some piety engenders a better possibility for an ongoing relationship with God than does none at all.

2. A Liturgical Formula

Praise Yahweh, for he is good	7	hdw yhwh ky ṭwb
For his *ḥesed* endures (forever) (from of old)	6	ky ḥsdw l'wlm

This formula occurs in essentially this form no less than eleven times.[28] In a shorter expression "Praise Yahweh for his *ḥesed* endures forever" (omitting *ky ṭwb*), it appears three additional times,[29] and the concluding phrase alone occurs 28 times.[30] The distribution pattern makes plain the reason for

---

28. I Chr. 16:34; II Chr. 5:13a; 7:3; Ezra 3:11a; Jer. 33:11; Ps. 100:5 (last vs.); 106:1; 107:1; 118:1,29 (last vs.); 136:1.

29. I Chr. 16:41; II Chr. 7:6a; 20:21.

30. Three is Ps. 118 in a list of those who should say

introducing this formula here rather than in Chapter III. Of the datable examples, six are in Chronicles, one in Ezra, and one in a collection of sayings inserted into Jeremiah.[31] But even though this usage appears in prose only in these late writings, it is quite possible that some of the psalms in which the formula appears may have been used during the era of the first temple.

The Chronicler's usage ties the formula dominantly to festive occasions at the temple. It is clearly associated with singing and especially with the duties of the special groups appointed to be in charge of temple music. It is used three times during the dedication of Solomon's temple (II Chr. 5:13a; 7:3,6a) and again in connection with the dedication of the second temple (Ezra 3:11a). It is also used in connection with the official singers as appointed by David for service before the tabernacle (I Chr. 16:41) and as the conclusion of a composite hymn attributed to the occasion of bringing the ark to Jerusalem (I Chr. 16:34). In only one text is the form (here short) separated from the cult center: the official singers lead Jehoshaphat's troops to battle against the Transjordanian forces with this refrain (II Chr. 20:21).

The Jeremiah usage explicitly ties the formula to the bringing of thank-offerings to the temple (33:11), and all the Psalms can be readily associated (several on internal grounds) with coming to or celebration in the temple.[32] It should also be observed that the full formula is found only as the opening or closing bicolon of these Psalms; it is never internal or

---

this; 25 in Ps. 136 as a refrain following each of a series of God's actions from creation through conquest of Transjordan.

31. Probably added after separate transmission. So Bright, *Jeremiah*, p. 298.

32. Cf. 100:4; 107:22,32, and internal structure; 118:19-20,24,27. Ps. 106 and 136 are less direct: 136 can be argued from its obvious antiphonal or responsive structure and also from its similarity to 135 in which vs. 3 specifies the temple occasion; 106 has no specific evidence except that vss. 47-48 are used by the Chronicler in connection with the temple dedication.

even the close of a sub-section. This placement suggests its importance as a refrain and may be a clue to its selection by the Chronicler for repeated use.

Can we say anything concrete about the meaning of *ḥesed* in this formula? The occurrence in temple-associated psalms and prose contexts, as well as the use in royal thanksgiving (Ps. 118), suggests the connection of the phrase with the theological tradition of Jerusalem and the Davidic covenant. Thus the general focus is more on God's free commitment to his people than on Israel's responsibility for covenant obedience as a "condition" for *ḥesed*. Glueck was correct in his observation that the presence of the word *ṭwb* in the formula cannot be used to undercut the importance of the covenantal basis for *ḥesed*, even though that relationship is not explicitly mentioned.[33] Yet as we have seen repeatedly before, it is the action of the powerful for the weak, not the mutuality of the relationship, which is in focus. Israel here is called upon only to praise Yahweh. That she should live uprightly is assumed and even urged (e.g. in the thrust of Ps. 106 generally), but her behavior does not earn God's *ḥesed*.

This liturgical expression is used in association with a great variety of circumstances, ranging from deliverance of individuals from sickness (Ps. 107:17ff.) or from perils of the high seas (Ps. 107:23ff.) all the way to a generalization to the *magnalia dei* for the community, including not only deliverance from Egypt and the Amorites but even the creation of the world itself (Ps. 136). This wide range of God's activity described as *ḥesed* continues to appear in other psalms contexts (see Chapter VI). *Ḥesed* thus is broadened in generalized

---

33. Glueck, p. 45. Glueck in this connection emphasized the restriction of *ḥesed* to Israel, and others have followed him in this. God's action of *ḥesed* for Israel may be destructive of her enemies. While the writer agrees with Glueck's observation, it must be kept in mind that the primary concern of the Old Testament is Yahweh's relationship to Israel. Hence Glueck's point is perhaps not so remarkable as it first appears. The question only arises if one attempts to force a universal application onto Israel's liturgical materials.

prayer and praise to encompass all manifestations of God's power in action for his people. Yet in this widening the term remains rooted in Israel's recognition of particular acts of deliverance of the helpless as manifestations of God's *ḥesed*.

CHAPTER V

ḤESED IN THE PROPHETIC LITERATURE

The occurrences of *ḥesed* in prophecy are evenly divided between *ḥesed* done by man (11x) and that done by God (11x).[1] As in the preceding chapters, this distinction will provide the primary basis for the analytical breakdown of the examples. Attention will be given to the general picture of usage for individual prophets, but the development in use of the word can best be seen by retaining the central division between God's action and man's.

A. *Man's* Ḥesed

Of the eleven examples, six are found in Hosea, with the remainder scattered through subsequent books.[2] Although there are textual questions which must be treated individually, it is apparent from the most superficial examination of the passages that we are dealing with a new category of usage for pre-exilic texts, that which has been called "religious," as opposed to "secular" or "theological."[3] As is to be expected, there are certain tensions which result in a "stretching" of the word as it is transferred from the secular to the religious realm, just as we have already seen "stretching" in the theological adaptation. To set the stage for the discussion of these difficulties, three of the most salient texts will be presented with brief contextual comment but with discussion of the word *ḥesed* itself reserved until all three texts have been set forth.

---

1. Excluding the strictly formulaic examples already discussed in Chapter III.

2. Hos. 2:21; 4:1; 6:4,6; 10:12; 12:7; Mic. 6:8; Jer. 2:2b-c; Isa. 40:6; 57:1; Zech. 7:9.

3. The only examples of "religious" usage outside of these prophetic texts are the three examples of the plural as "pious acts" discussed in the previous chapter. It will be suggested at the conclusion of this section that the meaning "pious acts" is probably the late offshoot or modification of the tradition seen developing here.

Hosea 4:1

Hear the word of Yahweh, O Israelites,
For Yahweh has a controversy *(rîb)* with the inhabitants of the land:
For there is no *ʾĕmet* and there is no *ḥesed*
And there is no knowledge of God in the land.

This verse introduces a "modified" or abbreviated *rîb* form in which the address to the heavens and earth is replaced by a call to Israel and the proclamation of the suzerain's acts is also absent.[4] The following verse goes on to catalogue the human sins rampant in the land. Several points are to be noted in anticipation of the discussion to follow. First of all, it is not self-evident whether the *ḥesed* lacking is of man to God, or of men to other men, or possibly both. Second, the word order in which *ʾĕmet* precedes *ḥesed* in the paired usage is unique,[5] suggesting the possibility of special emphasis on *ʾĕmet*. Third, *ḥesed* is also closely tied with "knowledge of God," as also in Hos. 2:21-22 and 6:6. The meaning of the latter phrase has been the object of debate, but it now seems possible to say that this usage is a refraction of a special ancient Near Eastern legal usage for the recognition of the suzerain by his vassal, as well as recognition of the binding

---

4. See Herbert B. Huffmon's brief article "The Covenant Lawsuit in the Prophets," *JBL* 78 (1959) 285-295, for the analysis of the *rîb* pattern in light of Mendenhall's work on covenant, and esp. p. 294 on Hos. 4:1-3. See also J. Harvey, "Le 'Rîb Pattern' réquisitoire prophétique sur la rupture de l'alliance," *Biblica* 43 (1962) 172-196. G. E. Wright has provided a needed corrective to Huffmon's interpretation of the role of heaven and earth in "The Lawsuit of God: A Form-Critical Study of Deuteronomy 32," in *Israel's Prophetic Heritage: Essays in Honor of James Muilenburg*, ed. by B. W. Anderson and W. Harrelson (New York: Harper & Brothers, 1962), pp. 46-47.

5. Although the words appear in reverse order in Mic. 7:20 (with God as subject), they are associated with Jacob and Abraham, also in obviously reversed order.

nature of the treaty stipulations.[6] Finally, the sins enumerated in vs. 2 ([false] swearing, lying, stealing, murder, adultery) are probably to be regarded as a review of the ethical requirements of the decalogue.

Jeremiah 2:2aβ-c

Thus says Yahweh:
I remember the *ḥesed* of your youth,
    Your bridal love,
How you followed after me in the desert,
    In a land not sown.

Several textual notes are in order. (1) There is disagreement between the Greek and Hebrew over the introduction of these words, but in each case it is clearly Yahweh who is addressing the people. (2) The Hebrew *lk* in the first colon is not represented by the Greek. Since the possessive suffix is separately represented, the Hebrew plus probably means "on your

---

6. Herbert Huffmon, "The Treaty Background of Hebrew *Yādaʿ*," *BASOR* 181 (1966) 31-37, esp. p. 36. This interpretation need not completely eradicate the connotation of the intimate conjugal relationship suggested by Eberhard Bauman, "*Ydʿ* und seine Derivate," *ZAW* 28 (1908) 22-41, particularly in Hosea where marriage imagery plays an important role. The prophet may well have used the expression with both images in mind, although the marriage imagery in Hosea may in itself be serving as an image for the covenant image. See Paul A. Riemann, "Desert and Return to Desert in the Pre-Exilic Prophets" (unpublished Ph.D. dissertation, Harvard University, 1964), p. 157. On the interpretation of "knowledge of God" as obedience to stipulations, see H. W. Wolff, "'Wissen um Gott' bei Hosea als Urform von Theologie," *EvTh* 12 (1952-53) 533-554, reprinted in H. W. Wolff, *Gesammelte Studien zum Alten Testament* (Munich: Chr. Kaiser Verlag, 1964), pp. 182-205, and the subsequent exchange between Wolff and Baumann in *EvTh* 15 (1955) 416-431. On the general use of the expression in the Old Testament, see also R. Bultmann, "γινώσκω" (Part C: The OT Usage), in G. Kittel (ed.), *Theological Dictionary of the New Testament* (Grand Rapids, Mich.: Wm. B. Eerdmans Publishing Company, 1964), I, 696-701.

behalf" and nuances the statement of fact with a thread of hope. The imperfect verbs of vs. 3b open the way for such a possibility by allowing the placing of the punishment of those who violate Israel in the present or future. (3) The Greek omits "in the desert, in a land not sown," and reads instead "The Holy One of Israel" as object of *'ḥry*. This may be a haplography followed by dittography in the Greek *Vorlage*, as the next line begins *qdš yśr'l*. Alternately, it might be regarded as a haplography followed by an explanatory expansion in the MT.[7] In either case, the meaning of *ḥesed* is not affected since the marriage imagery is not dependent upon the desert location.

The marriage imagery used here is probably related to the tradition of Hosea 1-3. Riemann has pointed out that the desert here is regarded as bad,[8] even though Israel's relation to Yahweh was good. Nevertheless, the passage has thematic and also verbal associations *(n'wrym, hlk, mdbr)* with Hos. 3:16-18, where in the context of marriage language the desert will be transformed into agrarian land.

Hosea 6:6

For I delight in *ḥesed*, not sacrifice
And in knowledge of God rather than *(mn)* burnt offerings.

Whether the use of *mn* is privative, indicating total rejection of sacrifice, cannot be determined on strictly grammatical grounds. The contrast is perhaps better understood when this most succinct statement is related to other similar texts. In Amos 5:21-24 Yahweh announces his rejection of feasts and sacrifices, concluding with an appeal for *mišpāṭ* and *ṣᵉdāqâ*.

---

7. Since this is not technically a zero-variant, it does not receive treatment in the work of J. Gerald Janzen, *Studies in the Text of Jeremiah* (Cambridge, Mass.: Harvard University Press, 1973).

8. Riemann, "Desert and Return to Desert," pp. 160-161. See also Shemaryahu Talmon, "The 'Desert Motif' in the Bible and in Qumran Literature," *Biblical Motifs: Origins and Transformation*, A. Altmann, ed. (Cambridge, Mass.: Harvard University Press, 1966), pp. 38-53.

In Micah 6:6-8 (see below) *mišpāṭ* and *ḥesed* are contrasted with sacrifices. In Jer. 7:21ff the commandment of obedience, not of sacrifice, is the one given to the fathers departing from Egypt. And on the individual level, Samuel declares to Saul that Yahweh's delight is in obedience, not sacrifice (I Sam. 15:22-23). In Isa. 1:10-20 sacrifice and prayers will receive no recognition without doing good, seeking *mišpāṭ*. Seen in this broader context, the sum and substance of the message must be that sacrifice without obedience, that is, without justice and righteousness, is worthless. If Harvey is correct that the secular *rîb* pattern included the rejection of offerings as a substitute for obedience,[9] then this tradition may be a religious extension of that form.

In Hos. 6:6, the parallel with "knowledge of God" coupled with the contrast to sacrificial offerings suggests that *ḥesed* is something directed toward God. At the same time, the related traditions suggest that whatever is desired (here *ḥesed*) involves behavior towards one's fellowmen.

With these three examples before us, we may examine the modification of the word *ḥesed* which takes place in "religious" usage. The term can be used both in the context of "primary," personal relationship (marriage imagery) and of "secondary," political relationship (suzerain-vassal imagery: discrete units), just as in the pre-exilic secular usage. Here much more than in secular contexts it refers to an ongoing behavior, although that aspect is not absent from the secular usage (e.g. Abner and Ishbaal/the Saulides; Abraham and Abimelech). The examples make clear that religious *ḥesed* is directed both to God (almost necessarily in Jer. 2:2, probably in all three examples) and also to fellowmen (possible in both Hosea texts, strongly suggested for 4:1 by the following catalogue of sins and for 6:6 by related usage, especially Mic. 6:8). With respect to God, it is clear that Israel has a responsibility, but it is to him, not for him. Since God is understood as all-powerful and self-sufficient, Israel's *ḥesed* obviously cannot

---

9. "Le 'Rîb Pattern'," p. 188. See also Harvey's *Le plaidoyer prophétique contre Israël après la rupture de l'alliance* (Montréal: Les Éditions Bellarmin, 1967), esp. pp. 103-105.

be an action of the powerful for the weak, an action of deliverance or rescue or protection. With respect to men, it is apparent that the boundaries of responsibility are here very much more generalized than in the secular usage where it is restricted to those with whom one is in a particular relationship. Furthermore, crimes such as murder or robbery are such as can be handled in the civil courts, whereas in secular *ḥesed* the failure to act would not normally be actionable except before God. Can these modifications in usage be accounted for in terms of the other parameters of the word and in terms of Israel's general religious self-understanding?

The extension of *ḥesed* to fellowmen can be readily understood when it is recognized that it is always spoken of within Israelite society, not the world of men as a whole. Thus the basis for responsibility, religiously speaking, is the membership of all Israelites in the covenant community.[10] On this level the responsibility for others is the same as for a personal intimate or a political ally. But what of the specific legal controls? The point here is that although obedience is required of each individual, it is the society *as a whole* or its *leadership* which lacks *ḥesed* or should display *ḥesed*. Although the Sinai Covenant is addressed to individuals, it is the community which is responsible to God:

...Society as a whole, and especially through its executive

---

10. This ideal of community solidarity is not to be regarded (as in the last century) as a primitive tribal notion happily rejected in the "individualism" of the later prophets. Although it is possible and even probable that the idea of covenant solidarity was in pre-settlement times built upon the secular understanding of inner-tribal solidarity, the coming of settled life and especially the movement from tribal to monarchical government led to a smaller sphere of responsibility (probably familial) on the secular level. At the same time, the concept of the covenant community bound all Israel together on the religious plane. On this issue, see Walther Eichrodt, *Theology of the Old Testament* (tr. by J. A. Baker from the 5th German ed., 1964; London: SCM Press Ltd., 1967), II, pp. 231-246, 319-322.

> and judicial apparatus, upholds the covenant pattern, enforces its terms, and effectively restrains or punishes evildoers. Individual violations of the stipulations of the Covenant become a threat to the stability and survival of the covenant community only when they are of such a grave nature or so widespread that the authorities cannot deal successfully with them or when the corruption extends to the governing body itself, with the leaders of Israel found to be in league with the covenant breakers (through weakness, indifference, tacit approval, or active collaboration).[11]

It is not, then, the sin of an individual punishable in the law courts which is at stake in the religious use of *ḥesed*. The absence of *ḥesed* is the wholesale abandonment of the stipulations of the decalogue; it is the absence of justice and righteousness within Israelite society. On this scale, the failure to do *ḥesed* is punishable only by God, just as is the extra-legal failure to act in the secular context.

The application of the word *ḥesed* to Israel's relationship to Yahweh is more complicated: as has been pointed out, Israel can never be in a position of power with respect to Yahweh so that she would be free from reprisal if she failed to meet her treaty obligations. In the secular usage both parties must maintain their responsibilities within a political relationship, but only the circumstantially superior party is said to do *ḥesed*. And even in the personal imagery of the marriage relationship one cannot escape Israel's subordination to Yahweh.[12]

---

11. D. N. Freedman, "Divine Commitment and Human Obligation," p. 428.

12. Because God does not need help from Israel, A. Jepsen attempted to treat all the occurrences of human *ḥesed* as referring only to interpersonal relationships ("Gnade und Barmherzigkeit," p. 269). But his proposal seems to stretch the sense of the passages more than Hosea's admittedly unusual usage stretches the meaning of the word itself.

Bright comments on Jer. 2:2 that *ḥesed* "does not properly describe a quality that men exhibit toward God." He suggests that its use here is "conditioned by the figure of marriage

There is a variety of factors which probably contributed to this stretching of the usage. Failure to do *ḥesed* on the individual, secular level was actionable by God; so also the covenant people's failure to do *ḥesed* was actionable by God. The two situations were not strictly analogous, but the source of blessing or retribution was the same. Further, Israel always had freedom of choice, if not freedom from reprisal. Yahweh could not force her to worship him alone and to establish a just society. He could threaten to bring the relationship to an end, to cut off the people from himself and from the land, but this action would be counter to his ultimate concern for the people. From the perspective of his genuine love and concern for Israel as his chosen, the people's action could be a source of pain and anguish for him - and herein lay the strength of the familial imagery. Israel was free to destroy the relationship with Yahweh. God desired her *ḥesed* rather than needing it; but he would not get what he really wanted by destroying Israel.

Third, in its use with respect to Yahweh, Israel's *ḥesed*

---

employed to describe the covenant relationship between Yahweh and Israel" (*Jeremiah*, p. 14). Although Bright is correct that the personal imagery does mitigate the strict inferior-superior relationship, the image is nevertheless not pervasive enough to account for the examples in which the covenant stands alone as the primary image. It is conceivably a matter of circumstance that there are no examples of *ḥesed* done by the weaker party in a secular relationship. In treaty relationship especially, faithfulness or obedience under threat of reprisal would not be something to be remarked upon. Yet as we have seen, there is no reference even to secular *violation* of relationship by a weaker party as *lack* of *ḥesed*. Freedom rather than coercion characterizes every example which is preserved in our texts. If the word could in fact refer to the meeting of the obligations of a relationship by the weaker party, then the discussion of "stretching" of usage in the subsequent paragraphs would be unnecessary. But since there are no secular examples which seem to fit this category, an explanation of the apparent shift must be provided.

is abstracted from specific actions and moves toward faithfulness or loyalty, sole recognition of the suzerain. Worship of Yahweh alone is a communal action, but it is an expression of faithfulness to him. Establishment of a just society is a communal action, but it is likewise an expression of faithfulness to Yahweh. It is in this connection that the repeated paralleling of *ḥesed* with *daʿat ʾĕlōhîm* in Hosea[13] is so significant. Much of the language of covenant, both in the biblical tradition and in the secular examples from the ancient Near East, could be used bi-directionally. This is quite to be expected so long as the words carry only general, abstracted connotations of meeting one's own responsibilities within the relationship. The root *ydʿ* is a particularly good example for which both the cognate secular traditions and the religious and theological uses in the Old Testament exhibit bi-directionality.[14]

So also the word "love" *(ʾhb)* can be used for a relationship between equals or between suzerain and vassal in both political and religious contexts.[15] It is not without interest that the book of Deuteronomy uses "love" primarily for Israel's duty to Yahweh (except for Yahweh's "election" love) and uses *ḥesed* only for God's response to Israel's love, in accordance with the formulaic (liturgical) tradition (see Chapter III). Hosea, on the other hand, uses *ḥesed* only with Israel as subject and does not speak of Israel's love for God either as fact or as ideal. Love in Hosea is tied primarily to conjugal and also to father-son imagery. As such, it is a response which cannot be commanded (unlike the Deuteronomic usage in which love is equated with obedience). By the same token, all which has been said about *ḥesed* suggests that it is a response which may be earnestly desired but not commanded, even in a political context. It may well be this nuance of the word which

---

13. 4:1; 6:6. Cf. also 2:21-22; 6:3-4 discussed below.

14. Huffmon, "The Treaty Background of Hebrew *Yādaʿ*," 31-37: "The most obvious technical usage of 'know' is that with reference to mutual legal recognition on the part of suzerain and vassal" (p. 31).

15. Cf. Moran, "Love of God in Deuteronomy," 77-87.

precipitates its frequent use in the religious sense precisely in Hosea.

Aside from the special use with "knowledge of God" in Hosea, the more general affinity of *ḥesed* with two other words, *'ĕmet* and *ḥāsîd*, probably provided additional impetus toward the use of the word for the fulfillment of the vassal's duty to the suzerain. *'ĕmet* is of course regularly coupled with *ḥesed* in secular and theological texts, as well as being a "B" word in theological usage in the Psalms.[16] The reversal of the usual order in the single use of *'ĕmet* in Hos. 4:1 is striking when set over against the general tradition, for it seems to emphasize the "faithfulness" aspect of *ḥesed* rather than particular actions. Although *'ĕmet*, like *ḥesed*, is most often used of God toward men, the reverse usage does occur,[17] again not surprisingly in view of the abstract level of the term.

There is substantial evidence that *ḥāsîd*, even more than *'ĕmet*, could normally be used of man (or in the plural, of the covenant community) as one faithful to God. Ps. 50:5 is perhaps the most striking example: "Gather to me my *ḥăsîdîm*, those who made a covenant with me in the presence of sacrifice...."[18] The *ḥăsîdîm* are those party to Yahweh's covenant,

---

16. The word order *ḥesed* (A) *'ĕmet* (B) is never violated in the Psalms, regardless of the specific pattern of usage (conjunction or parallelism). R. G. Boling, "Synonymous Parallelism in the Psalms," *JSS* 5/3 (1960) 231. From Boling's lists the same order appears to hold true for the related derivatives of the root *'mn* in parallel usage (but not in conjunction, cf., e.g., Ps. 89:25).

17. Principally in the Deuteronomic historian or his sources: Jos. 24:14; I Sam. 12:24; I Ki. 2:4; 3:6; II Ki. 20:3; also Jer. 4:2; Isa. 48:1. Since the antiquity of Jos. 24:12-14 is disputed, there is no certain example prior to Hosea. But the possibility for such usage was inherent in the word from the start.

18. Following Dahood's interpretation of the preposition *'ly*, but rejecting the *y* third person suffix (*Psalms* I, p. 307). The parallel with covenant-makers is remarkable in that only here are men rather than Yahweh the subject of *krt* with respect

even though here their behavior is being called into question. In II Sam. 22:26 = Ps. 18:26, Yahweh declares that he will act as *ḥāsîd* to the *ḥāsîd*. While one level of meaning here is simply that the practitioner of *ḥesed* in personal life will be the recipient of God's *ḥesed*, the more abstract connotation that faithfulness to God will be rewarded is also present and perhaps dominant.[19] The Hebrew of I Sam. 2:9 says that God will "guard the feet of his *ḥăsîdîm*," whereas "the wicked will be destroyed in darkness." Although the immediate parallelism suggests a contrast of good versus bad in human behavior, the larger context of the poor versus the rich, the weak versus the strong, suggests that the poem as a whole praises God's action for his people over against their adversaries not in the covenant.[20] Hence "faithful ones" or "covenant ones" is an appropriate rendering. Ps. 31:24 sets God's *ḥăsîdîm* alongside of "the faithful" *(ʾĕmûnîm)*. Although the parallelism is not exact, the thrust is that the covenant people are faithful ones in their loving of God. Once again the nuancing is ambiguous: the word is applied to the whole people and at the same time to the faithful (among the) people. This same parallel occurs

---

to his covenant. Although the consonantal text could be repointed as a first person perfect, the thrust of the sentence would be lost. Even *krt* can be bi-directional: here in a *rîb* context those who agreed to the covenant are called to account.

19. Vss. 26-27 contain a series of four such comments. While all involve qualities which may be exhibited in human relationships, it is easier to take them in the direct God-man relationship. This small section is only one of several older sources used by the psalmist, perhaps as early as the tenth century B.C. Cross and Freedman have dated the present written form "not later than the 9th-8th centuries B.C." ("A Royal Psalm of Thanksgiving," *JBL* 72 [1953] 20).

20. On the early date of this poem and its expression of Israel's view of God's relationship to the poor and weak, see Marvin Chaney, "*ḤDL*-II and the 'Song of Debora '" (unpublished Ph.D. dissertation, Harvard University, 1976) which also contains a detailed textual analysis. (Note that the lines cited here are not found in the Greek and Latin traditions.)

also in Ps. 12:2 (here with the singular *ḥāsîd*), where the emphasis must be on the *ḥāsîd* as faithful by his uprightness rather than simply as a member of the covenant community.

Although the dating of the individual psalms remains unsettled, it is clear that the tradition available to Hosea[21] did carry the word *ḥāsîd* with the triple nuances of covenant people, ones faithful to Yahweh, ones upright in their action. In his religious use of *ḥesed*, Hosea is saying that God desires both upright action and faithfulness from his covenant people: the community-directed and God-directed actions are two sides of a single coin.

The statement "Hosea is saying" is deliberate, even though an example from Jeremiah has been used to highlight the problem. It has already been pointed out that six of the eleven examples of religious *ḥesed* in prophecy are in Hosea. In the review of the group as a whole, it can be seen that the three remaining pre-exilic and exilic examples all appear in contexts so closely akin to Hosea's usage that it hardly seems accidental,[22] especially in view of the concentration of the word in such a short book and its unusual reservation to religious usage. This is not to say that the later prophets copied from Hosea but just to suggest the probability that they made selective use of a tradition to which he may have given the primary impetus.

To summarize: as behavior of men to other men, *ḥesed* could be given religious generalization through the concept of the covenant community. As behavior of the community toward God, *ḥesed* could be stretched to apply (despite God's power of reprisal and lack of need) because (1) as in secular tradition it was only God who punished; (2) although *ḥesed* was not needed, it nevertheless was desired and yet could not be forced out of the people; (3) *ḥesed* did in secular contexts refer to fulfilling of covenant responsibilities (even though from a position

---

21. I Sam. 2 and II Sam. 22 = Ps. 18 are almost surely earlier; some of the other examples could be. For further discussion of *ḥāsîd*, see Appendix.

22. The two post-exilic examples are a logical outgrowth of this usage but do not exhibit such specific affinities.

of power) and this is what was desired of Israel; (4) the bidirectional use of other covenant language may have lent impetus to the development of a religious usage; (5) the abstracting toward "faithfulness," by association with the closely related words *'ĕmet* and *ḥāsîd*, made the content of the word more appropriate for describing Israel's relationship to God.

The remarkable characteristic of *ḥesed* as a religious term in these texts is that it can be at once so closely associated with right behavior as a community on the one hand and with faithfulness to God on the other. The inseparability of these two is the essence of the suzerainty covenant, and the conjoining finds its clearest expression in the religious use of *ḥesed*. The word can be used in parallelism with *'ĕmet* and *'ĕmûnâ* which are primarily God-oriented; it can be used in parallelism with *ṣedeq/ṣedāqâ* and *mišpāṭ* which are primarily community oriented. It cuts in both directions, providing what might be called a one-word summary of the decalogue.[23]

The entire case for the understanding of the religious use of *ḥesed* has been presented on the basis of just three examples and sources related to them. In strictest methodological procedure, nothing should have been said about any of the occurrences until at least the eight pre-exilic instances had been presented, since these form a unified picture to which each contributes some part. But in the interests of clarity the problems and proposed solution have been presented early so that the reader may better follow the interpretation of the remaining examples. Inevitably the results have anticipated the larger group of texts which are now to be presented as confirmatory evidence.

Hosea 2:21-22

> And I will betroth you to me forever; and I will
> betroth you to me with (a bride-price of)

---

23. The closest approximation to this dual usage is perhaps the expression "knowledge of God" in the double sense of recognition of the suzerain and recognition of the stipulations as binding. But *ḥesed* is the stronger term insofar as it moves beyond recognition of the stipulations to their actual fulfillment.

> righteousness *(ṣdq)* and justice *(mšpṭ)* and *ḥesed* and mercy *(rḥmym)*; and I will betroth you to me with (a bride-price of) faithfulness *(ʾmwnh)*; and you shall know Yahweh.

A number of manuscripts read "and you shall know that I am Yahweh." This is probably an assimilation toward the usage of Ezekiel.[24]

The usage of *ʾrś b* in II Sam. 3:14 suggests that the payment was normally made by the prospective groom to the bride's father. Here the image is clouded since Israel herself as the bride must also stand as the recipient of the gifts. The inclusion of this text with the examples of "religious" rather than "theological" *ḥesed* is not self-evident. Rudolph states explicitly that since the five qualities are the groom's payment they cannot be regarded as human attributes, qualities of Israel. He then explains all the words as God's action toward Israel.[25] Wolff is less explicit, but seems to lean in the same direction.[26] Although this view is possible, the writer finds the alternate interpretation more plausible. This is not to say that Israel brings these items to the betrothal, which plainly is not the case. But it seems likely that in this instance Yahweh will give these qualities to Israel as "things" to possess, rather than doing them on her behalf. This interpretation is consonant with the image of a possession of value received by the bride's family.[27] More important, a major

---

24. Hans W. Wolff, *Hosea* (BK; Neukirchen Kreis Moers: Neukirchener Verlag der Buchhandlung des Erziehungsvereins, 1961), p. 57; Wilhelm Rudolph, *Hosea* (KAT; Gütersloh: Gütersloher Verlagshaus Gerd Mohn, 1966), p. 74.

25. Rudolph, *Hosea*, p. 81.

26. "22b nennt die zu erwartende *Wirkung* der Brautgaben Jahwehs" (*Hosea*, p. 65). (Italics mine.)

27. It might be countered that David paid for Saul's daughter by an action done on Saul's behalf. Two points counter this analogy: first, the story suggests that such was not the usual procedure; second, the idiom *ʾrś b* is used precisely with the foreskins, thus focusing on the actual thing received rather than on the action.

point of Hosea as a whole is the absence of these qualities from the life of the community. It is Israel who has played the harlot, who by the failure of her religious and ethical fiber has brought on the proclamation of divorce. Here, in a message of hope, Yahweh is saying that he will start over with a clean slate and will himself provide Israel with what she had been unable to achieve before. The bride payment is supposed to be that which legally takes care of the final obstacle to the marriage.[28] Theologically speaking, it is Israel's lack of these qualities which must be understood as the obstacle to the marriage. Perhaps this presses the image too far, but surely these qualities must be in Israel if the new marriage is to succeed as is expected.[29]

What has been said about *ḥesed* as faithfulness to Yahweh and justice in the Israelite society is evident in the usage here. The use of *rḥmym* does require comment, however, because the naming of Hosea's child "Not Pitied" suggests that this term (and hence all five) ought to be regarded as God's action. There is, however, evidence that *rḥmym* could also be used of relations among men, as in Amos 1:11 where it is associated with the failure to recognize a relationship of political brotherhood.[30] The word is not inappropriate for human relations; at the same time it must be recognized that all these five qualities of Israel are in fact well known as attributes which God displays in his relationship with his people. The emphasis here is that Israel will be able to respond in kind.

Hosea 6:4

What shall I do with you, O Ephraim?
    What shall I do with you, O Judah?

---

28. Wolff, *Hosea*, p. 64.

29. For another example of something given by Yahweh in which the central concern is Israel's possession of it, cf. Ezek. 11:19, the gift of the heart of flesh in place of the heart of stone.

30. In Zech. 7:9 the same pairing with *ḥesed* appears, obviously related to social responsibility for the weak in society. But that tradition is considerably later and cannot be given undue weight.

Your *ḥesed* is like the morning mist,
Like the dew which early is gone.

This verse begins the short word of Yahweh which climaxes in 6:6 discussed above. The *ḥesed* of the people of both parts of the original covenant community is described as ephemeral and the result is condemnation (vs.4) rather than the support which Yahweh would rather give. The cry of repentance attributed to the people in the preceding verses (6:1-3) is rejected as too transient and too superficial. The people do not take Yahweh's judgment seriously enough. It never occurs to them that he may not respond to their plea; they presume that "his going forth is sure as the dawn."[31]

Alt long ago proposed that all of 5:8-6:6 be understood in connection with the Syro-Ephraimite War, and most subsequent analyses have followed his lead with variations only in detail.[32] In understanding the overall form as lawsuit related material (with Good), it is not necessary to move away from the Syro-Ephraimite War into a cultic setting. (Indeed, Good admits that the highly structured presence of both Israel and

---

31. Edwin Good has proposed that this section may be associated with cultic theophany, perhaps in the autumnal festival, especially with the following rain motif ("Hosea 5:8-6:6: An Alternative to Alt," *JBL* 85 [1966] 280). G. E. Wright, on the other hand, has shown that the rain motif elsewhere may be associated with *rîb* traditions as well as with royal-theology ("The Lawsuit of God: A Form-Critical Study of Deuteronomy 32," pp. 54-55). In light of the response in vss. 4-6, both themes may be present, since failure to live up to the covenant has been accompanied by festival celebration. Nevertheless, against Good, the section 5:8-6:6 as a whole need not be drawn from cultic use.

32. Albrecht Alt, "Hosea 5:8-6:6. Ein Krieg und seine Folgen in prophetischer Beleuchtung," *Neue kirchliche Zeitschrift* 30 (1919) 537-568, reprinted in *Kleine Schriften zur Geschichte des Volkes Israel* (Munich: C. H. Beck'sche Verlagsbuchhandlung, 1953), II, pp. 163-187. For a brief bibliography of those who have followed Alt, see Good, "Hosea 5:8-6:6," p. 273.

Judah in 5:10-14 cannot be accounted for on his hypothesis.)[33] The structured references to Israel and Judah (which Alt overlooked in attempting perhaps too specific subdivision into sequential oracles), the transgression-of-covenant theme, and the invasion of Judah by Israel with Syria can be fitted into a unified theological interpretation. In the suzerainty treaty a basic obligation assumed by vassals is that they will not engage in hostilities with one another. In the Syro-Ephraimite War, we see the apex of disobedience of this obligation: not only is the covenant people divided within itself, but now the two factions are at war between themselves. The single vassal is living as two and is bent on destruction; Yahweh has called them to account. They repent but Yahweh knows their fickleness - at the least occasion they will be at it again. Thus *ḥesed* here involves faithfulness to Yahweh not only as social justice within Israel and Judah, but conceivably as political stability as well.[34]

Hosea 10:12a

Sow (for yourselves) what partakes of righteousness;
And you shall reap in accordance with *ḥesed*.

Despite the arguments of Wolff,[35] *ḥesed* here is best understood as human action. The text as well as grammar and syntax even of this portion of the verse is difficult, let alone that of the following cola. In the first colon, the

---

33. "Hosea 5:8-6:6," p. 283, n.42.

34. This emphasis on the political aspect of what Yahweh desires can be suggested only tentatively. It uses the covenant theme as now understood to push beyond Alt's suggestion that Hosea finally proposes a religious rather than political solution in the "return" theme. Although it seems possible that even the northern prophets regarded Jerusalem as the only legitimate cult center, it is more difficult to guess whether they would necessarily have extrapolated from this position to a theological support of political unity as well.

35. *Hosea*, pp. 234, 237. James L. Mays treats *ḥesed* here as human rather than divine. His interpretation of the term itself throughout Hosea is closely related to Glueck's perspective (*Hosea* [OTL; Philadelphia: Westminster Press, 1969], p.146).

Greek omits *lkm* which is metrically superfluous in the immediate bicolon but stands in parallel with 12bα. Meaning is not affected. In the second colon, the Greek reads *lpry* instead of *lpy*: "you shall reap what partakes of the fruit of *ḥesed*." In light of the references to fruit in 10:1,13, the LXX may well be correct; the case for the covenant community as the subject of *ḥesed* can be argued on either reading.

The function of the preposition *l* in the first colon (and in the second if the Greek text is followed) is difficult to assess. Neither *zrʿ* nor *qṣr*[36] ever appears elsewhere in such a construction; normally each takes the simple direct object. The meaning must be somewhere within the broad range of "in reference to," but the force of the image is perhaps best conveyed in English by omitting the preposition altogether. But this applies only to *l* in the first colon, not to the MT *lpy* in the second, and it is here that the interpretation becomes important for the understanding of the subject of *ḥesed*.[37]

If *lpy* is read, and recognized as distinct from *l* in the first colon, then *ḥesed* is the human action "in accordance with which, in proportion to which" the people will reap; no object is expressed for the verb *qṣr*. God's blessing or salvation (cf. 12cβ) is understood but is not expressed. If the Greek *lpry* is read, and it is the "fruit of *ḥesed*" which will be reaped, *ḥesed* is still to be regarded as human action. An examination of the usage of *pry* in construct shows that the second member of the phrase invariably names the source of the

---

36. On the second imperative as a statement of anticipated result, see C. Brockelmann, *Hebräische Syntax* (Neukirchen Kreis Moers: Verlag der Buchhandlung des Erziehungsvereins, 1956), Par. 3, p. 2, where he cites this example. Wolff follows this analysis (*Hosea*, p. 234), as does the translation given here.

37. The contrast between sowing and reaping has perhaps been the cause of the failure to take the particular usage here seriously enough. In Hos. 8:7, Prv. 18:22 especially, it is clear that one reaps what one sows. But the usage is modified in Hos. 10:12, either by *lpy* or by *pry*, and this shift must be accounted for.

fruit - the land, the vine, the earth, actions, work, wisdom - but not the fruit itself.[38] Thus here it is the *fruit* which is to be understood as *God's* blessing; but the *ḥesed* is *Israel's* action which will yield the fruit. *Ḥesed* is thus functionally in parallelism with the righteousness of the first part of the verse, as a societal expression of faithfulness which will lead to God's positive response.

Hosea 12:7

> . . . .
> Keep *mišpāṭ* and *ḥesed*,
> And wait continually for your God.

The literature on Hosea 12 and particularly on the Jacob materials (to which this verse apparently forms the conclusion) is plentiful,[39] but there is no consensus on the meaning of the pericope. It is not even agreed whether the references to Jacob are intended to be laudatory or condemnatory. The first colon of vs. 7, which has here been left untranslated, is widely agreed to be grammatically impossible, even though for once the Greek and versions seem to agree with the MT. A simple change from *b'lhyk tšwb* to *b'hlyk tšb* ("you shall sit in your tents") is usually proposed (cf. vs. 10b), but there is no agreement on whether this theme ought to be treated as blessing or curse. Wolff, however, argues that the expression *šwb b* is to be understood as a *constructio praegnans* with a further verb which takes *b* (e.g. *h'myn, bṭḥ*) implied.[40] The proposal is attractive, since the general sense "return to your God" would

---

38. The only possible exceptions are Ps. 107:37, with *tᵉbû'â*, where *pry* ought possibly to be excluded as an extra-metrical gloss, and Amos 6:12 where *pry ṣdqh* is changed to wormwood. But despite the parallel to simple *mšpṭ*, there is no reason that the Amos phrase could not mean the "results of righteous action," thus conforming to the normal pattern.

39. For bibliography, see Wolff, *Hosea*, p. 266, and especially Peter Ackroyd, "Hosea and Jacob," *VT* 13 (1963) 245-259, who gives a brief summary of the viewpoint of many of the more modern treatments of the problem. More recently, see Robert Coote, "Hosea XII," *VT* 21 (1971) 389-402.

40. Wolff, *Hosea*, p. 268.

seem appropriate here; but the solution must still be considered *ad hoc*.

These difficulties make it impossible to set the use of *ḥesed* in a context any broader than its own colon, and even this is metrically too short to fit comfortably with the preceding and following lines. It can only be said that the coupling with *mišpāṭ* as that which Israel ought to do is in accordance with the religious usage in other clearer texts. With the final colon focusing on stance before God, *ḥesed* again appears as the conjunction of attitude to Yahweh and communal behavior.

Micah 6:8

> He has showed you, O man, what is good *(ṭwb)*:
>
> And what does Yahweh require from you
>
> But to do *mišpāṭ* and to love *ḥesed*
>
> And to walk humbly with your God?

The close relationship in content with Hosea 12:7 is immediately apparent, but the relationship to Hos. 6:6 becomes evident only when the larger context (vss. 6-8) is examined. Yahweh asks *mišpāṭ*, *ḥesed*, faithfulness rather than a multitude of sacrifices.[41] The entire pericope, however, includes vss. 1-8, which as a unit is a variant on the covenant-lawsuit pattern. The concluding verse provides the warning (rather than the "sentence") to the vassal that he must live up to his covenant obligations.[42] Once again *ḥesed* conveys the inseparability of justice in the community and faithfulness to God as the covenant requirement. And even though the verb *drš* is used in the sense "to require" (cf. Dt. 23:22), it remains true that the warning can only serve as an exhortation. The vassal cannot be prevented from pursuing a course leading to his own destruction and the suzerain will not achieve his real aim by destroying the vassal.

The use of *ṭwb* is of interest here. It is possible that

---

41. For other parallels to this theme, see above, pp. 172-173.

42. Following the refinement of Harvey, "Le 'Rîb Pattern,' p. 178, on the work of Huffmon, "The Covenant Lawsuit," p. 287. See also Harvey, *Le plaidoyer prophêtique*, pp. 42-45.

rather than meaning "good" in the abstract or as right behavior in general the usage here is a technical one, namely, "the essence of friendly relations between the covenant parties." Moran's study of *ṭbtʾ* in the Sefire stelas suggests that such nominal forms could be used in this sense in parity treaties, and he suggests that they were probably used of vassals as well.[43] If this was in fact the case, and if *ḥesed* would regularly be associated with goodness in theological usage,[44] then the treaty sense of *ṭwb* may have offered yet another bi-directional term which could give impetus to the development of a religious use of *ḥesed* within the covenant framework.

Isaiah 40:6b-8

All flesh is grass
And all its *ḥesed* (?) is like the flower of the field.
The grass withers, the flower droops
When the wind of Yahweh blows against it;
The grass withers, the flower droops
But the word of our God shall stand forever.

These lines constitute the inaugural oracle given to Second Isaiah to proclaim. It is given him by a member of the Divine Council in the course of his inaugural vision, vss. 1-8.[45] Vs. 7c is regarded as a gloss. It disturbs the metric

---

43. "A Note on the Treaty Terminology of the Sefire Stelas," p. 175 and n.23. The only examples of usage of a vassal are from Hittite treaties, using the probable linguistic equivalent *atterūtu*. It should be noted that the common usage of the Semitic cognate forms is of parties in a parity treaty or of suzerain to vassal wherever the word is tied to one member of the relationship rather than standing as an abstraction for the friendly relationship itself. This is to be expected, since the weaker party can only ask for "friendship," not grant it. But once established, "friendship" in the abstract can be rebelled against by breaking the treaty terms, and it is here than an analogy to the religious use of *ḥesed* might come into play.

44. See the liturgical formula discussed in Chapter IV, pp. 165-168, and the discussion of other bi-directional terms

and poetic structure and has been excluded from the translation.

The usage here presents difficulties. The Greek translates δόξα, so that some have emended the text to *ḥmdw* or *hdrw*.[46] Others have followed the Targum, taking *ḥesed* as "strength" and pointing to passages such as Ex. 15:13 and Ps. 59:17 (where *ḥesed* appears in parallel with *kḥ* and *ʿz*), as well as to the sense of the passage.[47] Although the latter suggestion is attractive, it ought probably to be rejected: strength is never in itself a meaning of the word, for even in these parallels the nuance is clearly delivering power exercised on behalf of the covenant people.[48] Hence a third suggested emendation is to read *ḥsn* ("strength").[49]

In attempting to come to grips with the usage, it is necessary to consider the meaning of "all flesh," With the removal of the gloss, it is not necessary to refer the phrase to Israel. The meaning may simply be mankind in contrast to God, but a third possibility suggests itself. The proclamation of the overcoming of "all flesh," given in the image of God's breath on the flower, suggests that the overthrow of the Babylonians is what the oracle has in view. To the extent that an inaugural oracle expresses the prophet's message in summary form, such an interpretation would be highly appropriate as the specific expression of God's power on the human scene.

---

above, pp. 177ff.

45. See F. M. Cross, Jr., "The Council of Yahweh in Second Isaiah," *JNES* 12 (1953) 274-277; James Muilenburg, *Isaiah Chapters 40-66: Introduction and Exegesis* (IB; New York: Abingdon Press, 1956), p. 422.

46. To *ḥmdw*: Ludwig Koehler, ed., *Lexicon in Veteris Testamenti Libros* (Leiden: E. J. Brill, 1953), p. 318b. To *hdrw*: Bernhard Duhm, *Das Buch Jesaia* (*HkzAT*; Göttingen: Vandenhoeck & Ruprecht, 1892), p. 267.

47. Kuyper, "The Meaning of *ḥsdw* [in] Isa. XL 6," pp. 490-492.

48. See Chapter VI on poetic usage.

49. So Felix Perles, *Analekten zur Textkritik des Alten Testaments* (Munich: F. Straub, 1895), pp. 76ff.

What then of *ḥesed*? If Israel is not involved - and her failure is not an emphasis in Second Isaiah - then this example cannot be "religious" usage. As a secular term, *ḥesed* does not normally receive so generalized an application as to all mankind. Since Babylon has scarcely practiced *ḥesed* with respect to Israel or her other neighbors, this alternative is not attractive either. Hence a textual error seems likely,[50] and of the various proposals *ḥmdw* is the most probable on several grounds.

Graphically, the *m* to *s* change is the most likely error, since these two letters were easily confused in the orthography of the second century B.C.[51] The Greek uses δόξα principally for *kbwd* and not at all for *ḥmd* in sure texts, but the Greek word would be particularly appropriate for the imagery being conveyed here. If the interpretation of the oracle suggested above is correct, then the poet is referring to the splendor of the Babylonian empire under the image of the beauty of the flower. In usual usage, *ḥmd* would not refer to the splendor of a nation (as exhibited in Babylon's fine capital, for example, which was surely of a new magnitude compared to the Jerusalem which the exiles had known); but by the same token *kbwd* would not have been a usual description for a wild flower. The Greek translator has sensed what the oracle was trying to convey and has selected the word which best conveys both the immediate image (beauty) and that which it represents (splendor). The Israelites are assured that despite the apparent magnificence of Babylon, that nation will be swept away even as God's purpose will remain sure.

---

50. The word *ḥesed* could conceivably be applied to the international scene in a strictly political sense: treaty fulfillment on the human scale is fickle (and because of this Babylon will fall), but God will keep his word to Israel. If the Hebrew is to be retained, then this last interpretation of the word is likely.

51. F. M. Cross, "The Development of the Jewish Scripts," *BANE* (Garden City, N.Y.: Doubleday & Company, Inc., 1961), fig. 2 (p. 138), lines 1 and 2, and descriptions of the development of the Hasmonean *samekh*, p. 171, and medial *mem*, p. 170.

It is to be noted that here again even the mistaken use of *ḥesed* (which the glossator at least thought was "religious") is related to Hosea's usage: the text uses a nature image for the ephemeral character of *ḥesed*, just as in Hos. 6:4. Of course such images are widespread, but the similarity conceivably contributed to the occurrence or persistence of the textual error.[52]

Isaiah 57:1

> The righteous perishes and there is no one who
> gives it a thought *(śm ʿl lb)*,
> And men of *ḥesed* are being gathered up with no
> one giving heed.

This phrase climaxes a description (begun in 56:9) of the corruption of the post-exilic leaders of Third Isaiah's time. The parallelism shows once again the association of *ḥesed* with the concern for justice in society. In this usage, however, we can see the emergence of the application to individual piety rather than a specifically communal concern. The conception of a subgroup of faithful individuals perceived over against the dominant religious party of the community takes on new force.[53] The expression is like that of Micah 7:2, part of a lament over the corruptness of the people:

> The *ḥāsîd* has perished from the earth,
> And there is no upright *(yšr)* one among men.

Zechariah 7:9

> Thus says Yahweh of hosts, Judge true judgment and
> do *ḥesed* and mercy *(rḥmym)* each with his brother...

---

52. Then since the usual religious meaning of *ḥesed* in prophecy was well enough understood to cause some feeling of incongruity in the use with *kl bśr*, the explanatory gloss ("surely the people is grass") was added and crept into the text. Such a reconstruction can of course be made only hypothetically, but this seems the most satisfactory reason for the addition of the gloss and suggests further that the present Hebrew reading may actually be incorrect.

53. See Paul Hanson, "Old Testament Apocalyptic Reexamined," *Interpretation* 25 (1971) 468-74; also Hanson's *The Dawn of Apocalyptic* (Philadelphia: Fortress Press, 1975).

Here Zechariah recalls the message of earlier prophets.[54] From what precedes it is clear that he understands this requirement as the alternative to an excessive concern about fasting, just as earlier prophets focused on it in contrast to an excessive emphasis on cultic observance. Here the meaning is spelled out further in terms of the traditional command not to oppress the widow, orphan, poor, or sojourner (vs. 10).

In this instance as well as in the Isa. 57:1 usage, it is possible to see how the religious usage could move in the direction of individual good works once the changed political conditions (lack of independent nation) made the political imagery of covenant less viable. The possibility that individual good works or piety rather than national behavior would come to be called *ḥesed* was inherent in the religious use from the start, but the force of the view of the nation as Yahweh's vassal precluded the development of individual religious usage.

With the collapse of the nation, however, individual faithfulness became more important. We find a shift away from Hosea's covenantal focus. The question of moral behavior versus cult remained open and *ḥesed* is still primarily associated with social good deeds in these two texts of the early restoration period. In the writings of the Chronicler and Nehemiah, however, the word had apparently shifted to cultic good deeds, as witnessed by the religious usage discussed in Chapter IV. The possibility for this shift is probably to be explained by the assumption that the God-directed aspect of "faithfulness" persisted throughout the usage, while changing circumstances or the individual writer's viewpoint determined which type of good deeds, which aspect of the keeping of the law, should receive greater importance.

B. *God's* Ḥesed

The eleven theological occurrences of *ḥesed* in prophecy are limited to Micah, Isaiah, and Jeremiah. The two Micah

---

54. Vs. 8 is probably to be deleted so that the statement of vss. 9ff. is the continuation of the thought train of vs. 7. D. Winton Thomas, *Zechariah: Introduction and Exegesis* (IB; New York: Abingdon Press, 1956), p. 1084.

references, as well as Isa. 16:5, are exilic or post-exilic additions to the earlier sources. The three Jeremiah references (as well as the single instance of *ḥāsîd* with God as subject) are all generally considered authentic by modern commentators and thus are the earliest examples from prophecy. Of the remaining texts, three are in Second Isaiah, and two (both plurals) are in Third Isaiah. Although these are prophetic usage, a number of them are related to the occurrences in Psalms; appropriate references will be given as the occasion arises.

Jeremiah 31:3b

I have loved you with everlasting love
Therefore I have prolonged *ḥesed* to you.

The translation of the second colon is problematic because of the presence of two accusatives with the verb *mšk*. The traditional solution, and that of the Greek and versions, has been to take *ḥesed* as an adverbial accusative: "I draw you (to me) with *ḥesed*." This translation is supported by the parallelism with the preceding line, in which there is a cognate accusative which is taken adverbially, and also by the usage in Hos. 11:4 where Ephraim must be the direct object of *mšk*. Although this interpretation has much to commend it, the writer has opted for the alternate possibility most recently proposed by Dahood, in which the verbal pronominal suffix is taken in the dative sense. The grammatical possibility of such a construction has recently been reconsidered on the basis of usage in other northwest Semitic dialects and a number of possible examples in Biblical Hebrew have been adduced. The usage of Ps. 36:11 in which *ḥesed* must be the object of *mšk* is also noted.[55] While it is true that in Ps. 36:11 the recipient of *ḥesed* is expressed with the preposition *l*, as normally expected, it must also be recognized that the adverbial "means" used with *mšk* in Hos. 11:4 are expressed with *b*, not as adverbial accusatives, so that neither

---

55. Mitchell Dahood, "Ugaritic Studies and the Bible," *Gregorianum* 43 (1962) 67, and *Psalms I*, p. 223. See also Maurice Bogaert, "Les suffixes verbaux non accusatifs dans le sémitique nord-occidental et particulièrement en hébreu," *Biblica* 45 (1964) 238, n.2.

of the two texts provides an exact grammatical parallel for the line in question. Although affinities between Jeremiah and Hosea are not infrequent, the two passages here have in common only *mšk*, *ʾhbh*, and possibly the theme of God's patience with Israel, while the usage of the verbal image is quite different. No final decision is possible from the evidence now available.

The text is part of a pericope (31:2-6) which has been dated either early or late in Jeremiah's career; the concluding verse suggests that it most naturally belongs to the early period of Josiah's reform during the expansion of his hegemony into the former territory of the northern kingdom.[56] The inhabitants of the old northern kingdom will be invited to worship Yahweh in Jerusalem. The basis for this hope lies in God's ongoing love and *ḥesed* for the people: this new state of affairs is the evidence that he did not cast them off utterly with the destruction and deportation of a hundred years before. *Ḥesed* here then is God's persistent faithfulness to Israel: despite punishment the covenant relationship has not been ended.

The use of *ḥāsîd* in Jer. 3:12 evokes a similar picture:

> Go, proclaim these words toward the north, and say:
> Return, apostate one, Israel - oracle of Yahweh -
> I will not show displeasure against you
> For I am *ḥāsîd* - oracle of Yahweh -
> I do not stay angry forever.

This text also comes from an appeal to the old northern kingdom early in Jeremiah's career. Here the context is the imagery of adultery. Israel is asked only to admit her apostasy in ignoring Yahweh and going after others. As *ḥāsîd*, doer of *ḥesed*,[57]

---

56. Cf. Bright, *Jeremiah*, pp. 284-285. The extent and nature of Josiah's northern activity is disputed. Both Kings and Chronicles indicate such activity, but the range and timing vary. The religious purge may not have involved full political control. See, for example, H. Darrell Lance, "The Royal Stamps and the Kingdom of Josiah," *HTR* 64 (1971) 331-332.

57. The only other instance of *ḥāsîd* referring to Yahweh is Ps. 145:17, where it stands in parallelism with the regular appellation *ṣaddîq*. The psalm in general and particularly the

Yahweh is like the husband who does not put away his adulterous wife but instead maintains the relationship, sets aside his anger and invites her to return and start afresh. As in the liturgical formula of Ex. 34, Num. 14, *et al.*, his forgiveness is the concrete embodiment of his great *ḥesed*, his faithfulness despite the people's disobedience. The forgiveness will take concrete form in the restoration which can be made possible only by God himself who imposed the judgment and scattering. Yahweh is powerful and free, he takes sin seriously, yet he is ultimately committed and caring. The offer of *ḥesed* captures all these aspects of the situation.

Jeremiah 9:22-23

Let not the wise man boast in his wisdom,
    Let not the strong man boast in his strength,
Let not the rich man boast in his riches.
    But let him who boasts boast in this:
In understanding and knowing that I am Yahweh
    Doer of *ḥesed* and justice and righteousness in
        the earth.

The proposed versification omits the final phrase of vs. 23 ("for in these things I delight") as a secondary accretion and rearranges the lines to form six long cola (10/12/9/11/12/11) rather than four long plus four short as arranged in the Kittel text. Although the suggestion must remain just that, since the addition would have occurred early, at least two factors point in this direction. First, the division of the latter part of the saying into four short cola results in very awkward verse structure, quite in contrast to the high degree of structure in the first four lines. Although the separation of *yādōaʿ ʾōtî* from the *kî* clause is not impossible, the division in the middle of a series of closely connected objects for the following participle leaves the third short colon with no independent sense. The proposed solution obviates both problems by rejoining the phrases which properly belong together.

The second argument concerns usage. The two principal

---

last five verses exhibit a high degree of assonance; possibly this factor along with the occasional parallelism of *ḥesed* and *ṣedeq* precipitated the uncommon usage. (See Appendix.)

uses of *hll* in the hithp. are for false boasting in that which does not provide real security and for boasting in Yahweh who is the true source of security. This is precisely the thrust of the main part of the Jeremiah passage. The phrase "for in these things I delight" is usually taken to refer to behavior of man which is pleasing to God, as in Hos. 6:6 and the related passages discussed in Section A of this chapter.[58] But this idea has only a loose connection with the preceding theme and seems almost an afterthought. And to the extent that boasting in one's ethical behavior is suggested, it has no parallel in the usage of *hll*. It is true that God's behavior as described here is desired also of men, but the overall structure of the saying does not lend itself to the conjoining of the two ideas.

Several Psalms bring the same three words together to describe Yahweh's action. Particularly to be noted is Ps. 33:5: "He is a lover of righteousness and justice; the earth is filled with the *ḥesed* of Yahweh." This Psalm goes on to testify that armies, might, and war horses are vain hope but that those who trust in God's *ḥesed* will be saved. Although the verb *hll* is not used, the theme of the Jeremiah verses is certainly present. Likewise in Ps. 52 the man who sought refuge in wealth is contrasted to the one who made God his refuge, who trusted in God's *ḥesed*. And in Ps. 36 (cited also above in connection with Jer. 31:3) *ḥesed* and *ṣᵉdāqâ* are twice cited (once along with *ʾĕmûnâ* and *mišpaṭ*) as actions of the God in whom men find refuge.

It is difficult to make an absolute formal distinction in meaning among these words, and it is quite possible that the average worshipper using the Psalms did not concern himself with such theological niceties. The problem is compounded in that *ṣdqh* when used of Yahweh is often best understood as justification, vindication, salvation rather than as righteousness in the more usual English sense. The use of *ḥesed* involves the application to the people as a whole of that same meaning which

---

58. Contrast, however, Mic. 7:18 where "he delights in *ḥesed*" must mean that God himself prefers to do *ḥesed* rather than be angry. (Discussed below, pp. 210-212.) Nevertheless, even this would not be germane to the main point of the verse.

was seen in the prose narratives of the patriarchs: God's faithful actions or his faithfulness as expressed in his actions on behalf of his covenanted people. Their salvation from enemies without and the establishment of justice among the nations and within Israel are its concrete expressions.

Jeremiah 16:5

> For thus says Yahweh: "Do not enter a house of mourning, do not go to a house of wailing, do not lament for them: for I have removed my peace from this people (- oracle of Yahweh - the *ḥesed* and the mercy)."

The concluding portion shown in parentheses, as well as vs. 6a, is omitted in the Greek traditions. The final phrase following "oracle of Yahweh" appears under the asterisk in the Syrohexapla. The evidence for the source of this difference is conflicting, since the verse 5 omission looks very much like a gloss on *šelômî*, whereas vs. 6a seems essential to the train of thought.[59]

Whether original or supplement, the stringing on of *ḥesed* and mercy reinforces the removal of Yahweh's peace as an expressing of the impending doom of the nation. Jeremiah is commanded not to marry and not to mourn as a double sign that in the destruction to come there will be none left to lament the dead and no occasion for rejoicing as in a wedding celebration.

God will no longer have patience with the people in their worship of other gods and stubborn rejection of his law (vss. 10-13); hence he will no longer protect them against their enemies and they will suffer the horrors of slaughter, famine, and exile which come with devastation by a political enemy. The removal of God's *ḥesed* suggests the removal of his protective care which had persisted despite the ungrateful

---

59. Janzen, *Studies in Jeremiah*, p. 98. In accordance with his general argument that the Greek translator did not arbitrarily abridge the text, Janzen suggests that "possibly a line (of about 52 letters) fell out of Ǥ-*Vorlage*" (p. 98). This analysis still does not negate the possibility that the omitted part of vs. 5 was a very early gloss already introduced by the time of the Ǥ-*Vorlage*.

disobedience of the people. With the removal of this protective care, the peace (internal and external welfare) of the nation, which had its source in God's *ḥesed*, would come to an end as well.

The possibility exists that *šālôm* is here used with the further connotation of the friendship which is appropriate to a treaty relationship.[60] In this sense, the removal of peace could mean the abrogation of the covenant relationship, especially in association with the theme of removal from the land (vs. 13).[61] Such an interpretation cannot be pressed too far, however, for the regular use of *šālôm* in Jeremiah is clearly for the people's welfare, regarded as a gift from God.

Isaiah 54:7-8, 10

7 For a brief moment I abandoned you
But with great mercy I will gather you;
8 (In a flood of anger) I concealed my face (from you
for a moment)
But in everlasting *ḥesed* I will have compassion on
you -
Says your redeemer *(gō'ēl)* Yahweh.

10 For the mountains may depart
And the hills may totter
But my *ḥesed* will not depart from you
And my covenant of peace will not totter -
Says Yahweh, the one who has compassion on you.

The poetic structure of vss. 7-8 given above is based on

---

60. Cf. Biblical examples cited by W. F. Albright, "Abram the Hebrew," *BASOR* 163 (1961) 52, n.75.

61. The removal of *ḥesed* if understood with *šālôm* in this sense could likewise mean the complete end of the covenant relationship. However, the close coupling with *rḥmym* and the possibility of a late hand suggest that such a strong implication may not be called for here. Rather the combining of the three terms may reflect an attempt to make Jeremiah's word of doom contrast more specifically with the word of hope in Isa. 54:8, 10, where *ḥesed*, God's mercy (compassion) and the covenant of peace are brought together in an assurance to the people of his presence with them.

the possibility that the two phrases in parentheses in line three may be regarded as poetic alternates. The versification which the full text would require has several weaknesses: (1) the object *pny* is in a separate line from its verb *hstrty* (enjambement);[62] (2) the line *pny rgʿ mmk* is excessively short, having only five syllables; (3) "says Yahweh your redeemer" must be used to complete the structure, even though the comparable phrase stands outside the structure in the related vs. 10 and it might be expected to stand independently in any case; (4) the relationship of vs. 7 to vs. 8 is obscured. If this interpretation is correct, then the first phrase ("in a flood of anger") relates to the Noah theme of vs. 9[63] and also accords with the conjoining of *qṣp* and *hstr* in Isa. 57:17. The alternate, "from you for a moment" completes the full idiom with *hstr* and repeats the *rgʿ* of the preceding bicolon. There is no basis for judging either phrase to be clearly secondary to the other.

Vss. 7-8 and 10 form the double climax to a section which describes the restoration of Israel in terms of retaking of a rejected wife. The permanence of God's *ḥesed* is contrasted to the brevity of his abandonment of the people in his anger at their unfaithfulness. The close association of God's *ḥesed* with his mercy or compassion is to be noted, for here in the exilic use of the term we have the full exploitation of the meaning of the old liturgical formula, *ʾl ḥnn wrḥm, ʾrk ʾpym wrb ḥsd*.[64] The greatness of Yahweh's *ḥesed* is seen in its persistence which is everlasting, surer than the endurance of the

---

62. The idiom *hstr pnh (mn)* occurs a total of 16x in poetic texts (5x without *mn*), and in every case apart from this one the verb and object clearly belong to the same line. The *mn* likewise belongs in the single line wherever it occurs, the only possible exception being Ps. 102:3. But there the couplet as a whole is too short and it appears likely that a second verb has fallen out of the text. In that case, the *mn* would belong to the line of its own verb, as in all other examples.

63. Following the usual interpretation that the *hapax legomenon šṣp* does in fact stand for *šṭp*, "flood."

64. See discussion, Chapter III, pp. 119ff.

hills and mountains. Because of his faithfulness he does not cut off his people forever. Rather, he shows compassion, gathers them up in a covenant relationship[65] which cannot be shaken. Although even in the early usage forgiveness and the continuation of *ḥesed* could only be hoped for, never deserved, here the emphasis on Israel's undeserving state is heightened. The exile demonstrated to Israel that God's forgiveness is not to be presumed upon; the loss of the land and end of kingship ought to have signified the complete end of Israel's relation with Yahweh, and it certainly showed her that any claim which she may have thought she had on Yahweh's protection had been abrogated by her disobedience. The threat of the Mosaic covenant tradition had been enforced with the loss of the land. The supposedly sure promises to David had collapsed with the exile of Jehoiachin and destruction of the temple. There was no reason for hope. In Jeremiah's terms, peace had been removed, *ḥesed* and mercy were no more.

To that desperate situation Second Isaiah proclaimed the occasion for rejoicing: the "divorce" was really only a separation, the "final dissolution" of the relationship was only a temporary chastisement, the removal from the land will be ended by a new exodus greater than the first. Renewed *ḥesed* (as saving action) now has its source in freely extended mercy in a situation in which there is seemingly no longer a covenant basis for appealing to God for *ḥesed*. At the same time, mercy even as in the past still has its source in ongoing *ḥesed* (as faithfulness), for God, despite the destruction of the nation, had not abandoned his people.

Isaiah 55:3b-5

I will establish with you an everlasting covenant

---

65. The exact nuance of *bᵉrît šālôm* cannot be established with certainty, although the expression as such appears essentially in exilic texts (Num. 25:12 [P]; Ezek. 34:25; 37:26; also Mal. 2:5 which reflects the Num. tradition). It is possible that both the themes of general welfare and political friendship (suggested above for the use of *šālôm* in Jer. 16:5) are present in the Isaiah and Ezekiel usage. The Num. and Mal. texts concern the priesthood and may be a special usage.

The trustworthy *ḥesed*s which were for David
Behold I made him a witness to the peoples
A leader and commander for the peoples
Behold you will summon a nation you do not know
Those who do not know you will run to you
On account of Yahweh your God
And of the Holy One of Israel: because he has glorified you.

The line containing *ḥesed* presents various difficulties. First of all, this is the only instance[66] in which the second member of a construct chain with *ḥesed* must be regarded as the recipient of *ḥesed* rather than the actor. Elsewhere some preposition invariably is used to express the recipient.[67]

Second, and more difficult to assess, is the dangling nature of the *ḥesed* line itself as it stands in the MT. English editions and commentators regularly translate the line without comment, but the difficulty cannot be so easily passed over since a literal translation does not make sense in English. The verb *krt* is normal usage with *b^{e}rît* but is never used with *ḥesed* in the singular, let alone plural. If the text is correct as it stands (and there is no Greek or versional evidence to the contrary), then the expression is highly elliptical. The full sense would be: "I will establish my covenant with

---

66. Aside from the dual meaning of II Chr. 6:42 which is surely dependent on the tradition here. See Chapter IV, p. 156. Pronominal suffixes likewise uniformly refer to the actor.

67. André Caquot has argued that David should be regarded as the actor in accordance with normal usage ("Les 'Graces de David' à propos d'Isaie 55/3b," *Semitica* 15 [1965] 45-59). The statistics which he amasses to show this text as a solitary exception are impressive; yet grammatical analogies alone cannot override what seems to be the clear sense of the tradition from which this text arises: David has *ḥesed*s which God provides. On the possibility of such datival constructions in Psalms and elsewhere, see Dahood, *Psalms I*, pp. 88, 127, 156, 307. It must be admitted, however, that this example is less amenable to the dative understanding in the English feel for a double object than are the examples cited by Dahood.

you; I will establish for you the *ḥesed*s which were trustworthy for David." There is evidence from Psalm texts that Hebrew poets used ellipsis[68] but the fact of its presence here has not received comment. The structure of this bicolon is then understood as analogous to the following bicolon in which the object of the verb is further described in the second colon.

The theme of this pericope, the "democratization" of the Davidic covenant, encapsulates Second Isaiah's response to the question posed in Ps. 89:50: "Where are your former *ḥesed*s, O Lord, (which) you swore to David in your faithfulness?"[69] In both texts the plural *ḥesed*s comes near to the English "promises," although the word continues to convey the nuance of the free benevolent actions of the more powerful party of the covenant relationship. Here Israel as a whole replaces David as party to the covenant. The role of the Davidic ruler in relation to the people[70] is now transferred to the people in relation to the nations.[71] Second Isaiah contains no reference

---

68. Dahood, *Psalms I*, p. 8. Normally, one would expect a separate sentence using *ḥesed* in its line. Such could be obtained by omitting the *h* of *hn'mnym* as mistaken anticipation of the *hn* which immediately follows. The participle then would lack the definite article and the line could be read: "The *ḥesed*s of David are trustworthy." The sense of the bicolon, however, would remain that suggested for the elliptical interpretation.

69. Vss. 39-52 of this Psalm are regarded by most scholars as an exilic addition, despite occasional attempts to assert the unity of the poem. It is not to be supposed that Second Isaiah must have had this specific line in mind; but the problem raised was certainly an important concern for the exiles who came from the school which had believed in God's absolute support of the Davidic dynasty.

70. Note especially the use of the traditional title *nāgîd*, as well as the thematic affinities between this passage and Ps. 18:44, although that verse is set in the context of a warrior's victory.

71. If (as the writer believes) the "Servant" of Second Isaiah is most often Israel herself, then this particular

to the reestablishment of the Davidic rule as part of the anticipated new salvation, thus standing in contrast to the traditions of Jeremiah and Ezekiel and especially of Haggai and Zechariah.[72]

What then can be the content of *ḥesed*s, if it does not refer to the establishment of the royal line in the traditional sense? It becomes generalized to promises of an enduring special role or function for the people (as an "elect" or "chosen" one of Yahweh) within the established order of human affairs. Israel, like David, is to be God's witness (cf. 43:10; 44:8). As the king had been "mediator" of God's blessing to Israel, so Israel will be "mediator" to the nations.[73] God's *ḥesed*, even

---

passage accords well with what may be an overall theme of the prophet. The royal theology used the servant language (among others) to describe the king's relationship to Yahweh (e.g. Ps. 89:4,21,40) and this language too is "democratized" to Israel as a whole. Cf. Otto Eissfeldt, "The Promises of Grace to David in Isaiah 55:1-5," *Israel's Prophetic Heritage*, ed. Anderson and Harrelson (New York: Harper and Brothers Publishers, 1962), pp. 202-203 and n.9.

72. Eissfeldt, "The Promises of Grace to David," p. 203. Also Muilenburg, *Isaiah Chapters 40-66*, p. 646; John L. McKenzie, *Second Isaiah* (AB; Garden City, N.Y.; Doubleday & Company, Inc., 1968), p. 144; Claus Westermann, *Isaiah 40-66* (tr. by D. Stalker from the 1966 German ed.; OTL; London: SCM Press, Ltd., 1969), pp. 284-285; C. R. North, *The Second Isaiah* (Oxford: The Clarendon Press, 1964), p. 258; all against the view of earlier commentators (Duhm, Skinner, Torrey). Even within Jeremiah and Ezekiel, references to a renewal of the Davidic line are infrequent and guarded. For a full discussion of the way in which Second Isaiah uses the exodus but not Sinai from the Mosaic tradition and Zion but not kingship from the Davidic tradition, see Bernhard W. Anderson, "Exodus and Covenant in Second Isaiah and Prophetic Tradition," *Magnalia Dei. The Mighty Acts of God*, ed. Cross, Lemke and Miller (Garden City, N.Y.: Doubleday & Company, Inc., 1976), pp. 339ff.

73. The passage is supported by and serves to clarify the conception of the servant as covenant to the people // light to

more enduring than the people had dared to hope, takes on a new shape as it undergirds a covenant understanding different from either of the major covenant traditions which had gone before.[74]

Isaiah 16:5

(then) A throne will be established in *ḥesed*
And there shall sit upon it in *ʾĕmet* (in the tent of David)
One judging and seeking *mišpāṭ*
And prompt in *ṣedeq*.

The text is problematic in many respects. The meter is irregular, with the second line being too long (possibly the words in parentheses are a gloss) and the fourth line too short. The sentence probably begins with vs. 4b which, despite multiple textual difficulties, must anticipate the end of foreign military oppression. With such an occasion for the establishment of a Davidic throne, this small pericope should probably be regarded as an exilic or post-exilic piece. But the reason for its present position remains a mystery. It has no obvious connection to vss. 1-4a to which it is attached, in which Moabites are seeking refuge in Judah. That unit in turn is out of character with the main body of the dirge over Moab (15:1-16:11) and may itself be an insertion. And if the dirge as a whole is to be set at about 650 B.C.,[75] then the poem as a

---

the nations (42:6; cf. 49:8). Cf. Muilenburg, *Isaiah Chapters 40-66*, p. 468. It may also be noted that the construct usages *bryt ʿm* and *ʾwr gwym* both provide grammatical parallels for the unusual *ḥsdy dwd*.

74. In developing this theme more generally, Second Isaiah roots his new understanding in a fresh use of the patriarchal traditions. For a detailed study, see the work of Edgar W. Conrad, "Patriarchal Traditions in Second Isaiah" (unpublished Ph.D. dissertation, Princeton Theological Seminary, 1974).

75. W. F. Albright, review of R. H. Pfeiffer's *Introduction to the Old Testament*, *JBL* 61 (1941) 119. Albright associated the poem with the end of Moab as a nation due to an Arab irruption ca. 652-648 B.C. This position is asserted over against Pfeiffer and Duhm who had placed the poem a century later. There is no comment on the possibility of secondary intrusions into the basic poem.

whole must be secondary to the work of the prophet and his immediate school. Thus from the most immediate to the broadest level there is no clear context in which to place vss. 4b-5, nor is it apparent why they appear in their present location. Conceivably the theme of Moab's tribute (16:1) brought to mind the old Davidic hegemony and this in turn evoked the theme of messianic restoration even though a king ought properly to be presumed for the bringing of tribute. But even this can only be conjecture.

Scholars have disputed whether *ḥesed* is to be done by God or the king, and again we are confronted with the artificiality of strict divisions between theological, religious, and secular usage. Quite probably the verse may be read on all three levels, as also in Prov. 20:28. For it is certainly God who will establish and maintain the Davidic line, and the tradition of the words *ḥesed* and *ʾĕmet* or *ʾĕmûnâ* for his doing so is plainly attested (Ps. 89). At the same time, there is the tradition of David's practice of *ḥesed* which is secular in its own narrative but which could easily become projected into a "religious" usage by being joined with *ʾĕmet*, *mišpāṭ* and *ṣedeq*, as is the religious *ḥesed* of the people as a whole in the prophetic literature. Without a definite context, we can do little more than place the verse in the tradition of the royal theology and messianism and add the note that if this is a genuine messianic example, it is remarkably the only messianic text in which the word *ḥesed* actually appears, despite the apparent importance of the word for the royal theology of the monarchy.

Isaiah 63:7

I will recount the *ḥesed*s of Yahweh
The praiseworthy deeds of Yahweh
According to all which Yahweh has bestowed upon us
And the greatness of [his] goodness to the house of Israel
Which he bestowed upon us according to his mercy
And according to the abundance of his *ḥesed*s.

Although the syllable counts are quite uneven, a general pattern of three 1:b pairs can be identified. The Greek *Vorlage* evidently had a dittography of the *yhwh* at the end of line three which led to the reading of *rb* as a participial form of the root *ryb*. In the fifth line the LXX first plural verbal suffix is to be preferred over the MT third plural. The vocalization of *rab-ṭûb* is problematic; BDB suggests reading the expected nominal vocalization *rōb* or *rob*.[76] In any case, the meaning is clear.

This verse forms the hymnic introduction to a long song of intercession which continues through 64:11. The opening section recalls God's deliverance of the people from Egypt, his protection in the wilderness despite their disobedience, and the gift of the land (he "gave them rest"). The poet then mourns the fact that the holy people through their hardheartedness (inflicted by Yahweh!) have become as the peoples whom Yahweh never chose. He prays for forgiveness and a new manifestation of God's power on behalf of his people.

As in the individual petitions of the patriarchs, God's past acts of *ḥesed* are acknowledged as the preface to petition for renewed assistance. Here, however, it is clear that the people are regarded as completely undeserving from start to finish. As in Isaiah 54:8,10 God's *ḥesed* is closely associated with his mercy or compassion. Because the people were false to God despite his high hopes for them (63:8,10) they cannot assume that he has any moral obligation to save them. So the basis for their appeal is only his mercy and the fact that they are his people (64:8). The fact of the particular relationship of the people to Yahweh provides a ground for hope for future salvific acts. The hope that he will continue to recognize the relationship and act from a sense of responsibility for his people is held in tension with the recognition that

---

76. The only other occurrences of these two words in sequence (Ps. 31:20; 145:7) both use the identical *a-û* vocalization with the *maqqēph*, and one of these (Ps. 145:7) must be read as a construct. It is conceivable, then, that in this particular phrase an *o-ū* sequence dissimilated in pronunciation to *a-ū* and that the Masoretes simply had a rare pronunciation of a nominal form. The sequence *kl-ṭwb* is invariably vocalized *o-ū* (5x), however, and the regular occurrence of *lōʾ-ṭôb* (8x, 4 in Prv.) shows that no general rule can be made.

there can be no claim upon him.

The double use of the plural *ḥesed*s in Isa. 63:7 provides occasion for a summary presentation of all of the plural occurrences not previously discussed. The usage in 63:7 suggests two possible meanings for the plural form. The parallelism of the first two cola suggests that the plural with God as subject was used simply for his many delivering and protective acts on behalf of his covenant people. The second use with *rb* and in association with the formally plural *rḥmym* suggests an alternate usage of the plural in an intensive sense. Since the particular combination of the plural with *rb* and *rḥmym* has concrete affinities with several of the other plural occurrences, it is possible that the latter interpretation may be correct.[77]

In three texts the MT reads the plural after *rōb*.[78] In each of these instances and also in Isa. 63:7, the Greek translates with the singular, which is perhaps original unless the *Vorlage* was here written defectively. In Ps. 106:45 and Lam. 3:32 (both *kerōb*, as in Isa. 63:7), the MT itself has a singular *ketīb*, although there are manuscripts and versions which do indicate the plural reading. Such fluidity is hardly surprising, since there is no sharp line between the usage of the singular and plural.

Ps. 106:7

Our fathers in Egypt ( )
They did not give attention to your wondrous acts;
They did not remember the greatness of your *ḥesed*s;
But they rebelled against Elyon at the Red Sea.

The last part of the first line appears to have been lost. God's *ḥesed* is paralleled with his wondrous acts, much as they are with his praiseworthy deeds. Here too the poet focuses on

---

77. The second possibility was suggested to the writer by F. M. Cross, who pointed out the comparable late development of the intensive plural *ʿwlmym*. Normally a noun has either an ordinary plural or an intensive plural, so that one interpretation or the other should be chosen (private communication, August 1970).

78. Ps. 106:7,45; Lam. 3:32. In Neh. 13:22 and Ps. 5:8; 69:14, *berōb* is followed by *ḥesed* in the singular.

Israel's early failure to act in correspondence with his goodness to her.

Ps. 106:45

He remembered on their behalf his covenant

And he took pity according to the greatness of his *ḥesed*s.

Perhaps this should be read as singular as the MT *k^e tîb*; it may be under the influence of the plural with *rōb* earlier in the Psalm or of the identical phrase in Isa. 63:7. On the other hand, the specific action mentioned in vs. 46 (he made them the object of mercy before their captors) may be understood to be the new act of *ḥesed* in accordance with his long series of actions.

Lam. 3:32

For though he causes grief he will have compassion

According to the greatness of his *ḥesed*s.

This example too might well be taken as singular, although if the Isaiah text is reliable it could just as easily be plural. The theme that there is yet hope for his compassion may be based either in his past deeds regarded individually or regarded collectively as the expression of his faithfulness.

Ps. 25:6

Remember your mercy (O Yahweh) and your *ḥesed*s

For they are from of old.

The verse is followed by a plea that Yahweh remember the suppliant according to his (Yahweh's) *ḥesed* (singular) rather than according to the petitioner's transgression. The use of the plural in vs. 6 may be evoked by the plural *rḥmym*, again drawing attention to the long history of good actions which Yahweh has done for his people. Lam. 3:22 again parallels the plural form with *rḥmym*, claiming their continual nature as a source of hope in a time of distress.

Ps. 89:2 forms the introduction to the Psalm and may be associated with the plural use in connection with the royal theology. However, the themes of continuity to all generations and singing (cf. recounting) are widely used and make an appropriate general introduction to the Psalm.

Ps. 107:43

Whoever is wise, let him observe these things,

And let men consider the *ḥesed*s of Yahweh.

As the conclusion to vss. 33-43[79] the verse suggests the importance of recognizing God's action in the world and presumably implies that one would do well to act in harmony with God's purposes. The preceding verses describe his *ḥesed*s in terms of rescue and benevolence to the downtrodden (righteous) and bringing low of those in high places who have attained their station by wickedness. As elsewhere, *ḥesed* for the immediate recipient can mean disaster for those outside the context of the relationship.

It may be noted here that in the main section of Ps. 107 *ḥesed* is used four times in a liturgical refrain (vss. 8,15,21, 31) in parallelism with *npl'wtyw* ("his wondrous deeds," cf. Ps. 106:7). Here the Greek consistently translates with plurals, while the Hebrew traditions consistently show singular in both *k^e^tīb* and *q^e^rē*. This reversal of the pattern seen before (in which the MT plurals are singular in Greek) shows even more clearly the necessity to allow for fluidity in the tradition, especially in usage with plural parallels.

In Ps. 17:7 the verb should perhaps be taken from *pl'* (cf. Ps. 31:22),[80] and possibly the verb has given rise to the plural here (cf. *npl'wt*), although the other, certain example uses the singular. Again no fixed pattern is apparent.

Ps. 119:41

Let your *ḥesed*(s) come to me, O Yahweh,

Your salvation according to your promise.

This final example ought probably to be read as a singular despite the Masoretic tradition of vocalization. The Greek reads the singular. The Hebrew *k^e^tīb ḥsdw* is singular and furthermore the noun in this instance is the subject of the verb which itself is singular in the *k^e^tīb*. The parallel is "thy salvation" (singular) and the psalmist is requesting Yahweh's help for himself, not reviewing his actions in general or in the past.

---

79. Which appear to be a separate section of this psalm.

80. Dahood has proposed a completely different approach to these lines which should receive serious consideration (*Psalms I*, pp. 92, 96). See Chapter VI, p. 220, n.9.

In summary, the MT *k^e tîb* and *q^e rē* and also the Greek and versions exhibit considerable variation in the appearance of the plural of *ḥesed*. The frequent occurrence of the plural form in conjunction with emphasis on God's mercy and compassion and with concern for his forgiveness suggests that the form may have been intensive, related to the connotation of *rab ḥesed* that God's faithfulness is far greater than that experienced in human relationships.

Micah 7:18,20

18 Who is a God like you: one who forgives iniquities
And one who passes over transgression (to the remnant of his inheritance)
He does not retain his anger forever
For he is one who delights in *ḥesed*.

20 You will give *'ĕmet* to Jacob
And *ḥesed* to Abraham
As you have sworn to our fathers
from days of old.

These verses form a part of the conclusion to what is generally regarded as an exilic or post-exilic addition to Micah's work.[81] The odd usage of Abraham (rather than Israel) with Jacob[82] and the unique reversal of *'ĕmet* and *ḥesed* in poetic parallelism suggest that the writer was not intimately at home with traditional "canons" of prosodic usage or else was deliberately innovative. The unevenness of line length (within what seems to be intended as an l:b pattern) inclines the writer

81. Eissfeldt, however, has argued for a seventh century date. See "Ein Psalm aus Nord-Israel," *Zeitschrift der Deutscher Morgenländischen Gesellschaft* 112 (1962) 259-268. One source of difficulty is in identifying the beginning of the poem. It is possible that vss. 18-20 were not an integral part of the preceding poem and should in any case be regarded as a later addition. The constant shift of person within the poem and within these final lines as well further compounds the difficulty in assessing the material.

82. The closest parallel is Ps. 105:6, but even there the people are described as "offspring of Abraham, sons of Jacob" so that Abraham does not stand directly for the people.

toward the first explanation.

The opening with *'ēl* followed by the *nś' 'wn* and the use of *pš'* in 18a, *'p* and *ḥsd* in 18b, along with the use of *rḥm* and *ḥṭ't* in 19 and the general theme of the section, suggest that it may be a reflection on the tradition of Ex. 34:6-7. Although God is slow to become angry, he does not ignore persistent wrongdoing. But in his *ḥesed* he does not permanently cut off the guilty; rather, he forgives their sins and restores them. So in these verses *ḥesed* is that great faithfulness which finds expression in the ending of punishment, the renewal of compassion. Deliverance is anticipated as the concrete sign of God's forgiveness. The deliverance itself will be an act of *ḥesed*; at the same time, deliverance/forgiveness is the concretizing of God's ongoing *ḥesed* as faithfulness to the people in accordance with his oath of ancient times.[83]

Summary of Section B

In reviewing the prophetic references to the *ḥesed* of God, it can be seen that the major concerns of theological usage developed in Chapter III persist in the prophetic texts. God's faithfulness to his covenant people is the central concern, his faithfulness as one who is sovereign yet caring; whose ever new acts of succor are a continuing surprise in the face of the people's unfaithfulness; whose continued support can be comprehended only in terms of the greatness of his commitment to his people, a commitment which extends beyond all expectations based on ordinary human interaction.

Because the message of the prophets concentrates on interpreting God's work in the world as he judges and restores Israel, the connotation of forgiveness (which we have seen was

---

83. There is no mention of *ḥesed* in connection with God's covenant with Abraham or the promises to the fathers in the patriarchal narratives themselves. This text may be a late refraction of the tradition reflected in Dt. 7:12: "...the covenant and *ḥesed* which he swore to your fathers to keep." The Dt. usage is plainly conditional, however, so it is only the Dt. motif of continuity from the beginning which appears in the Micah passage.

already present in the old liturgical formula of Ex. 34) is very much in the picture here. Forgiveness is mentioned or else clearly in view in Jer. 31:3b; Jer. 3:12; Jer. 16:5 (negatively); Isa. 54:7-8,10; and Micah 7:18. The prophets recognize that it is Yahweh's persistent faithfulness to the people which is the sole basis for any future hope. *Ḥesed* is the covenantal ground for forgiveness and also the delivering act of succor in which the rescue from judgment takes form. While it is not insignificant that the word "mercy" appears several times in connection with *ḥesed* in these texts, the two words are not simply to be collapsed into a single idea. *Ḥesed* retains always its responsibility-in-relationship connotation even when the particular manifestation of God's self-imposed responsibility is a free and compassionate act of forgiveness.

These passages suggest that the prophets insisted upon God's persistent faithfulness to his people - his covenant *ḥesed* - even while they saw the foundations of traditional Israelite theology crumbling around them. It was God's *ḥesed*, not one particular form of its expression, which remained constant. A covenant dependent solely upon the people's obedience was doomed ultimately to fail, yet the monarchy and its covenant seemed not to embody God's full intention either. So in the exile the patriarchal traditions could take on new importance. Promises of progeny, land, and purpose in God's larger kingdom had been made to the forefathers, without condition. Second Isaiah could speak of democratization of the Davidic promises to the people in the context of a new emphasis on Abraham and Jacob; the addition to Micah 7 brought this new perception to explicit expression.

CHAPTER VI

ḤESED IN PSALMS, PROVERBS, AND RELATED LITERATURE

A substantial number of the occurrences of *ḥesed* in Psalms have already been discussed in connection with narrative and prophetic usage dealt with in earlier chapters. The understanding of *ḥesed* which can be gleaned from the texts to be discussed here accords well with what has been said of *ḥesed* in the foregoing chapters and the picture is enhanced and enriched. Yet, because of the difficulty of dating and absence of concrete contexts, these examples cannot in themselves provide an independent basis for establishing the parameters of *ḥesed*.

There are additional difficulties. Many of these passages do not in themselves give any clue as to the content of the word. In secular usage, examples include Prv. 31:36b ("the teaching of *ḥesed* is upon her tongue") and Prv. 3:3 ("let not *ḥesed we'ĕmet* abandon you"). Other proverbs say little more than that *ḥesed* brings its own reward: "A man of *ḥesed* benefits himself, but the cruel man stirs up trouble for himself" (Prv. 11:17); "He who pursues righteousness and *ḥesed* will find life and honor" (Prv. 21:21). In theological usage the most frequent type of uninstructive passage is the psalm in which God is simply praised for his *ḥesed* without further comment or in which the greatness of his *ḥesed* is compared to the height of heaven or the like (57:11; 63:4; 66:20; 92:3; 108:5; 117:1; 138:2,8). In these and a number of other passages (25:10; 26:3; 48:10; 85:10; 101:2; 103:4; 115:1; 119:64) *ḥesed* can carry any and all of the various nuances to be suggested in the section below on theological usage.

Further, there are some examples in which the text does not make clear sense or seems ungrammatical as it stands, yet there is no emendation which commends itself as the "obvious" solution. These include Prv. 14:22; Job 6:14, 10:12; Ps. 52:3. Prv. 19:22 probably should not read *ḥsdw* at all. *Ḥsnw* and *sḥrw* ("the desire of man is for his gain") have been proposed,[1] but

---

1. By R. B. Y. Scott, *Proverbs, Ecclesiastes* (AB; Garden City, N.Y.: Doubleday & Company, Inc., 1965), p. 116, and G.

the writer would suggest *ḥsrw* as the least difficult graphically and also on the grounds of sense ("the desire of man is for what he lacks").

A. *Human* Ḥesed *in Psalms and Wisdom Sources*

With the bypassing of texts which cannot confirm or contribute further to the understanding of *ḥesed* we are left with just three examples in which man is the subject - one each in Job, Psalms, and Proverbs.

Job 6:14 is difficult textually: Hebrew manuscripts do not agree on the first word and the Greek also seems to represent a different reading. Although the text and translation of the line as a whole are not clear,[2] it is evident from the context that *ḥesed* is something which Job feels he ought to have from his friends but is not receiving from them. *Ḥesed* here involves sticking by a friend in troubled times. Job's friends have not done this; they have faded as the wadi stream fades in the dry season. Job points out how little he has asked of them - no financial help or rescue from dangerous enemies (vss. 22-23), the type of action one might more often associate with *ḥesed*. Rather, he has only asked for support in trouble, for help in understanding his plight. But his "friends" have not accepted his protestation of innocence and worked with that fact; they have instead insisted that he must be guilty and in this breach of confidence they have failed to do *ḥesed*.

The proud but fickle nature of men is recognized also in the tradition of Proverbs 20:6: "Many a man proclaims his own *ḥesed*; but a faithful man, who can find?" Here we see once again the close connection between *ḥesed* and faithfulness as the attitude and action aspects of reliability in a relationship

---

Beer, apparatus to Proverbs, *BH*[3], *ad loc*, respectively.

2. For a summary of various proposals, see S. R. Driver and George B. Gray, *A Critical and Exegetical Commentary on the Book of Job* (ICC; New York: Charles Scribner's Sons, 1921), Pt. II, pp. 39-40. Pope (*Job* [AB; Garden City, N.Y.: Doubleday & Company, Inc., 1965], p. 52) may be correct in regarding the Hebrew as a terse but sensible text, in which case the other traditions were attempting to guess the meaning.

Much of what has been said of human *ḥesed* is caught up in this brief saying. *Ḥesed* is something which is tested out in one's actions; it is action performed in accordance with and because of one's relationship to another; it is something easy not to do and often easier left undone.

The lone occurrence of human *ḥesed* in the Psalter is found in 109:12, 16. The dominant theme of the prayer is the wishing for all manner of ill to befall the man who has unjustly tried to harm the petitioner and others: let the most dire straits come upon him (vss. 6-11, 13-15), and in these straits "let there be none to prolong *(mšk) ḥesed* to him (vs. 12)....for he did not remember to do *ḥesed* (vs. 16)." Here the content of *ḥesed* is similar to that expressed in Zech. 7:9. The man who did not remember to do *ḥesed* is one who "pursued to death the poor and needy and broken in spirit." The text could partake of both the "secular" and "religious" spheres. The failure to do *ḥesed* is the strong taking advantage of the weak for whom he has moral obligation to show special concern; the level of application could vary from one petitioner to another.

B. Ḥesed *of God in Psalms and Other Hymns*

The dominant source here is of course the psalms, with two examples from hymnic material preserved outside the psalter (Ex. 15:13; Jon. 2:9) to be incorporated into this section. Because of the large number of texts and considerable duplication in theme and mode of expression, the text-by-text procedure of the previous chapters will not be continued in this section. Rather, a variety of themes and motifs discernible in the material as a whole will be presented with illustration from key examples and notation of other relevant passages. It is hoped that this approach will provide a more coherent picture of the usage than would otherwise be possible. The discussion will in the main be restricted to passages which have not been previously introducted.

An analysis of the use of *ḥesed* by the classic form-critical categories of the Psalms has not proved productive. As Thordarson showed, the word appears dominantly in psalms of the "lament" category.[3] But this is scarcely surprising, since

---

3. "The Form-Historical Problem of Ex. 34:6-7," pp. 150ff.

we have seen that *ḥesed* regularly involves rescue from dire straits as its specific action content. The obtaining of such assistance is normally the object of the petitioner in a lament. The word can equally well appear in a hymn extolling God for his faithfulness or in a royal psalm seeking the maintenance of the Davidic line. For this reason, the presentation of examples will cut across all types, with brief notations about particular usage as it contributes to the larger picture.

1. The Specific Action Content of *Ḥesed*

As has just been suggested, *ḥesed* in the psalms as elsewhere is predominantly associated with deliverance rather than any special blessing.[4] God's faithfulness (to his people or to the individual suppliant) always is understood as the background of this deliverance, which is the concrete expression of and testimony to his faithfulness. Within this broad category of *ḥesed* as faithful deliverance the narrower nuancings of power to deliver (strength) and willingness to deliver can be discerned. Absolute distinctions are of course impossible to maintain, and numerous examples in the following presentation can be seen to cross such analytical boundaries.

Deliverance

Perhaps the best example of *ḥesed* as "deliverance" in the narrow sense is in the refrain of Ps. 107 (vss. 8,15,21,31), where it is paralleled with "his wonderful works."[5] Each section of the psalm describes some disaster from which Yahweh has provided rescue: desert wandering, bondage, illness, a storm at sea. In Ps. 57:4 God's sending to save is followed by "God will send his *ḥesed* and his *ʾĕmet*,"[6] his sure deliverance. In

---

4. In fact, as Claus Westermann has observed, the requests in psalms generally fit this picture. Supplication in time of trouble rather than petition for particular "things" is the dominant character of the requests. *The Praise of God in the Psalms* (tr. by K. Crim from the 1961 German ed.; Richmond, Va.: John Knox Press, 1965), pp. 33-34.

5. In these texts, the Greek tradition reads the plural of *ḥesed*; cf. Chapter V, pp. 209-210.

6. Dahood here and elsewhere (23:6; 40:11; 85:11; 89:15)

Ps. 119:41, the psalmist asks that Yahweh's *ḥesed*[7] will come to him, God's salvation *(tšwʿh)* in accordance with his promise. Through God's help, the psalmist will be able to confront his persecutors. A similar theme appears in vss. 76-77 of the same psalm, in which the psalmist prays for the promised comfort of God's *ḥesed* by which he may survive and his persecutors be shamed. In Ps. 77 the psalmist remembers God's former deeds and wonders whether his *ḥesed* has ceased forever (vs. 9), whether he has forgotten to be gracious and merciful.[8] He

---

regards the two words as "personified attendants," observing that "in Canaanite mythology the gods or dignitaries are often accompanied by two attendants." He suggests "that 'kindness' and 'fidelity' also belonged to the larger Canaanite pantheon, but in Hebrew theology they are demythologized and reduced to attendants of Yahweh" (*Psalms II*, p. 52). Although the idea is imaginative, this writer has serious reservations about its ultimate probability, especially since the word *ḥsd* has not yet appeared in any Canaanite source other than neo-Punic. The two words exist as a standard pair in Hebrew independent of the interpretation Dahood proposes. And while there is some degree of personification involved in the imagery, it does not seem necessary to refer every "personification" to a background in a pantheon.

7. Plural in MT *qᵉrē*, but probably should be singular; see Chapter V, p. 210.

8. MT points the *ʾmr* parallel to *ḥesed* as "promise"; Dahood suggests "vision" (*Psalms II*, p. 228). Although the alternate meaning "to see" for *ʾmr* had definitely been found in some biblical texts, the usage does not especially illuminate the text here. Conceivably, Dahood is influenced here by his interpretation of the very difficult 42:9 in which he reads *šyrh* (usually "his song") also as "vision" (*Psalms I*, p. 259), following the proposal of T. H. Gaster ("Critical Note on Ps. 42:8," *JBL* 73 [1954] 237-238) who proposed an identification with Ugaritic *śrt* and Akkadian *šīru*. Neither Dahood nor Gaster gives any suggestion of how such a reading improves the sense of the text. The presence of day and night as a pair does not especially call for a (night) "vision," which seems to be

wonders whether there is yet hope for deliverance from his distress.

Ability to Deliver

More frequently *ḥesed* is nuanced as delivering power or the ability to deliver: "Let your face shine on your servant; save me by your *ḥesed*." This colon (Ps. 31:17) summarizes a plea for deliverance from enemies and persecutors. In a different vein, God is praised for his *ḥesed* which upheld the suppliant when his foot was slipping (Ps. 94:18). In Ps. 109:26 the prayer is "help me...,save me by your *ḥesed*." The rescue of the suppliant and the shaming of his accusers is urged so that the opponents may recognize God's saving power at work. Ps. 17:7, a plural form in the MT tradition, may also exemplify the theme of God's *ḥesed* as his saving power.[9]

A noteworthy illustration of this nuance appears in Ps. 143:12: "And by your *ḥesed* exterminate my enemies, and destroy all who harass my life." Early commentaries proposed emendations for *ḥesed* on the ground that extermination and destruction could scarcely be considered an expression of God's mercy. Glueck made the key step toward the correct understanding of the text when he argued that emendations "are superfluous if we understand *ḥesed* as conduct corresponding to the covenant by

---

Gaster's starting point. Despite the unusual usage, it does not seem impossible that the psalmist here is saying that because God sends forth *ḥesed* to him a song in praise of Yahweh is on his lips. The text is problematic, nonetheless, as is suggested at once by its general metric and syntactic difficulties.

9. The verse is problematic, however, and Dahood has proposed reading *ḥsdyk* as "those who revile you" paralleling "those who rise up against (you)" with a double-duty use of the *k* suffix. Although this Aramaic meaning for the root is quite rare in Biblical Hebrew, the improved meter and syntax possible on Dahood's reading are impressive and his translation of the entire verse may well be correct: "Fell those who revile you, O Savior, with your right hand muzzle your assailants" (*Psalms I*, pp. 92, 96).

which God helps his faithful."[10] In his emphasis on conduct within the covenant, however, Glueck glosses over the connotation of "strength" which, as he notes, had already been suggested by Perles.[11] Perles was not correct that *ḥesed* could mean simply "strength," but as a characteristic of the action of a powerful party on behalf of a weak one this nuance should certainly be recognized. Two additional points shed further light on the passage. First, attention should be called to Ps. 57:4 in which the psalmist prays that God will "exterminate" his enemies "in faithfulness" *(ʾĕmet)*. Clearly the same type of thought is present here. Indeed, the broad spectrum of "lament" psalms presents a similar picture. Although God is usually asked in his *ḥesed* or *ʾĕmet* to deliver the psalmist, he is regularly to do this by shaming or destroying the enemy. Thus Ps. 143:12 brings together in succinct form what is typical of many psalms when the overall theme is considered. Second, this theme of protection or deliverance of the one within the relationship with corresponding misfortune to those on the outside has affinities with the secular use of *ḥesed* (David and Hushai vs. Absalom; Abraham and Sarah vs. Abimelech), although this is not an essential characteristic of the term. In the same way, it is present in theological usage where there are actual enemies or oppressors but need not be present when the prayer emerges out of some other affliction such as sickness.

This nuancing of *ḥesed* as "delivering power" reaches its height in a series of texts in which it paralleled with *ʿz*, "strength." Prominent among these is Ex. 15:13:

You led in your *ḥesed*
    The people whom you redeemed;
You guided in your strength *(ʿz)*
    To your holy encampment.

A second example is Ps. 62:12b-13a: "Strength *(ʿz)* belongs to God, and to you, O Lord, *ḥesed*." The precise parallel appears also in Ps. 59:17: "I will sing your strength *(ʿz)*, in the morning I will ring forth your *ḥesed*." Ps. 59:11 and its

---

10. Glueck, p. 55.

11. Perles, *Anelekten zur Textkritik des Alten Testaments*, pp. 76ff.

doublet in vs. 18 are difficult textually, but it does seem probable that the poem originally used *ʿz* and *ḥesed* alongside of *mśgb* as figurative "titles" for Yahweh.[12] A similar usage appears in Ps. 144:2 where *ḥsdy* appears without *ʿz*, but with *mṣwdty*, *mśgby*, *mplṭy* and *mgny* as a description of Yahweh who subdues peoples and in whom the psalmist takes refuge. The sequence of epithets is similar to but not identical with Ps. 18:3 (cf. II Sam. 22:2b-3a), in which *slʿy* appears in the position occupied by *ḥesed* in Ps. 144:2. A final example which is perhaps to be associated with this group is Jonah 2:9: "Those who give regard[13] to vain idols forsake their *ḥesed*," that is, they forsake Yahweh who is their *ḥesed*.

Kuyper has proposed the simple meaning "strength" for *ḥesed* in these passages.[14] Dahood, who usually translates *ḥesed* as "kindness," proposes "rampart" for the epithet series and "firmness" for the other texts.[15] The difficulty with Kuyper's analysis, as suggested earlier, is his failure to

---

12. Dahood (*Psalms II*, pp. 70-71) argues that the final *w*'s on *ʿz* and *ḥsd* in vs. 11 are archaic nominative endings; this view is not impossible. The clear *y* (first person possessive suffix) on *mśgb* suggests that the readings on all three nouns might be *y*, as in vs. 18, even though one would normally expect the text to move toward a clear reading rather than in the opposite direction. Dahood's reading of *ʾlyk* as *ʾēlî kî* (rather than MT *ʾēlèkā*) improves the sense and his corresponding rearrangement of the metric structure ought probably to be followed.

13. This is the only pi. occurrence of the verb *šmr*. For the same phrase expressed with the qal, cf. Ps. 31:7, in which the rejection of idolaters is coupled with trust in Yahweh and the receiving of *ḥesed*. It is on the basis of this text that the Jonah passage is here taken as an example of theological rather than religious usage.

14. "The Meaning of *ḥsdw* [in] Isa. XL 6," p. 491. As the title suggests, he then extends this interpretation to explain Isa. 40:6. (See Chapter V, p. 190, for the writer's critique of this proposal.)

15. *Psalms II*, pp. 71, 94.

recognize that "strength" is not an additional, independent meaning of the word but rather a particular emphasis within the larger framework of meaning evoked by the term. It is for this reason that the English "strength" cannot be used alone to explain Isa. 40:6, nor can it be used to explain the appearance of *ḥsdyw* in II Chr. 32:32 as opposed to *kl gbwrtw* in II Ki. 20:20.[16] Dahood's usage likewise fails to give sufficient attention to the connecting link between such disparate connotations. In his comment on these passages, Glueck suggests that "God's might, set in motion for the sake of his own, is virtually identical with his *ḥesed*," and adds that the two "are not synonymous, but the showing of *ḥsd* can lead to the exercise of *ʿz*."[17] Although his two remarks seem at first contradictory, Glueck's perception once again points in the right direction. The meaning of *ḥesed* lies in the connection between strength and faithfulness, between kindness and power. It takes concrete form in deliverance or protection of one to whom one has a special, socially and/or legally recognized relationship. The action may require strength and display power, but as a freely performed deed it also is based in faithfulness and displays kindness or love.

In several texts the nuances of power or ability to deliver and that of deliverance itself are not clearly distinguishable. Among these is Ps. 13:6, "But I have trusted in thy *ḥesed*, I shall rejoice in thy salvation *(yᵉšûʿâ)*." In Ps. 98:1-3 *ḥesed* and *ʾĕmûnâ* are set alongside *yᵉšûʿâ* and *ṣᵉdāqâ*. Either deliverance itself or the power which gives deliverance may here be understood as the expression of God's faithfulness. It is of course unnecessary and even improper to suppose that these are either/or situations which have been obscured for the modern exegete. Rather, the "ambiguity" here is really a matter of multiple senses in which the richness of the word is expressed.

---

16. In the summary of Hezekiah's reign. As suggested in Chapter IV, p. 153, if *ḥsdyw* was original, then the Chronicler wished to make a different point about Hezekiah; he was not selecting a synonym.

17. Glueck, p. 46.

Willingness to Deliver

A third major nuance of *ḥesed* is God's willingness to deliver, and it is this focus which is most directly related to the idea of faithfulness which permeates the entire spectrum of the word. There are no "unambiguous" examples of this type, but a number of texts probably encompass this thought, including Pss. 13:5 and 98:1-3 just cited in connection with the first two themes. In a prayer for rescue from enemies, especially death, come the lines "With your great *ḥesed* answer me, with your reliable help *(b'mt yšʻk)* deliver me" (Ps. 69:14). Again the parallel suggests willingness, as well as power and the deliverance itself. Ps. 44:27 urges God to remember the people upon whom he has allowed affliction to come: "Arise, help us, ransom us for the sake of *(lmʻn)* your *ḥesed*." The use of *lmʻn* is unusual; Dahood's translation "as befits" best captures the sense here. An act of deliverance is appropriate; it is in accordance with God's faithfulness to his people, his readiness to maintain his relationship with them. Although Ps. 119 is extremely variegated, four of its seven uses of *ḥesed* can be placed with this type. Three times (vss. 88,149,159) the petitioner asks that his life be spared in accordance with God's *ḥesed* (cf. vs. 124). The psalm as a whole is not so much concerned for God's power as for his willingness to support the man who delights in the law. Repeatedly there is appeal for action in accordance with God's word or promise (vss. 38,41,49, 50,58,74,76,81,82,107,114,116,123,133,147,154,169,170). God's *ḥesed* is nuanced as his justice (vs. 149) expressed in his willingness to hear and answer the prayer of the obedient, to provide him with discernment so that he may live in more perfect obedience (cf. vss. 125,135,144,146).

Protection

A fourth nuance of *ḥesed* in the psalms might be described as maintaining of the favorable *status quo*. On the broad plane this constitutes "protection": it is the ongoing aspect of faithful action which prevents distress,[18] just as "deliverance"

---

18. In secular usage, cf. Abner's words to Ishbaal, "this day I keep doing *ḥesed*...and have not given you into David's power..." (II Sam. 3:8; see Chapter II, pp. 27-31.

involves rescue from distress already present. Two passages exemplify this theme particularly. Ps. 36:11, "Prolong your *ḥesed* to those who know you," introduces a plea for protection from the arrogant and wicked who would do harm to the faithful. And in Ps. 32:10 *ḥesed* could almost be translated "protective care": "Many are the pains of the wicked; but the one who trusts in Yahweh, with *ḥesed* he [Yahweh] surrounds him."[19]

A special variant on the theme of protective maintenance has to do with the preservation of the royal line on the throne. This aspect of the usage of *ḥesed* has already been discussed in connection with II Sam. 7 and Ps. 89;[20] several additional texts may be cited here. Ps. 18 (= II Sam. 22) ends with an ascription of praise to Yahweh who "increases the victories of his king, who does *ḥesed* to his anointed, (to David and his seed forever)."[21] Ps. 23 is in praise of God's protection and may be regarded either as a general or a royal psalm. The psalmist is convinced that goodness and *ḥesed* will follow him: blessing and protection from harm will be his, so that he can worship in the temple. (Cf. Ps. 5:8 in which the greatness of

---

19. Following the analysis of Hermann Gunkel (*Die Psalmen* [HkzAT; Göttingen: Vandenhoeck & Ruprecht, 1926], p. 135) and Dahood (*Psalms I*, pp. 197-198, 35) that *ḥesed* preceding the verb is here an accusative of means. If the nominative interpretation is preferred (as RSV translates), the meaning is not substantially affected. It is Yahweh's *ḥesed* for the trusting one in either case.

20. See Chapter III, pp. 139-145. Cf. also Isa. 16:5 and Prov. 20:28, Chapter V, pp. 205-206; and Ps. 61:7.

21. Cross and Freedman argue on orthographic grounds (non-representation of diphthongs indicating their contraction) that the poem took written form in the Northern Kingdom during the ninth-eighth centuries B.C. (*Ancient Yahwistic Poetry*, pp. 273ff.). If this is so, then the final line may represent a later adaptation to the specific tradition of the Davidic promises. While the poem in oral form could go back to the period of the United Monarchy, one cannot know whether the ideology of Davidic kingship was firmly enough entrenched to appear even in a northern record of the poem.

God's *ḥesed* enables the upright to enter God's house.) Finally, Ps. 21:8 asserts, "For the king trusts in Yahweh; and in the *ḥesed* of the Most High he shall not be moved."[22] This verse climaxes the description of Yahweh's care for the king in crowning him and seeing to his material prosperity, longevity, and military victory. It leads naturally into the next section of the poem which describes a battle in which Yahweh gave victory to the king, hence maintaining him on the throne.

Forgiveness

A final and important nuance of *ḥesed* in the psalms, one which stands somewhat apart from those previously discussed, is Yahweh's faithfulness given expression in his forgiveness. Yet this aspect of *ḥesed* cannot be completely divorced from deliverance and the willingness to deliver, for misfortune was often regarded as an indication of God's displeasure and change of fortune was in turn seen as an expression or sign of forgiveness.[23] This conjoining of deliverance and forgiveness appears most clearly in Pss. 85 and 90, two communal laments. In Ps. 85 the people pray for restoration, reviving and the putting away of anger. Clearly their distress is occasioned by sin; they ask for *ḥesed* and salvation (*yšʿ*, vs. 8). Likewise in Ps. 90 the people recognize their plight as the expression of God's wrath at their sins. In another context, 90:14 ("Satisfy us in the morning with thy *ḥesed*...") could easily be the plea of the falsely accused upright worshipper. Here, however, deliverance cannot be understood apart from forgiveness. In Ps. 40 the individual plea is primarily for deliverance; vs. 13 ("My iniquities have overtaken me...") is the only indication that the suppliant sees himself at fault for his distress. Three other psalms show greater emphasis on the blotting out of sins as an expression of *ḥesed*: Ps. 130:7 parallels Yahweh's *ḥesed* with his redemption *(pdwt)* of Israel from her sins. In Ps. 25:7 the

---

22. Dahood (*Psalms I*, p. 133) reads the *b* preposition as "from," hence: "he shall not swerve from the *ḥesed* of the Most High." But *ḥesed* is not used elsewhere in such a sense, and the receiving of God's *ḥesed* is regularly the counterpart of the petitioner's trust (see below, p. 228).

23. Cf. Chapter III, pp. 112-125 on Ex. 34 and Nu. 14.

penitent prays that he will be remembered according to God's *ḥesed* rather than according to his sins. Here *ḥesed* might best be described as that great depth of faithfulness, freely extended, by which God is able to overlook the repeated human violation of their relationship. And in Ps. 51:3, in a free adaptation of the formula of Ex. 34:6, the psalmist asks for mercy, moral cleansing in accordance with God's great *ḥesed*.

Finally, Ps. 103:6ff. is of interest for this category, as it seems almost to be an extended comment on the conflated formulaic tradition of Ex. 34:6-7. Ps. 103:8 cites the opening statement *verbatim*, and vs. 9, "he will not always chide, nor will he keep his anger forever," can easily be regarded as a restatement of "forgiving iniquity and transgression and sin, but he will by no means clear the guilty." Vss. 10-14 then comment that the greatness of God's *ḥesed* consists in his removal of transgression, in his not giving out what is justly deserved - but even here forgiveness and pity are for "those who fear him," those who have sincere intention of living within the covenant. The next section of the psalm is more loosely connected to the old formulaic usages; yet vss. 17-18 seem to be a refraction of the tradition of Ex. 20 = Dt. 5 which is also partially preserved in Ex. 34. *Ḥesed* is assured to all generations of those who fear him, "to those who keep his covenant and remember to do his commandments." With the theme of the endurance of God's *ḥesed* there is no comment on the fate of the stubbornly rebellious, but one feels God's requital of those who hate him lurking behind the scene of the carefully restricted assurance of *ḥesed*. These last verses are particularly important as concrete confirmation that on the national level *ḥesed* was definitely a part of the covenant tradition and specifically was the expression of God's faithful action on behalf of the people within the covenant relationship. As such, the text forms an appropriate bridge to the final section of this chapter.

2. The Relationship of the Recipients of *Ḥesed* to Yahweh

With the exception of Pss. 51, 106 and 130, the psalms which contain *ḥesed* place little emphasis upon the abject unworthiness of the recipients. In fact, quite the opposite is true. The psalms often preface or follow up a request for *ḥesed* with a statement indicating that the suppliant's relationship to God is in good repair.[24] While this need not imply that the petitioner has a claim on God or a hold over him - indeed, a prime feature of *ḥesed* is the actor's freedom not to act - the petitioner still may hope and even expect to receive *ḥesed* because he is fulfilling his part of the relationship. It may even be suggested that these statements of the "deserving" behavior of the suppliant form the backdrop for the confident statements of praise or assurance of deliverance which often conclude the lament form.

"Trust" *(bṭḥ)* is a primary word by which the petitioner describes his relationship to Yahweh: "But I trust in Yahweh, and I shall rejoice and be glad in your *ḥesed*" (Ps. 31:8). "But in you have I trusted, Yahweh...rescue me by your *ḥesed*" (31:15a,17b). "He who trusts in Yahweh, he will surround him with *ḥesed*" (32:10). "Let me hear of your *ḥesed* in the morning, for in you I trust" (143:8). "Let your *ḥesed* come to me...for I trust in your word" (119:41a,42b). "For the king trusts in Yahweh, and by his *ḥesed* he shall not be moved" (21:8). In an

---

24. Von Rad deals with this form of expression in "'Righteousness' and 'Life' in the Cultic Language of the Psalms," *The Problem of the Hexateuch and Other Essays* (New York: McGraw-Hill Book Company, 1966), pp. 243-267 (tr. by E. W. T. Dicken from the German which first appeared in *Festschrift für Alfred Bertholet* [Tübingen, 1950], pp. 418-437). He suggests that the worshipper states his perfect trust and obedience as "something prescribed by the cultus as a means of obtaining the favour God has offered to Israel" (p. 250). While his general observation is relevant, here it should be noted that von Rad is especially concerned for the more extended descriptions of moral perfection of the psalmists. With *ḥesed*, however, the vocabulary used focuses more on the petitioners' dependence on God and exclusive worship of him than on the details of their moral rectitude. And as von Rad himself says (following Cremer and Fahlgren), even *ṣdqh* is centrally a relationship term: fulfilling the requirements of a relationship is counted as "righteousness."

alternate mode of expression, the psalmist may state his confidence in God's *ḥesed* itself: "But I trust in your *ḥesed*, my heart will rejoice in your salvation" (13:6). "I trust in the *ḥesed* of the eternal and everlasting God" (52:10b).[25]

Related to trust is the use of hope *(yḥl)* in God or his *ḥesed*. The word expresses confidence in God's response but also indicates that the suppliant places himself in Yahweh's hands rather than turning to some other (false) source of help. God responds to those who are in right relation to him: "Yahweh takes pleasure in those who fear him, those who hope in his *ḥesed*" (147:11). "Behold the eye of Yahweh is on those who fear him, those who hope in his *ḥesed*" (33:18).[26] "Let your *ḥesed* be upon us, O Yahweh, according as we hope in you" (33:22). "Hope, O Israel, in Yahweh, for with Yahweh is *ḥesed* and plenteous redemption" (130:7). This last psalm opens with the recognition that no one is perfect before Yahweh. Yet the psalmist expresses the assurance that if he waits for the Lord he will be heard and forgiven, and he calls on Israel to join him in this stance before God. The receiving of *ḥesed* as forgiveness is contingent upon a right relation to God, just as is deliverance for the man who is portrayed as fully obedient.

Ḥesed is also asked for those who are Yahweh's servants: "By your *ḥesed* exterminate my enemies...for I am your servant" (143:12). "Let your face shine on your servant; save me by your *ḥesed*" (31:17). "Answer me, O Yahweh, for your *ḥesed* is good...hide not your face from your servant" (69:17-18). "Let

---

25. For this translation, see Dahood, *Psalms II*, p. 16, and *Psalms I*, pp. 66, 272-273. It may be noted here that the occurrence of *ḥesed* in vs. 3 of this psalm is extremely problematic. Some have attempted to read a form of the Aramaic *ḥsd* "to revile"; see most recently C. Schedl, "'ḥesed ʾēl' in Psalm 52 (51), 3," *Biblische Zeitschrift* 5 (1961) 259-260. Dahood proposes reading *ḥāsīd ʾel* taken sarcastically and contrasted with the true *ḥāsîd* at the conclusion of the psalm. This interpretation is certainly plausible, but no solution is fully convincing.

26. The provision of *ḥesed* for those who fear him is found also in 103:11,17. Cf. above, p. 227.

your *ḥesed* be ready to comfort me according to your promise to your servant" (119:76). In this servant language, just as with trust, hope, and fear, even those who are being punished for their sin are described in relational vocabulary as they come in penitence seeking deliverance: "Have pity on your servants: satisfy us in the morning with your *ḥesed*...let your work be manifest to your servants" (90:13b-14a,16a).

A variety of other expressions of the relationship between God and those desiring or receiving *ḥesed* are found scattered through the texts. In addition to 103:17, covenant-keepers appears also in 25:10. *Ḥesed* is for those who "know" Yahweh, for the "upright in heart" (36:11). It is for those who love his precepts (119:159), for those who take refuge in Yahweh (57:2-4; cf. Chapter V, pp. 196-197). And finally it is for those who express their trust, hope, reverence, servanthood by the very act of calling upon Yahweh for assistance: "Save me by your *ḥesed*; let me not be put to shame, for I call on you" (31:17b-18a). "But as for me, my prayer is to you...answer me in the greatness of your *ḥesed*" (69:14).[27]

3. Summary

A brief review of God's *ḥesed* in Israel's hymnic literature has shown the principal features of God's *ḥesed* to individuals (as in the patriarchal narratives) and to the covenant community as a whole (as in the prophetic literature) are found here also. *Ḥesed* is God's faithfulness given expression as protection, deliverance, or forgiveness. The relational vocabulary which is used (e.g. trust, hope, know, servant) suggests the importance of the covenant imagery in which the suppliant expects and hopes that his trust is not misplaced and that he will receive freely given protection and support. As in the theological usage examined in earlier chapters, this succor may be promised or surprising, it may be seen as deserved because

---

27. Cf. 106:44 in which the rebellious people are answered when they cry to Yahweh. A number of other psalms in which *ḥesed* occurs include a statement of relationship to Yahweh which is not directly linked with the *ḥesed* section. Cf. Pss. 44, 57, 59, 62, 63, 85, 86.

of uprightness or undeserved yet offered as a compassionate act. God's *ḥesed* is the providential exercise of his power on behalf of the needy people with whom he has established a special relationship.

SUMMARY OF RESULTS

The study of the many contexts in which the word *ḥesed* appears can only heighten one's appreciation of the flexibility of the term not only over the long time span of biblical writing but also within any given period or author. The lack of an adequate English equivalent and the difficulty (and danger) of selecting even a single phrase to convey the concept in all cases also becomes increasingly apparent. The word may often be summarized as "deliverance or protection as a responsible keeping of faith with another with whom one is in a relationship." But such a statement is extremely cumbersome and even so does not cover the full range of meaning, notably in its omission of forgiveness as an aspect of *ḥesed* in theological usage. In the summary, then, as in the analysis throughout, the Hebrew term will be retained while various English words will be used to describe its shades of meaning.

In secular usage in texts from the pre-exilic period *ḥesed* is used to describe a particular or ongoing action either between persons in an intimate personal relationship (husband-wife, father-son, king-counsellor, king-military leader) or between persons in a voluntary but non-intimate relationship, often one between rival political factions or individuals (spies-residents of enemy city, rival kings). In the case of intimate relationships, *ḥesed* is simply requested or offered. The fact of the relationship is presumed as the basis for the request. Where the relationship is not intimate, however, where the parties may be described usually as "discrete" units who have entered into a voluntary agreement, there is regular reference to some prior action as the basis for an act of *ḥesed* requested or offered. The fact that the party in need has shown his good faith when not in need is offered as the basis for his deserving of assistance in his time of trouble.[1] While

1. It must be emphasized again that these summary statements and those to follow cannot be applied in detail to every case. For modifications in particular examples, the reader should and must consult the discussion of the passage in question.

ḥesed is regularly used for the immediate action, the second of the two mentioned, it is only sometimes used for the first action. The use of *ḥesed* for the first action has been described as an extended or dependent usage. The situation from which the first action emerged did not confront the actor with the same degree of responsibility as does the second situation to its actor. At the same time, the prior action itself as a freely performed rescue or deliverance which could not be obtained elsewhere was congruent with the content of a *ḥesed* action. The David and Jonathan narrative provides a special case in which the relationship was personally intimate and yet the two remained politically discrete units, so that features of both types are present.

All these secular examples, whether or not in intimate relationships, have certain principal features in common which provide the parameters for the use of the word. *Ḥesed* is never a special favor; rather it is always the provision for an essential need. In the form of a specific action, it normally provides deliverance from dire straits (broadly conceived; ranging from death to end of the family name to burial in a foreign land). As an ongoing behavior (series of actions) it constitutes protection from similar dangers. *Ḥesed* is an action performed for the weak party by the powerful one, for the situationally inferior party by the situationally superior one. Because of his powerful status, the superior party is always free not to perform the act of *ḥesed*; the weak party will have no future opportunity to "get even" and no outside recrimination or interference (as from legal authorities) is to be feared. Nevertheless, the potential actor has a privately and even publicly recognized responsibility to do *ḥesed* because of the relationship in which he stands. In the case of "discrete units," the mention of a previous action serves to show that the relationship is in good repair and hence a valid basis for recognition of responsibility. Furthermore, the superior party is normally the sole source of assistance available to the party in need; if the powerful one does not act, the needy will meet with certain disaster. This fact increases the freedom not to act; yet it also increases the sense of responsibility to act. The actor may or may not have a measure of self-interest in his action, and the action may or may not be difficult to perform - these are occasional but not essential features of the *ḥesed* action.

Except for the late meaning "favor" or "beauty" (in which *ḥesed* seems to have fallen together with *ḥēn*) found in Esther, there are no new examples of secular usage of the word in exilic or post-exilic sources. The possible exception, II Chr. 24:22, appears to be from an earlier source. The post-exilic usage with a human subject includes religious usage, something which is not found in the pre-exilic narratives. It should be pointed out that the absence of secular examples in post-exilic texts does not necessarily mean that the word had dropped out of use or become very rare. Since a good portion of the Chronicler is dependent upon the Deuteronomic history, there is actually relatively little narrative material preserved from the exilic and post-exilic period. Nonetheless, a shift in the balance of emphasis toward the religious usage seems probable, especially since the secular meaning in Esther is so far removed from the earlier tradition.

The post-exilic use of *ḥesed*(s) for "pious acts," acts which are pleasing to God and which he requires of men (although they do not always comply), seems to have emerged as a generalized adaptation of the religious use of *ḥesed* which is earlier encountered in prophecy. This prophetic usage appears primarily in Hosea and in subsequent utterances which show a relationship with Hosea's usage. In this usage, *ḥesed* is understood as proper action of all Israelites to one another and also as Israel's collective responsible action towards God. In religious usage, the basis for recognition of responsibility is extended from immediate relationships to the covenant society as a whole. The use of *ḥesed* to describe Israel's behavior toward God involves a more complicated adaptation, however, for it is the action of the inferior party toward the superior. Despite Yahweh's power of reprisal and lack of need, the word could be "stretched": Israel's faithfulness as given expression in an upright society was still something which God desired but could not force from the people; as in the secular realm, the keeping of covenant responsibilities is what is desired, even though not from a position of power; other covenant vocabulary was bi-directional; the traditional coupling with *ʾĕmet* and the semantic relationship to *ḥāsîd* allowed for an abstracting of *ḥesed* to "faithfulness," a meaning which could readily be predicated of men in relation to God. In pre-exilic usage "religious" *ḥesed* as faithfulness and as societal justice and righteousness is specifically a communal concern. It is only in post-exilic texts that the word used religiously receives individual application so that there is a distinction drawn between men who practice *ḥesed* and those who do not. This individualizing of religious usage sets the stage for the eventual development of the meaning "pious acts."

The theological use of *ḥesed* in the pre-exilic tradition includes examples which are patterned both on the analogy of the intimate personal relationship and on the analogy of discrete parties in a formalized voluntary relationship. These are not clearly distinguished, however, and sometimes both may be involved (as in Hosea's and Jeremiah's use of marriage as an image for covenant which is in turn an image for describing God's relationship with Israel). In the patriarchal narratives the *ḥesed* of Yahweh to particular individuals is most like that of intimate personal relationships on the human scale. God fulfills his responsibility in freely given personal acts of deliverance and protection. He is called upon to do *ḥesed* at a point when the suppliant has exhausted his human resources and can rely only on God to save him; if God does not respond, there is no hope for a solution for the difficulty. The person's right relationship to God is not stated as a basis for the *ḥesed*, but it is always clear that the individual is acting in obedience to God or is doing the morally upright against difficult odds and hence is "deserving" of divine assistance.

This individual usage of the patriarchal tradition is reflected in psalms in which the upright man seeks God's protection or deliverance from persecutors. In the Psalms, however, the suppliant is often careful to point out his upright behavior. (This is probably to be regarded as a device of cultic usage rather than as personal boasting.) In late literature, this form reappears in Nehemiah's prayer that God will do *ḥesed* for him because of his zealous activity on behalf of Jewish faith and practice. Here, however, the word seems to have taken on the connotations of mercy granted despite unworthiness. Nehemiah seems to be offering his deeds as a small token over against his general behavior which might not be deserving of *ḥesed*.

A second area of theological usage, which appears only three times, appears to be a technical means for bringing a relationship to an end when adverse circumstances require it. This ending of the relationship may be offered by the weaker party to the powerful; it involves committing the powerful to God's *ḥesed* and suggesting that the powerful should shift his primary personal or political responsibility to another person.

A third and major area of theological usage is that of God's *ḥesed* for his covenanted people in the Mosaic tradition. This usage finds expression primarily in pre-exilic (and probably very ancient) liturgical titles of Yahweh and in the theological usage of prophecy. In this usage, two seemingly contradictory themes are held in tension: God's *ḥesed* is delivering, protective power exercised on behalf of those who are obedient; God's *ḥesed* is also surprising forgiveness offered to the disobedient when they are penitent. Two factors hold these disparate themes together. First, forgiveness is expressed in terms of deliverance, since trouble regularly comes with disobedience. God is the only sure source of deliverance (forgiveness) since he is the source of the trouble (punishment). Second, both forgiveness for the penitent and assistance for the obedient are regarded as expressions of God's faithfulness to his covenanted people, his willingness to meet fully his responsibility for the people with whom he initiated a relationship. In the old liturgical titles and their hymnic reuse, the forgiveness aspect of this faithfulness is associated with the expression *rb ḥsd*, not simply *ʿśh ḥsd*. The use of *rb* is most appropriate, for it is in the greatness of God's willingness to maintain the covenant relationship that he does not cast aside the people in their disobedience but goes beyond the limits of what can be called *ḥesed* in normal human usage.

One may ask why *ḥn* or *rḥmym* was not used instead, and a glance at the formulaic pattern *ḥnwn wrḥwm* indicates how closely these have come together. The point is that even forgiveness itself was seen as an expression of covenant faithfulness, and only *ḥesed* could express this idea. It is true, nevertheless, that in the exile and beyond *ḥesed* seems to have become more and more associated with mercy, *rḥm*, in theological language. Once the people were removed from the land, the Mosaic covenant tradition required radical reinterpretation. The final covenant threat had been realized and forgiveness rather than "deserved" assistance for the people of the covenant became the dominant concern.

A final area of theological application was in the special understanding of God's preservation of the Davidic dynasty. The maintenance of the dynasty in accordance with the promise which God freely made to David was regarded as a special instance of God's *ḥesed* for an individual and through him and his successors to the nation. The main Jerusalem theological tradition evidently regarded this as a covenant relationship (Ps. 89); yet the Deuteronomic historian used the word only briefly in order to recognize the fact of the continuing Davidic line and give it a theological setting. Although he has hope for the future of the line, it is based on Josiah's reform, conditioned on continuing faithfulness, rather than a presupposition of unconditional kingship no matter what. With the coming of the exile and the collapse of the monarchy, the tradition of unconditional *ḥesed* to the Davidic line was suddenly ended. Here too reinterpretation was needed. With the possible exception of Isa. 16:5, which is completely divorced from its context, there is no mention of *ḥesed* in connection with the exilic or post-exilic messianic expectations. Instead, there emerges the fresh synthesis of Second Isaiah, who democratized the Davidic covenant to all Israel and thus in a sense brought the usage full circle to the ancient tradition of the old liturgical formula: God's *ḥesed* will yet be for all Israel and that fact will make Israel a light to the nations.

The term *ḥesed* thus proves to be one which throughout the tradition was remarkably rich in its theological meaning. Here the sovereign freedom of God and his strong commitment to his chosen people were held together in a single word. A single word expressed the utter dependence of the people upon Yahweh and his willingness and ability to deliver them. A single word communicated the promised faithfulness of God upon which the people could base their cry for help and the surprising faithfulness of God which transcended even his own declarations of judgment upon his people. God preserved the covenant community even in its failure, in accordance with his own commitment to the people - a sure and everlasting *ḥesed*, great beyond any human expectation.

And so Israel could proclaim in varied forms throughout her history:

> Praise Yahweh
> for he is good
> for his *ḥesed* endures forever. (Ps. 107:1)

APPENDIX

ḤĀSÎD

A number of brief comments about the possible background and content of the term *ḥāsîd* have been gathered into an Appendix for convenience. Much of what is said here has been adumbrated in the main text of the study. There is no intention of presenting an exhaustive study of the term.

Grammatically, the word is best understood as a survival of an old passive form on a *qatîl* pattern. The suggestion of a passive background here is analogous to the suggestion of W. F. Albright for Hebrew *nābîʾ*.[1] The earlier theory of an old active *qātil* form is rejected because this form regularly developed into the normal Hebrew active participle *qôtēl*. The *qatîl* pattern has been recognized for other words besides *nābîʾ*, among them *nāśîʾ*, *pāqîd*, and *māšîaḥ*. Since these terms designate an office or function, an original passive form could easily acquire a stative or active meaning. In the case of *ḥāsîd*, the dominant usage is stative.[2]

The occurrences of *ḥāsîd* are concentrated in the Psalms (26x), with only two instances in prophecy (Jer. 3:2; Mic. 7:2) and one in Proverbs (2:8). II Chr. 6:41 is a quotation from Ps. 132; II Sam. 22:26 duplicates Ps. 18:26; the two remaining occurrences are within poetry preserved outside the Psalter (Dt. 33:8; I Sam. 2:9).[3] Given this distribution, the reader

---

1. "The Archaeological Background of the Hebrew Prophets of the Eighth Century," *Journal of Bible and Religion* 8 (1940 132-133. See also his *From the Stone Age to Christianity*, pp. 231-232.

2. The verb (with the lone exception of hithp. II Sam. 22:26 = Ps. 18:26) is no longer attested. Cf. *nābîʾ*, for which the extant Hebrew verb forms must be regarded as denominative even though the verb from which the passive form originally came is attested in Akkadian.

3. Although both the Blessing of Moses and the Song of Hannah are archaic poems, in each of these cases the *ḥāsîd* material may be intrusive. On Dt. 33:8-9 see Frank M. Cross,

will not be surprised to find that there are no strictly "secular" uses of the word. Since *ḥesed* itself was commonly used in a "secular" way, we must assume that *ḥāsîd* became fixed very early as a religious technical term and hence became restricted in its usage.[4] Those who were the recipients of God's *ḥesed* (as the one called is the recipient of a call, the one appointed is the recipient of an appointment) were designated *ḥāsîd(îm)*. The word came then to describe one in a relation to God (which led to the granting of *ḥesed*). It is of interest that *ḥāsîd* is used "theologically" (of God as opposed to men) only twice, in Jer. 3:12 and Ps. 145:17 (where it is in parallelism with *ṣaddîq*). The rarity of this usage may further reinforce the overall interpretation of a passive turned stative, for only in these instances does the term come full circle to describe the (original) giver rather than the recipient of the *ḥesed*.[5]

Jr., *Ancient Yahwistic Poetry* (Baltimore: Johns Hopkins, 1950), p. 220. In I Sam. 2 it should simply be noted that the Greek tradition does not preserve the line. For discussion, see Marvin L. Chaney, "*ḤDL*-II and the 'Song of Deborah.'"

4. No date can be assigned to this restriction, although the form suggests an early development rather than a late innovation. This analysis thus rejects the view, espoused most recently by Julian Morgenstern ("The *Ḥasîdîm* - Who Were They?" *HUCA* 38 [1967] 59-73), that the word "evolved only shortly before, or, quite possibly, during the Exile, or perhaps even in the early post-Exilic period" (p. 59). Morgenstern's primary concern is to push back the date of emergence of the term *ḥăsîdîm* - from the Greek or Maccabean period (to which he says "most scholars" assign the pertinent psalms) to approximately 485 B.C., where he dates Pss. 89 and 132, along with 97 and 149. But ever since Gunkel's work, the trend in Psalms scholarship has been toward earlier dates generally and towards greater openness in recognizing that many psalms cannot be identified with a particular period. In any case, the writer would certainly regard Psalms 89 and 132 as pre-exilic. For a cross-section of the wide variety of opinion on Ps. 149, see Hans-Joachim Kraus, *Psalmen II*, p. 966.

5. Morgenstern seems to believe that the theological use

In its religious usage, the plural of *ḥāsîd* appears to connote three different "groups" of people. On the broadest level, the *ḥăsîdîm* are apparently all Israel, the entire people as recipients of God's *ḥesed*. This use is found in Ps. 148:14, in which it is in parallelism with "his people" and "the people of Israel" and in Ps. 149:1 (parallel to "Israel") and 5 (parallel to "his people"). It also appears in Ps. 50:5 where the parallel is "those who made a covenant with me by sacrifice" and probably in Ps. 79:2, using "your servants" in a description of the fate of the people in the destruction of Jerusalem.

The second group is the faithful and/or the upright. Here the word seems to be used to point to a particular subgroup of Israel which has remained loyal to Yahweh and expressed its loyalty in its social behavior. Yet it does not seem necessary to associate this subgroup with a particular sect or party, even though a party called *ḥăsîdîm* did flourish briefly in the late post-exilic era. Even the term "subgroup" is misleading insofar as it connotes some recognized or organized body rather than a collection of individuals who possess the traits in question. Ps. 37:28-29 suggests that God will protect the *ḥăsîdîm*, who are the righteous as opposed to the wicked. Ps. 97:10-11 reiterates this theme, as does Prv. 2:8.[6] In Ps. 31:24 the *ḥăsîdîm* are pictured as the faithful, in contrast to the haughty, and in 85:9-10 they are the ones who fear Yahweh and as penitents will be the recipients of his salvation. In this last example, the word also is paralleled with "his people." The text demonstrates again the impossibility of any absolute demarcation between the nation as a unit and individuals within it in the use of *ḥāsîd*.

---

emerged before the religious, largely because Jer. 3:12 is fixed in date prior to his date for the Psalm texts. ("The *Ḥasîdîm*," pp. 59-60). The writer believes his view improbable on linguistic as well as chronological grounds.

6. The contrast of the *ḥăsîdîm* with the wicked in I Sam. 2:9 may be added to this group. But it seems likely in terms of the poem as a whole that here the contrast is properly Israel vs. non-Israel. Such fluidity may well exist throughout the spectrum of usage.

The third "group" described as *ḥăsîdîm* appears in only two examples and is somewhat puzzling. In Ps. 132:9 and 16 (quoted in II Chr. 6:41) *ḥăsîdîm* is clearly paralleled with "priests" *(khn)*. It might be possible to regard this as synthetic rather than synonymous parallelism so that all Israel or all worshippers could be meant by *ḥăsîdîm*. But the usage in Dt. 33:8 suggests that the *ḥāsîd* parallel in Ps. 132 and II Chr. 6 may in fact be restricted to a priestly class. In Dt. 33:8 we may reconstruct:

Give to Levi your urim
To your man of *ḥesed* your thummim.

In the first line, the reconstruction "give to Levi" is based on the Greek and on a Qumran reading *hbw llwy*.[7] The translation of the second line presumes (again following the Greek) that *l'yš ḥsdk* was the original reading. The Mt *l'yš ḥsydk* does not make good sense. The single word *lḥsdyk* could be an alternate reading conceptually. But the two-word phrase yields exact 8/8 meter; also, it would be difficult to regard *'yš* as a secondary intrusion. It may be suggested that the reading *ḥsydk* came into the text under the influence of the related passages in Ps. 132 and II Chr. 6:41. The parallelism with Levi cannot be set aside here, nor can the mention of urim and thummim which likewise suggests a limited priestly referent. Although parts of vss. 8-10 are probably intrusions into the Blessing, it is likely that at least this opening couplet is old.[8] Thus conceivably we have here and in Ps. 132 an old special usage of *ḥāsîd/'îš ḥesed* which the Chronicler and perhaps the religious tradition he knew attempted to reemphasize.[9]

One would then hypothesize that the more general application of *ḥāsîd* to all of God's people in covenant existed

---

7. 4Q Dt^{h}, F. M. Cross, private communication, August 1970.

8. F. M. Cross, *Ancient Yahwistic Poetry*, p. 220; and on the antiquity of these two lines (private communication, August 1970).

9. Note that urim and thummim also disappear from our sources between early texts and the sudden reappearance in Ezra 2:63 (cf. Neh. 7:65).

alongside of a use for special religious functionaries which only occasionally came into the foreground. The special emphasis on perfect obedience was also present and provided a background for special application to those loyal under persecution in the intertestamental period. Such an interpretation must remain conjectural but it can account for the surprising range in usage from designation of a function or office all the way to a simple adjective meaning faithful or upright.[10]

---

10. For this unspecified adjectival usage, Micah 7:2 (where the parallel is *yšr*) provides a good example. The complex picture is further compounded by the apparent application of the term to the Davidic line or David himself (Ps. 89:20).

INDEX OF PASSAGES DISCUSSED[1]

1. The Index is not intended to serve as a complete catalogue of passages in which *ḥesed* occurs, for which the reader is referred to standard concordances. Nor are all texts referred to in this study (or even all those using *ḥesed*) listed here. Only passages discussed in some detail are included. For unlisted Psalms passages, the reader is referred especially to pp. 165ff. (liturgical), 208ff. (plural forms), and to Chapter VI, *passim*.

SELECTED BIBLIOGRAPHY

Texts, Lexicons, and Grammars

Brockelmann, Carl. *Grundriss der vergleichenden Grammatik der semitischen Sprachen.* Vol. I: *Laut- und Formenlehre.* Vol. II. *Syntax.* Hildesheim: Georg Olms Verlagsbuchhandlung, 1961.

______. *Hebräische Syntax.* Neukirchen Kreis Moers: Verlag der Buchhandlung des Erziehungsvereins, 1956.

Brooke, Alan England and McLean, Norman. *The Old Testament in Greek According to the Text of Codex Vaticanus. Supplemented from other Uncial Manuscripts, with a Critical Apparatus Containing the Variants of the Chief Ancient Authorities for the Text of the Septuagint.* Vol. I (in 4 Parts): *The Octateuch.* Vol. II (in 4 Parts): *The Later Historical Books.* Vol. III, Part 1: *Esther, Judith, Tobit.* Cambridge: Cambridge University Press, 1906-1940.

Brown, Francis, Driver, S. R., and Briggs, Charles A. *A Hebrew and English Lexicon of the Old Testament.* Oxford: Clarendon Press, 1966. (Corrected reprint of the 1907 edition.)

Gesenius, Guilielmus. *Thesaurus Philologicus Criticus Linguae Hebraeae et Chaldaeae Veteris Testamenti.* Tomi primi fasciculus prior. Editio alter secundum radices digesta priore germanica longe auctior et emendatior. Lipsiae: Sumtibus Typisque Fr. Chr. Guil. Vogelii, 1829.

Gesenius' Hebrew Grammar as Edited and Enlarged by E. Kautzsch. 2nd English edition revised in accordance with the 28th German edition (1909) by A. E. Cowley. Oxford: Clarendon Press, 1960. (Reprint of corrected 1910 edition.)

Harris, Zellig S. *A Grammar of the Phoenician Language.* American Oriental Series, Vol. 8. New Haven: American Oriental Society, 1936.

Hatch, Edwin, and Redpath, Henry A. *A Concordance to the Septuagint and the Other Greek Versions of the Old Testament (Including the Apocryphal Books).* 3 vols. in 2. Graz, Austria: Akademische Druck.-U. Verlagsanstalt, 1954. (Reprint of the 1897 Oxford Edition.)

Jastrow, Marcus. *A Dictionary of the Targumim, the Talmud*

Babli and Yerushalmi, and the Midrashic Literature. 2 vols. New York: Pardes Publishing House, Inc., 1950. (First published 1903.)

Jean, Charles F. (and) Hoftijzer, Jacob. *Dictionnaire des inscriptions sémitiques de l'ouest.* Leiden: E. J. Brill, 1965.

Joüon, Paul. *Grammaire de l'Hebreu Biblique.* 2d ed. Rome: Pontifical Biblical Institute, 1947.

Kittel, Rudolph *et al.*, eds. *Biblia Hebraica.* 12th ed. (emended printing of 7th ed., a rev. and expanded version of 3d ed., 1937). Stuttgart: Württembergische Bibelanstalt, 1961.

Koehler, Ludwig, and Baumgartner, Walter. *Hebräisches und Aramäisches Lexikon zum Alten Testament.* I: ʾ - *ṭebah.* 3d ed., newly revised by W. Baumgartner. Leiden: E. J. Brill, 1967.

Lane, Edward William. *An Arabic-English Lexicon.* Book I, Parts i-viii. London: Williams and Norgate, 1863-1893.

Liddell, Henry George, and Scott, Robert. *A Greek-English Lexicon.* New (9th) rev. and expanded ed. Ed. H. S. Jones *et al.* Oxford: Clarendon Press, 1961. (Reprint of 1940 ed.)

Lisowsky, Gerhard. *Konkordanz zum hebräischen Alten Testament.* Stuttgart: Privileg. Württ.Bibelanstalt, 1958.

Mandelkern, Solomon. *Veteris Testamenti Concordantiae Hebraicae atque Chaldaicae.* 5th expanded and rev. ed. Tel-Aviv: Schocken Publishing House Ltd., 1962.

Margolis, Max L., ed. *The Book of Joshua in Greek.* Parts I-IV. Paris: Librairie Orientaliste Paul Geuthner, 1931.

______. "Specimen of a New Edition of the Greek Joshua." Reprinted from *Jewish Studies in Memory of Israel Abrahams.* Vienna, 1927. 307-323.

Payne Smith, Jessie, ed. *A Compendious Syriac Dictionary.* Founded upon the *Thesaurus Syriacus* of Robert Payne Smith. Oxford: Clarendon Press, 1903.

Septuaginta: Vetus Testamentum Graecum. Auctoritate Societatis Litterarum Gottingensis editum. Vol. VIII, 3: *Esther.* Ed. R. Hanhart. Vol. X: *Psalmi cum Odis.* Ed. A. Rahlfs. Vol. XIII: *Duodecim Prophetae.* Vol. XIV: *Isaias.* Vol. XV: *Ieremias, Baruch, Threni, Epistula Ieremiae.* Ed. J.

Ziegler. Göttingen: Vandenhoeck und Ruprecht, 1931-1966.

Sperber, Alexander, ed. *The Bible in Aramaic based on Old Manuscripts and Printed Texts.* Vol. II: *The Former Prophets according to Targum Jonathan.* Leiden: E. J. Brill, 1959.

Wagner, Max. *Die lexikalischen und grammatikalischen Aramaismen im alttestamentlichen Hebräisch.* Berlin: Töpelmann, 1966.

Wright, William. *Lectures on the Comparative Grammar of the Semitic Languages.* Ed. W. R. Smith. Cambridge: The University Press, 1890.

Other Works

Ackroyd, Peter R. "Hosea and Jacob," *VT* 13 (1963) 245-259.

Aharoni, Yohanan. "Three Hebrew Ostraca from Arad," *BASOR* 197 (1970) 16-41. (Originally published in *Eretz Israel* 9 [1969] 10-21 [Hebrew].)

Albright, William Foxwell. "Abram the Hebrew: A New Archaeological Interpretation," *BASOR* 163 (1961) 36-54.

______. "The Archaeological Background of the Hebrew Prophets of the Eighth Century," *Journal of Bible and Religion* 8 (1940) 131-136.

______. Review of *Introduction to the Old Testament*, by Robert H. Pfeiffer, *JBL* 61 (1942) 111-126.

______. *From the Stone Age to Christianity.* Baltimore: Johns Hopkins Press, 1940.

______. "The Israelite Conquest of Canaan in the Light of Archaeology," *BASOR* 74 (1939) 11-23.

______. "A Votive Stele Erected by Ben-Hadad I of Damascus to the God Melcarth," *BASOR* 87 (1942) 23-39.

Alt, Albrecht. "The God of the Fathers," *Essays in Old Testament History and Religion.* Translated by R. A. Wilson. Oxford: Basil Blackwell, 1966. 3-77. (Originally published as "Der Gott der Väter," *Beiträge zur Wissenschaft vom Alten und Neuen Testament* III, 12 [1929].)

______. "Hosea 5:8-6:6. Ein Krieg und seine Folgen in Prophetischer Beleuchtung," *Neue kirchliche Zeitschrift* 30 (1919) 537-568. (Reprinted in *Kleine Schriften zur Geschichte des Volkes Israel* II, 163-187. Munich: C. H.

Beck'sche Verlagsbuchhandlung, 1953.)

______. "The Origins of Israelite Law," *Essays in Old Testament History and Religion.* Translated by R. A. Wilson. Oxford: Basil Blackwell, 1966. 78-132. (Originally published as "Die Ursprünge des Israelitischen Rechts," Bericht über die Verhandlungen der Sächsischen akademie der Wissenschaften zu Leipzig. Philologisch-historische Klasse, Band 86, Heft 1. Leipzig: S. Hirzel, 1934.)

Anderson, Bernhard W. "Exodus and Covenant in Second Isaiah and Prophetic Tradition," *Magnalia Dei. The Mighty Acts of God.* F. M. Cross, W. Lemke, and P. Miller, eds. Garden City, N.Y.: Doubleday & Company, Inc., 1976. 339-360.

Asensio, Felix. *Misericordia et Veritas, el Ḥesed y 'Emet divinos. su influjo religioso-social en la historia de Israel. Analecta Gregoriana* 48, Sec. 3, No. 19. Rome: Apud Aedes Universitas Gregorianae, 1949.

Bailey, L. "Israelite *ʾĒl Šadday* and Amorite *Bêl Sadê*," *JBL* 87 (1968) 434-438.

Baumann, Eberhard. "*Ydʿ* und seine Derivate," *ZAW* 28 (1908) 22-41.

Berger, Philippe. "Mémoire sur la grand inscription dédicatoire et sur plusieurs autres inscriptions néo-puniques du temple d'Hathor-Miskar à Maktar," *Mémoires de l'Academie des Inscriptions et Belles-lettres.* Vol. XXXVI, Pt. 2. Paris: Impr. nat., 1899.

Bogaert, Maurice. "Les suffixes verbaux non accusatifs dans le sémitique nord-occidental et particulièrement en hébreu," *Biblica* 45 (1964) 220-247.

Boling, Robert G. *Judges.* AB. Garden City, N.Y.: Doubleday & Company, Inc., 1975.

______. "'Synonymous' Parallelism in the Psalms," *JSS* 5/3 (1960) 221-255.

Bowen, Boone M. "A Study of *ḥsd.*" Unpublished Ph.D. dissertation, Yale University, 1938.

Bright, John. *A History of Israel*². Philadelphia: Westminster Press, 1972.

______. *Jeremiah.* AB. Garden City, N.Y.: Doubleday & Company, Inc., 1965.

Bultmann, Rudolph. "γινώσκω." Part C. The OT Usage. In G.

Kittel, ed., *Theological Dictionary of the New Testament.* Grand Rapids, Mich.: Wm. B. Eerdmans Publishing Company, 1964. I, 696-701.

______. "ἔλεος, ἐλεέω; ἐλεημοσύνη." G. Kittel, ed., *Theological Dictionary of the New Testament.* Grand Rapids, Mich.: Wm. B. Eerdmans Publishing Company, 1964. II, 477-486.

Caird, George B. *The First and Second Books of Samuel: Introduction and Exegesis.* IB. New York: Abingdon Press, 1953.

Campbell, Edward F. Unpublished paper on the Book of Ruth. Presented at the meeting of the Biblical Colloquium, Washington, D.C., November 8, 1969.

Caquot, André. "Les 'graces de David.' À propos d'Isaie 55/3b," *Semitica* XV (1965) 45-59.

Chaney, Marvin L. "ḤDL-II and the 'Song of Debora'." Unpublished Ph.D. dissertation, Harvard University, 1976.

Clermont-Ganneau, Charles. *Recueil d'Archéologie Orientale.* Paris, 1900.

Conrad, Edgar W. "Patriarchal Traditions in Second Isaiah." Unpublished Ph.D. dissertation, Princeton Theological Seminary, 1974.

Cooke, G. A. *A Text-book of North-Semitic Inscriptions.* Oxford: Clarendon Press, 1903.

Coote, Robert B. "Hosea XII," *VT* 21 (1971) 389-402.

Cross, Frank Moore. *Canaanite Myth and Hebrew Epic: Essays in the History of the Relition of Israel.* Cambridge, Mass.: Harvard University Press, 1973.

______. "The Council of Yahweh in Second Isaiah," *JNES* 12 (1953) 274-277.

______. "The Development of the Jewish Scripts," *The Bible and the Ancient Near East: Essays in Honor of William Foxwell Albright.* G. Ernest Wright, ed. Garden City, N.Y.: Doubleday & Company, Inc., 1961. 133-202.

______. "The Structure of the Deuteronomic History," *Perspectives in Jewish Learning* III (1967) 9-24.

______. *Studies in Ancient Yahwistic Poetry.* Reprint of Ph.D. dissertation. Baltimore: Johns Hopkins University, 1950.

______. "Yahweh and the God of the Patriarchs," *HTR* 55 (1962) 225-259.

______, and Freedman, David N. "A Royal Psalm of Thanksgiving," *JBL* 72 (1953) 15-34.

Dahood, Mitchell. *Psalms I*. AB. Garden City, N.Y.: Doubleday & Company, Inc., 1966.

______. *Psalms II*. AB. Garden City, N.Y.: Doubleday & Company, Inc., 1968.

______. "Ugaritic Studies and the Bible," *Gregorianum* 43 (1962) 55-79.

Dentan, R. C. "The Literary Affinities of Exodus 34:6f.," *VT* 13 (1963) 34-51.

Driver, Samuel Rolles. *The Book of Genesis with Introduction and Notes*. 2d ed. WC. London: Methuen & Co., 1904.

______. *Notes on the Hebrew Text of the Books of Samuel*. Oxford: Clarendon Press, 1890.

______, and Gray, George B. *A Critical and Exegetical Commentary on Job*. ICC. New York: Charles Scribner's Sons, 1921.

Ehrlich, Ernst Ludwig. *Der Traum im Alten Testament*. Beiheft zur *ZAW* 73. Berlin: Alfred Töpelmann, 1953.

Eichrodt, Walther. *Theology of the Old Testament I*. Translated by J. A. Baker from the 6th German ed., 1959. Philadelphia: Westminster Press, 1961.

______. *Theology of the Old Testament II*. Translated by J. A. Baker from the 5th German ed., 1964. London: SCM Press Ltd., 1967.

Eissfeldt, Otto. "The Promises of Grace to David in Isaiah 55:1-5," *Israel's Prophetic Heritage: Essays in Honor of James Muilenburg*. Bernhard W. Anderson and Walter Harrelson, eds. New York: Harper & Brothers, Publishers, 1962. 196-207.

______. "Ein Psalm aus Nordisrael. Micha 7,7-20," *Zeitschrift der Deutschen Morgenländischen Gesellschaft* 112 (1962) 258-268.

Farr, G. "The Concept of Grace in the Book of Hosea," *ZAW* 70 (1958) 98-107.

Février, J. G. "La grande inscription dédicatoire de Mactar," *Semitica* VI (1956) 15-31.

Freedman, David Noel. "Divine Commitment and Human Obligation," *Interpretation* 18/4 (1964) 419-431.

______. "God Compassionate and Merciful," *Western Watch* 6 (1955) 6-24.

______. "A Limited Study of the Root *nś'* in Connection with Isaiah 52:13-53:12, and its Bearing on the Theology of Forgiveness and Reconciliation and the Doctrine of the Atonement." Typescript of paper presented at the meeting of the Biblical Colloquium, Pittsburgh, Pa., November 29, 1952.

Galling, Kurt. *Die Bücher der Chronik, Esra, Nehemiah.* ATD. Göttingen: Vandenhoeck und Ruprecht, 1954.

Gaster, T. H. "Critical Note on Ps. 42:8," *JBL* 73 (1954) 237-238.

Gese, Harmut. "Der Davidsbund und die Zionserwählung," *ZTK* 61 (1964) 10-26.

Giesebrecht, Friedrich. *Das Buch Jeremia.* HkzAT. Göttingen: Vandenhoeck und Ruprecht, 1907.

Glueck, Nelson. *Das Wort* ḥesed *im alttestamentlichen Sprachgebrauche als menschliche und göttliche gemeinschaftgemässe Verhaltungsweise.* Giessen: Alfred Töpelmann, 1927. (Published in English as Ḥesed *in the Bible.* Translated by Alfred Gottschalk. Cincinnati: Hebrew Union College Press, 1967.)

Good, Edwin M. "Hosea 5:8-6:6: An Alternative to Alt," *JBL* 85 (1966) 273-286.

______. "Love in the Old Testament," *The Interpreter's Dictionary of the Bible.* George A. Buttrick *et al.*, eds. New York: Abingdon Press, 1962. III, 164-168.

Goodman, A. E. "*Ḥsd* and *twdh* in the Linguistic Tradition of the Psalter," *Words and Meanings: Essays presented to David Winton Thomas.* Peter W. Ackroyd and Barnabas Lindars, eds. Cambridge: University Press, 1968.

Gray, George. *A Critical and Exegetical Commentary on Numbers.* ICC. Edinburgh: T. & T. Clark, 1903.

Gray, John. *Joshua, Judges and Ruth.* CB. London: Thomas Nelson (Printers) Ltd., 1967.

______. *I & II Kings: A Commentary.* OTL. Philadelphia: Westminster Press, 1963.

Gunkel, Hermann. *Einleitung in die Psalmen: Die Gattungen der religiösen Lyrik Israels.* Completed by Joachim Begrich.

2d ed. Göttingen: Vandenhoeck & Ruprecht, 1966. (Reprint of 1933 ed.)

______. *Genesis übersetzt und erklärt*. HkzAT. Göttingen: Vandenhoeck & Ruprecht, 1917.

______. *Die Psalmen*. HkzAT. Göttingen: Vandenhoeck & Ruprecht, 1926.

Hanson, Paul. "Old Testament Apocalyptic Reexamined," *Interpretation* 25 (1971) 454-479.

______. *The Dawn of Apocalyptic*. Philadelphia: Fortress Press, 1975.

Harvey, Julien. *Le plaidoyer prophétique contre Israël après la rupture de l'alliance*. Montréal: Les Éditions Bellarmin, 1967.

______. "Le '*Rîb*-pattern,' réquisitoire prophétique sur la rupture d l'alliance," *Biblica* 43 (1962) 172-196.

Hertzberg, Hans Wilhelm. *Die Bücher Josua, Richter, Ruth übersetzt und erklärt*. ATD. Göttingen: Vandenhoeck & Ruprecht, 1953.

______. *I & II Samuel: A Commentary*. Translated by J. S. Bowden from the 2d rev. German ed., 1960. Philadelphia: Westminster Press, 1964.

Hillers, Delbert R. "A Note on Some Treaty Terminology in the Old Testament," *BASOR* 176 (1964) 46-47.

Hills, Sidney. "*Ḥesed* and *Berîth* and their Interrelationships." Outline of talk presented at the meeting of the Biblical Colloquium, Drew University (Madison, N.J.), November 25, 1960.

______. "The *Ḥesed* of Man in the Old Testament" and Part II "The *Ḥesed* of God." Unpublished paper presented at the meeting of the Biblical Colloquium, Pittsburgh, Pa., November 29, 1957.

Huffmon, Herbert B. "The Covenant Lawsuit in the Prophets," *JBL* 78 (1959) 285-295.

______. "The Treaty Background of Hebrew *Yādaʿ*," *BASOR* 181 (1966) 31-37.

______, and Parker, Simon B. "A Further Note on the Treaty Background of Hebrew *Yādaʿ*," *BASOR* 184 (1966) 36-37.

Hyatt, J. P. "The God of Love in the Old Testament," *To Do and to Teach: Essays in Honor of Charles Lynn Pyatt*. Roscoe

M. Pierson, ed. Lexington, Ky.: College of the Bible, 1953. 15-26.

Janzen, J. Gerald. *Studies in the Text of Jeremiah.* Cambridge, Mass.: Harvard University Press, 1973.

Jellicoe, Sidney. *The Septuagint and Modern Study.* Oxford: Clarendon Press, 1968.

Jepsen, Alfred. "Gnade und Barmherzigkeit im Alten Testament," *Kerygma und Dogma* 7 (1961) 261-271.

Jenks, Alan W. "The Elohist and North Israelite Tradition." Unpublished Th.D. dissertation, Harvard Divinity School, 1965.

Johnson, Aubrey R. "*Ḥesed* and *Ḥasīd*," *Interpretationes ad Vetus Testamentum Pertinentes Sigmundo Mowinckel.* Oslo: Fabritius and Sønner, 1955. 100-112.

Kittel, Rudolph. *Die Bücher Chronik.* HAT. Göttingen, 1902.

Kraus, Hans-Joachim. *Psalmen.* BK. Neukirchen Kreis Moers: Neukirchener Verlag der Buchhandlung des Erziehungsvereins, 1960.

Kuyper, Lester J. "Grace and Truth," *Reformed Review* 16/1 (1962) 1-16.

______. "The Meaning of *ḥsdw* [in] ISA XL 6," *VT* 13 (1963) 489-492.

Lampe, G. W. H. "Saint," *The Interpreter's Dictionary of the Bible.* George A. Buttrick *et al.*, eds. New York: Abingdon Press, 1962. IV, 164-165.

Lance, H. Darrell. "The Royal Stamps and the Kingdom of Josiah," *HTR* 64 (1971) 315-332.

Langlamet, F. "Israël et 'l'habitant du pays' (à suivre)," *RB* 76 (1969) 321-350.

Lemke, Werner. "Synoptic Studies in the Chronicler's History." Unpublished Th.D. dissertation, Harvard Divinity School, 1963.

Lewy, Julius. "Les textes paléo-assyriens et l'Ancient Testament," *Revue de l'histoire des religions* 110 (1934) 29-65.

Lidzbarski, Mark. *Ephemeris für semitische Epigraphik.* 3 vols. Giessen: Alfred Töpelmann, 1902-1915.

Lofthouse, W. F. "*Ḥēn* and *Ḥesed* in the Old Testament," *ZAW* 51 (1933) 29-35.

McCarthy, Dennis J. *Old Testament Covenant: A Survey of Current*

Opinion. Richmond, Va.: John Knox Press, 1972.

______. *Treaty and Covenant: A Study in Form in the Ancient Oriental Documents and in the Old Testament*. Rome: Pontifical Biblical Institute, 1963.

McKenzie, John L. *Second Isaiah*. AB. Garden City, N.Y.: Doubleday & Company, Inc., 1968.

McNeile, A. H. *The Book of Exodus*. WC. New York: Edwin S. Gorham, 1908.

Marsh, John. *The Book of Numbers: Introduction and Exegesis*. IB. New York: Abingdon Press, 1953.

Masing, Uku. "Der Begriff *Ḥesed* im Alttestamentlichen Sprachgebrauch," *Charisteria Iohanni Kõpp: Octogenario oblata*. Papers of the Estonian Theological Society in Exile, No. 7. Holmae: November 9, 1954.

Mays, James L. *Hosea: A Commentary*. OTL. Philadelphia: Westminster Press, 1969.

Mazar, Benjamin. "The Aramean Empire and its Relationship with Israel," *BA* 25 (1962) 98-120.

Mendenhall, George E. "Covenant," *The Interpreter's Dictionary of the Bible*. George A. Buttrick *et al*., eds. New York: Abingdon Press, 1962. I, 714-723.

______. *Law and Covenant in Israel and the Ancient Near East*. Pittsburgh: The Biblical Colloquium, 1955.

Montgomery, James A. *A Critical and Exegetical Commentary on the Books of Kings*. Henry S. Gehman, ed. ICC. Edinburgh: T. & T. Clark, 1950.

______. *A Critical and Exegetical Commentary on Daniel*. ICC. New York: Charles Scribner's Sons, 1927.

______. "Hebrew *ḥesed* and Greek *charis*," *HTR* 32 (1939) 97-102.

Moran, William L. "The Ancient Near Eastern Background of the Love of God in Deuteronomy," *CBQ* 25/1 (1963) 77-87.

______. "A Note on the Treaty Termonology of the Sefire Stelas," *JNES* 22 (1963) 173-176.

Morgenstern, Julian. "David and Jonathan," *JBL* 78 (1959) 322-325.

______. "The *Ḥ*^{a}*sîdîm* -Who were they?" *HUCA* 38 (1967) 59-73.

Muilenburg, James. *Isaiah Chapters 40-66: Introduction and Exegesis*. IB. New York: Abingdon Press, 1956.

Myers, Jacob M. *II Chronicles*. AB. Garden City, N.Y.:

Doubleday & Company, Inc., 1965.

______. *Ezra, Nehemiah*. AB. Garden City, N.Y.: Doubleday & Company, Inc., 1965.

Napier, B. Davie. "Prophet, Prophetism," *The Interpreter's Dictionary of the Bible*. George A. Buttrick *et al.*, eds. New York: Abingdon Press, 1962. III, 896-919.

Nöldeke, Theodor. *Neue Beiträge zur Semitischen Sprachwissenschaft*. Strassburg: K. J. Trübner, 1910.

North, Christopher R. *The Second Isaiah*. Oxford: Clarendon Press, 1964.

Noth, Martin. *Das Buch Josua*. 2d ed. HAT. Tübingen: J.C.B. Mohr, 1953.

______. *Exodus: A Commentary*. Translated by J. S. Bowden from the 1959 German ed. OTL. Philadelphia: Westminster Press, 1962.

______. *Numbers: A Commentary*. Translated by J. D. Martin from the 1966 German ed. OTL. London: SCM Press Ltd., 1968.

______. *Überlieferungsgeschichtliche Studien*. Halle: Max Niemeyer Verlag, 1943.

Oppenheim, A. Leo. *The Interpretation of Dreams in the Ancient Near East*. Transactions of the American Philosophical Society, New Series, Vol. 46, Pt. 3. Philadelphia: The American Philosophical Society, September, 1956.

Paton, Lewis B. *A Critical and Exegetical Commentary on Esther*. ICC. New York: Charles Scribner's Sons, 1908.

Peckham, J. Brian. *The Development of the Late Phoenician Scripts*. Cambridge, Mass.: Harvard University Press, 1968.

Pedersen, Johannes. *Israel: Its Life and Culture, I-II*. London: Oxford University Press, 1926.

Perles, Felix. *Analekten zur Textkritik des Alten Testaments*. Munich: F. Straub, 1895.

Pope, Marvin H. *Job*. AB. Garden City, N.Y.: Doubleday & Company, Inc., 1965.

Pritchard, James B., ed. *Ancient Near Eastern Texts relating to the Old Testament*. 2d ed. Princeton, N.J.: Princeton University Press, 1955.

Procksch, Otto. *Die Genesis übersetzt und erklärt*, zweite und dritte Auflage. KAT. Leipzig: A. Deichertsche

Verlagsbuchhandlung, 1924.

Rad, Gerhard von. *Genesis: A Commentary*. Translated by John H. Marks from the 1956 German ed. OTL. Philadelphia: Westminster Press, 1961.

______. "'Righteousness' and 'Life' in the Cultic Language of the Psalms," *The Problem of the Hexateuch and Other Essays*. Translated by E. W. T. Dicken. New York: McGraw-Hill Book Company, 1966. 243-267. (Originally published in *Festschrift für Alfred Bertholet*. Tübingen, 1950.)

Rawlinson, George. *The Five Great Monarchies of the Ancient Eastern World*. 2d ed. New York: Dodd, Mead, and Company [1881].

Reed, William L. "Some Implications of *ḥēn* for Old Testament Religion," *JBL* 73 (1954) 36-41.

Renaud, Bernard. *Je suis un dieu jaloux*. Paris: Les Éditions du Cerf, 1963.

Richter, Wolfgang. *Traditionsgeschichtliche Untersuchungen zum Richterbuch*. Bonn: Peter Hanstein verlag GMBH, 1963.

Riemann, Paul A. "Desert and Return to Desert in the Pre-Exilic Prophets." Unpublished Ph.D. dissertation, Harvard University, 1964.

Robinson, Henry Wheeler. *Inspiration and Revelation in the Old Testament*. Oxford: Clarendon Press, 1964.

Rost, Leonhard. *Die Überlieferung von der Thronnachfolge Davids*. Stuttgart: Verlag von W. Kohlhammer, 1926.

Rudolph, Wilhelm. *Das Buch Ruth; Das Hohe Lied; Die Klagelieder*. KAT. Gütersloh: Gütersloher Verlagshaus Gerd Mohn, 1962.

______. *Chronikbücher*. HAT. Tübingen: J. C. B. Mohr, 1955.

______. *Esra und Nehemiah*. HAT. Tübingen: J. C. B. Mohr, 1949.

______. *Hosea*. KAT. Gütersloh: Gütersloher Verlagshaus Gerd Mohn, 1966.

______. *Jeremia*. 2d ed. HAT. Tübingen: J. C. B. Mohr, 1958.

Rylaarsdam, J. Coert. *The Book of Exodus: Introduction and Exegesis*. IB. New York: Abingdon Press, 1952.

Sarna, N. M. "Psalm 89: A Study in Inner Biblical Exegesis," *Biblical and Other Studies*. Alexander Altmann, ed. (Lown Institute Studies I) Cambridge: Harvard Univ. Press, 1963.

Scharbert, Josef. "Formgeschichte und Exegese von Ex. 34,6f und seiner Parallelen," *Biblica* 38 (1957) 130-150.

Schedl, Claus. "'ḥesed 'ēl' in Psalm 52 (51), 3," *Biblische Zeitschrift* 5 (1961) 259-260.

Schulthess, Friedrich. *Homonyme Wurzeln im Syrischen.* Berlin: Reuther and Reichard, 1900.

Scott, R. B. Y. *Proverbs, Ecclesiastes.* AB. Garden City, N. Y.: Doubleday & Company, Inc., 1965.

Skinner, John. *A Critical and Exegetical Commentary on Genesis.* 2d ed. ICC. Edinburgh: T. & T. Clark, 1930.

Smart, James D. *The Book of Jonah: Introduction and Exegesis.* IB. New York: Abingdon Press, 1956.

Smith, Louise Pettibone. *The Book of Ruth: Introduction and Exegesis.* New York: Abingdon Press, 1953.

Smith, W. Robertson. *Kinship and Marriage in Early Arabia.* First published 1885, reprinted 1903 with additional notes by the author and Ignaz Goldziher. Stanley A. Cook, ed. London: Adam & Clarles Black, 1903.

Snaith, Norman H. *Distinctive Ideas of the Old Testament.* London: Epworth Press, 1944.

______. "Lovingkindness," *A Theological Wordbook of the Bible.* Alan Richardson, ed. New York: Macmillan, 1951. 136-137.

Speiser, Ephraim A. *Genesis.* AB. Garden City, N.Y.: Doubleday & Company, Inc., 1964.

______. "I Know Not the Day of My Death," *JBL* 74 (1955) 252-256.

______. "The Wife-Sister Motif in the Patriarchal Narratives," *Biblical and Other Studies.* Alexander Altmann, ed. (Lown Institute Studies I) Cambridge: Harvard University Press, 1963. 15-28.

Stamm, J. J. with Andrew, M. E. *The Ten Commandments in Recent Research.* London: SCM Press Ltd., 1967.

Stapleton, M. P. Review of *Misericordia et Veritas* by Felix Asensio, *CBQ* 14 (1952) 288.

Stoebe, Hans Joachim. "Bedeutung und Geschichte des Begriffes *ḥäsäd.*" Unpublished doctoral dissertation, Münster, 1951.

______. "Die Bedeutung des Wortes *Ḥäsäd* im Alten Testament," *VT* 2 (1952) 244-254.

______. "Gnade, I," *Evangelisches Kirchenlexikon.* Vol. I: A-G, pp. 1604-1605. Heinze Brunotte and Otto Weber, eds. Göttingen: Vandenhoeck & Ruprecht, 1956.

Talmon, Shemaryahu. "The 'Desert Motif' in the Bible and Qumran Literature," *Biblical Motifs: Origins and Transformations*. Alexander Altmann, ed. Philip W. Lown Institute of Advanced Judaic Studies, Brandeis University, Vol. III. Cambridge, Mass.: Harvard University Press, 1963. 31-64.

Thomas, D. Winton. *Zechariah: Introduction and Exegesis*. IB. New York: Abingdon Press, 1956.

Thompson, John A. *The Book of Joel: Introduction and Exegesis*. IB. New York: Abingdon Press, 1956.

Thordarson, Thorir K. "The Form-Historical Problem of Ex. 34:6-7." Unpublished Ph.D. dissertation, University of Chicago Divinity School, 1959.

Tournay, R. J. Review of *Misericordia et Veritas* by Felix Asensio, *RB* 57 (1950) 290.

Tsevat, Matitiahu. "Studies in the Book of Samuel, III: The Steadfast House: What Was David Promised in II Sam. 7:11b-16?" *HUCA* 34 (1963) 71-82.

Vaux, Roland de. *Ancient Israel: Its Life and Institutions*. New York: McGraw-Hill Book Company, Inc., 1961.

Ward, J. M. "The Literary Form and Liturgical Background of Psalm LXXXIX," *VT* 11 (1961) 321-339.

Wellhausen, Julius. *Der Text der Bücher Samuelis*. Göttingen: Vandenhoeck und Ruprecht's Verlag, 1871.

Westermann, Claus. *Isaiah 40-66: A Commentary*. Translated by David M. G. Stalker from the 1966 German ed. OTL. London: SCM Press Ltd., 1969.

______. *The Praise of God in the Psalms*. Translated by K. Crim from the 1961 German ed. Richmond, Va.: John Knox Press, 1965.

Wiéner, Claude. *Recherches sur l'amour pour Dieu dans l'Ancien Testament*. Paris: Letouzey et Ane, 1957.

Wolff, Hans W. *Hosea*. BK. Neukirchen Kreis Moers: Neukirchener Verlag der Buchhandlung des Erziehungsvereins, 1961.

______. "'Wissen um Gott' bei Hosea als Urform von Theologie," *EvTh* 12 (1952-53) 533-554. Reprinted in H. W. Wolff, *Gesammelte Studien zum Alten Testament*. Munich: Chr. Kaiser Verlag, 1964. 182-205.

Wright, G. Ernest. "The Lawsuit of God: A Form-Critical Study of Deuteronomy 32," *Israel's Prophetic Heritage: Essays in Honor of James Muilenburg*. Bernhard W. Anderson and Walter Harrelson, eds. New York: Harper & Brothers, Publishers, 1962. 26-67.

______. "The Literary and Historical Problem of Joshua 10 and Judges 1," *JNES* 5 (1946) 105-114.

______. "The Nations in Hebrew Prophecy," *Encounter* 26 (1965) 225-237.

Yarbrough, Glenn. "The Significance of *ḥsd* in the Old Testament." Unpublished Ph.D. dissertation, Southern Baptist Theological Seminary, 1959.

Zimmerli, Walther. *Gottes Offenbarung: gesammelte Aufsätze zum Alten Testament*. Munich: Chr. Kaiser Verlag, 1960.